D0359700

THE THIRD REICH
DAY BY DAY

THE THIRD REICH
DAY BY DAY

General Editor: Peter Darman

Grange
BOOKS

This edition published in 2004 by Grange Books
Grange Books plc
The Grange
1–6 Kingsnorth Estate
Hoo
Near Rochester
Kent ME3 9ND

www.grangebooks.co.uk

© 2004 The Brown Reference Group plc

ISBN 1-84013-675-8

The Brown Reference Group plc
8 Chapel Place
Rivington Street
London
EC2A 3DQ
UK
www.brownreference.com

Printed in China

Editors: Stephen Crane, Peter Darman
Picture research: Antony Shaw
Design: John Woolford
Production: Matt Weyland

Page 1: The SS Long Service Cross.

CONTENTS

INTRODUCTION

Deutschland Erwache

The Third Reich, which was spawned on January 30, 1933, was born out of the National Socialist Workers' Party, which was the very embodiment of Adolf Hitler himself. On April 20, 1889, its Führer (Leader) was cast upon the unsuspecting world at Braunau, Upper Austria. At the age of nine he became a choirboy in the Catholic Church at Lambach, and claimed in later years that his great vocal power had developed while singing hymns. He was an average, lazy and rebellious student, with a talent for drawing. This talent decided him on a career in art. His oratorical rehearsals were not overlooked. August Kubizek, his close boyhood friend, recalled young Adolf practising elocution in an open field. From his schooldays Hitler was a fanatical German Nationalist with a rancorous hatred of others, mostly Slavic races which made up the Austro-Hungarian Empire.

With the aim of entering the Academy of Art or the School of Architecture, Hitler moved to cosmopolitan Vienna in 1907, which at the time housed a large Jewish community. His failure in the entrance examinations was to have dire consequences for the future of Europe. Angry at his rejection, Hitler also caught the infection of anti-Semitism and became a prey to a morbid loathing of the Jews, which affected his whole outlook on life. A fierce nationalism and a corresponding intolerance of other races soon furnished Hitler with a distorted view on life from then on. His German nationalism was derived from Fichte, Hegel, Treitshed, Nietzsche and Richard Wagner. Wagner's operas, with their emphasis on Teutonic and German mythology, had an enormous influence on him, while the writings of the philosopher Nietzsche also attracted him.

▶ **Adolf Hitler, the extremist who founded the Third Reich, which he regarded as the greatest of all German Empires.**

Nietzsche expounded the notion of the "superman" (*Ubermensch*), a being perfect in mind and body who disdained man-made laws and goals, and who discarded morality for the virtue of "hardness". In this way Nietzsche extolled the ideas of force and strength. Hitler and the Nazis would later appropriate and pervert these ideas to create a ruthless totalitarian state. In Hitler's eyes the Nordic German hero was the archetypal superman, but he had to be freed from the shackles of Christian morality, which Hitler condemned for its Judaistic origins.

In May 1913 Hitler was 25 and had moved from Vienna to Munich. By this time, he was to claim later, his character was fully formed and his fundamental philosophy was already worked out, though materially he was little better than a vagrant, making a living from selling his paintings. In January 1914, and overdue for Austrian military service, he was summoned to military service in Austria and the Munich police obliged him to return. At Salzburg he was found to be medically unfit, though, and was allowed back to Munich. In August he joined the crowds demanding action

▼ *At the end of World War I, a Hessian regiment marches back across the Rhine at Koblenz to a Germany in chaos.*

against Russia and calling for a pan-German movement against both Russia and Serbia. The Austrian Empire had already declared war against Serbia since the heir to its throne had been assassinated in the town of Sarajevo. August 1914, with the outbreak of World War I, gave the wandering Hitler an opportunity. He threw himself into it with an ardour extraordinary even in those euphoric first days. He promptly addressed

▲ *Revolution in Germany, October 1918. Troops loyal to the Kaiser battle with communists on the streets of Hamburg.*

a petition to the Kaiser seeking permission, although he was an Austrian, to join a Bavarian regiment.

The disability which had kept him out of the Imperial Austrian Army having been apparently overlooked, Hitler's wish was

granted. He served during World War I as an infantry volunteer in the 1st Company of the 16th Bavarian Regiment known, after its founding colonel, as the *List* Regiment. By October Hitler's regiment was at the front before the town of Ypres. By his own choice he served in the dangerous role of regimental message runner for the duration of the war, refusing promotion beyond the rank of corporal. In 1914 he won the Iron Cross second class. In the regiment were Lieutenant Wiedemann and Sergeant Max Amann, both of whom later became prominent Nazi Party members. In October 1916 Hitler was injured in the thigh and sent to a military hospital in Berlin. On recovery he was sent to the reserve

▲ *The very first SS members, whose task was to be Hitler's bodyguard.*

◄ *Two SA members. The Sturmabteilung (Brownshirts) was the Nazi Party's private army of ex-servicemen.*

battalion in Munich, returning to his regiment in March 1917. The *List* Regiment participated in Ludendorff's April 1918 offensive, when Hitler was awarded the Iron Cross first class for his bravery. The act of heroism for which he received his award is not known, but apparently he captured an enemy officer and about a dozen soldiers. The award to a soldier of his rank was unusual, and marked him out as a distinguished frontline soldier. In the fighting near Ypres he was blinded by gas in October 1918 and sent to hospital in Pasewalk in eastern Germany, until discharged fit and posted back to the Munich barracks in November 1918

World War I ended on November 11, 1918, leaving Hitler not yet having reached Munich and Germany in chaos and revolt under the frail Weimar Republic. The chancellor of Germany was the social democrat Friedrich Ebert, who in 1919 would become president of the country. Under the terms of the armistice, the army was reduced to a 100,000-man force called the *Reichswehr*.

Germany was far from a united country. On the one hand, the disbanded troops and their officers viewed the new republic with distaste, while the socialists and communists were fomenting revolution, culminating in January 1919 when the Spartacist revolt broke out at the beginning of that month.

The new republic's army decided to defend itself against subversion. Munich, for example, was first under the rule of a Bavarian socialist government, which was subsequently crushed by central government troops with the aid of its *Freikorps* allies. The *Freikorps* were groups of right-wing ex-soldiers which sprang up all over Germany following the end of the war. Essentially gangs of brutalized men

▲ *An early SA and Nazi Party member and later editor of the* Völkischer Beobachter, *Max Amann.*

normality and felt himself drawn to exploit the chaos which engulfed Germany after her defeat. This unusual combination produced a detestable personality that was to be his ultimate undoing. He had remained in the army after the war and fought in Ritter von Epp's Freikorps to crush the revolutionary Bavarian socialist government. He was also at this time secretly employed by the army to establish ammunition and weapons dumps in the Munich region for monarchist and nationalist groups, and to organize a special political intelligence unit for the army. Hitler, still a corporal awaiting his discharge from service, was selected for training in this new unit as an education officer in February 1919. Hitler's deeply held nationalistic views and anti-Semitic prejudices were bolstered by the political instruction that he received during his training. In September 1919, his army intelligence masters sent him to investigate this small group. Drexler's ideas appealed to Hitler, for he was bitterly opposed to the "capitalist Jews" and the "Marxist conspiracy" (these ideas were to form the very core of Nazi ideology). Hitler joined Anton Drexler's German Workers' Party in

1919. Drexler wrote confidentially to a colleague about Hitler, describing him as, "An absurd little man", and commenting on how in such a short time Hitler had become steering committee member No 7 of the party. Drexler's position in the party was under threat by Hitler's forceful personality and his persuasive oratory. Hitler later wrote of Drexler in *Mein Kampf*: "His whole being was weak and uncertain, nor did he have the ability to use brutal means to overcome the opposition to a new idea inside the party. What was needed was one fleet as a greyhound, smooth as leather, and hard as steel." In less than a year the "absurd little man" had become the dominant force in the party. Soon afterwards, Hitler had created the *National Sozialistische Deutsche Arbeiter Partei* (National Socialist German Workers' Party – NSDAP) to succeed the DAP.

To inflate its importance and size, Hitler massaged the membership numbers, but the party desperately needed a kick-start. Ernst Röhm, who was chief of staff to the

▼ *German Army troops in Berlin in 1919 during the Spartacist revolt. The Freikorps assisted in the suppression of this uprising.*

whose allegiance was to their commanders only, the *Freikorps* fought for the elimination of all "traitors to the Fatherland". They brutally suppressed the Spartacist revolt in Berlin, and then helped to put out the embers of left-wing revolt that had spread to other parts of Germany (ironically, the *Freikorps* fought with British and French approval when they fought against the Bolsheviks in Lithuania and Latvia in 1919).

Onto the political stage during this turbulent time appeared two luminaries, both of which Hitler would eclipse. The first was an insignificant railway locksmith, Anton Drexler. He was a harmless-looking, bespectacled man who worked with the Fatherland Party during and after World War I, whose aim was to get a fair peace for Germany. Drexler merged two tiny groups of malcontents into the *Deutsche Arbeiterpartei*, the German Workers' Party, or DAP, in January 1919. It was an organization with no assets except a cigar box in which to put contributions. The second was a far more sinister character named Ernst Röhm, who could be best described as short, overweight and bullet-scarred, with flushed cheeks and a savage smile. He was a non-conformist, a roistering lecher, homosexual and adventurer who by his own admission detested bourgeois

▲ **The Reichswehr, the 100-000 man post-Versailles Treaty German Army, was forced to train with dummy tanks.**

commandant of the Munich military region, now chose to support Hitler, thus helping the fledgling Nazi Party to grow. Röhm fancifully considered himself a revolutionary and had heady ambitions of forming a revolutionary army with himself at its head. His chosen vehicle was the Bavarian Home Guard, which possessed clandestinely secreted weapons, which Röhm hoped he could use in his revolution. The Berlin government, having collected intelligence about revolutionary activity, disbanded this and other military groups who were covertly gathering in various districts of Germany in early 1921. This thwarted Röhm's ambitions. Hitler's embryonic Nazi Party acted as a magnet and seemed the obvious receptacle for his inflated ego (Röhm was confident he could mould Hitler to his will and usurp his powers). He courted Hitler with introductions to influential persons like General Erich Ludendorff, World War I hero and right-wing nationalist, and General Franz Ritter von Epp, the commandant of the Munich military region. These introductions subsequently bore fruit. Hitler and his party gained credibility and

financial help began to materialize. Money equates to power, a fact not wasted on Hitler. He now needed to improve the party's programme, and its visual aspect would be its best advert. Men were now used to military life and uniforms and the pageantry that went with it. What was more natural than to harness these patriotic feelings, which had been instilled and burned into them during the four years of carnage? Hitler chose the female form of the ancient swastika emblem as his symbol, and planned the design of the Nazi flag, which he described as "something akin to a blazing torch".

With a visual political message and growing financial support, Hitler's party was making progress, but he needed a major confrontation with his political enemies to attract more attention. This occurred on November 4, 1921.

Hitler was informed that at the Hoffbrauhaus, the venue for a speech he was going to make that evening, the left-wing social democrats and the communists were going to try to crush his party. The meeting went ahead, but during his speech fighting broke out in the hall. Hitler later

described the event poetically: "The dance had not yet begun when my stormtroopers, for so they were called from this day on, attacked like wolves. They flung themselves in packs of eight or 10 again and again on their enemies, and little by little actually began to thrash them out of the hall. After five minutes, I hardly saw one of them who was not covered with blood. Then two pistol shots rang out and now a wild din of shouting broke out from all sides. One's heart almost rejoiced at this spectacle which recalled memories of the war."

THE BIRTH OF THE SA

In the early days of Nazism, Hitler was surrounded by the unwieldy *Sturmabteilung* (Storm Detachment), or SA, who were in the main tough, unemployed ex-soldiers who frequented Munich beer halls such as the Torbräukeller near the Isar Gate. They were recruited by Röhm to protect Nazi speakers at public meetings. The Brownshirts, as they became

that was to be a folk festival to encourage German rural life. Coburg's geographical position is some 192km (120 miles) east of Frankfurt on Main and about 64km (40 miles) from Schweinfurt. The city had a population of approximately 30,000, was Marxist controlled and was largely insignificant – until October 1922.

COBURG, OCTOBER 14–15, 1922

Hitler with his party were invited to the gathering (one wonders by whom considering the political persuasion of those who controlled the city), which afforded him the public platform that he so desperately needed to publicize his fledgling party. The chances of political violence were high, but the greater the disturbance, the more media attention it would attract. First, though, Hitler had to overcome an initial problem: transportation to the venue. Although without visible funds, he managed to hire a train, and the tickets bought by almost every party member who boarded the train defrayed the cost. With what was virtually the entire membership of the party – some 700 accompanied by a 42-piece band – set off from Munich in the "special train". Such was the devotion of some of the Nazi membership that many had bought tickets with their last Reichmarks.

The Marxist city officials were far from elated when they perceived the full

▲ *Ernst Röhm (second from left), homosexual, bully and freebooter, turned the SA into a powerful arm of the Nazis.*

▼ *The Stosstrupp (Shock Troop) Adolf Hitler provided the Nazi leader with protection in Munich in the early 1920s.*

known, were party uniformed supporters who acted as bodyguards. They were to grow in number, acting under Röhm's orders rather than Hitler's.

The Nazi Party, being small and relatively insignificant, needed the oxygen of publicity to keep its cause alive. In 1922 there occurred an incident that kept the Nazis in the public mind and was later to become part of party folklore. Coburg's city fathers had decided to hold a "German Day"

STOSSTRUPP-HITLER
MÜNCHEN

INTRODUCTION

ramifications of what was descending on the carefully controlled Coburg festival. A police captain was dispatched to greet the train, who pronounced that the Nazis could not enter the city with flags flying and band playing, as this was contrary to the law. The police officer was brushed aside by Hitler, and the Nazi Party marched off in formation. Eight massive Bavarians carrying Alpenstocks and clad in lederhosen led the cortege, and formed an escort for Hitler and his confidants: Max Amann, Hermann Esser, Dietrich Eckhart, Christian Weber, Ulrich Graf, Alfred Rosenberg and Kurt Ludecke.

Word had spread concerning the approach of the Nazis and a crowd, some thousands strong, threatened to bar their way. One of its Marxist members began to throw projectiles, sparking off a furious fight which lasted approximately 15 minutes. A curious thing now happened, for the crowd began to go over to the Nazis, who proceeded to march into the town. Hitler addressed a meeting in the town hall that evening attended by the Duke and

▼ The swastika flies at the 1st Nazi Party Day on January 28, 1923, held in the snowy streets of Munich.

▲ *SA men carry Deutschland Erwache (Germany Awake) standards at the 1st Nazi Party Day, January 1928.*

Duchess of Coburg, who were later to become active Nazis. This speech was to be hailed as one of his triumphs, and after it fights raged between Marxists and the Nazis long into the night. In the morning the city was festooned with notices calling for a "People's Demonstration" that would eject the Nazis. The Marxists had made their move. Hitler grouped his men and marched them into the city's main square. Here, it was thought, would be gathered as many as 10,000 townsfolk waiting to annihilate them. Instead, there were only a few hundred die-hard Marxists, whose stranglehold over the city was broken before the day was out. Imperial flags were festooned from windows and the rock-throwing crowds were replaced by cheering throngs. The Marxists, reeling from the defeat, announced that they would not let the "special train" leave. Hitler, buoyed up by his victory, told the officials that he would take hostages of every communist he could find and transport them to Munich on his train. The outcome was not lost on the Marxists, who capitulated to Hitler's demands. Hitler had won his first decisive

victory. In Nazi circles the event entered folklore and led to the expression in later years: "But were you at Coburg?"

The mass meetings continued. A party rally to be held on the outskirts of Munich on the Marsfeld was planned by Hitler during 1922 and proposed for January 27-29 the following year. It was to be the NSDAP's largest rally to date, with 5000 SA men from all over Bavaria converging on Munich. To increase popular appeal, bands and traditional dance groups had been hired, in addition to 12 meeting halls. Also planned were marches of SA and party supporters through the streets of the city on the way to the massed meetings. This *Parteitage* (Party Day) was to be all-important, as Hitler's first four *Deutschland Erwache* ("Germany Awake") standards were to be consecrated on the Marsfeld along with other NSDAP flags. The government, however, became increasingly uneasy upon hearing rumours of a *Putsch* (*coup d'état*), and so a ban was issued against the outdoor ceremony of consecrating the flags and standards, plus half of Hitler's publicly announced meetings throughout Munich. Upon hearing of these bans, Hitler flew into a rage and went to the Munich police commissioner, Eduard Nortz. Hitler demanded that the ban to be lifted, but Nortz would not be moved and reiterated that the ban would remain. Hitler shouted at the commissioner that the rally would still take place in its original

▼ *A lone voice in the political wilderness: Hitler speaks to Nazi Party members outside Munich on April 15, 1923.*

form and, in the defiance of the ban, he would march at the front of the SA through the streets of Munich. Nortz convened a session of the Council of Ministers. They proclaimed a "state of emergency" which automatically banned all the activities planned for the party rally. Hitler now had only one possible solution – the *Reichswehr* – which was sympathetic to the National Socialists. Hitler arranged for Röhm and Ritter von Epp to persuade Lossow, its commander in Bavaria, to meet with him to discuss the situation. After the meeting Lossow informed the government that he considered "the suppression of the Nationalist Socialist organisation unfortunate for security reasons". The ban was subsequently lifted. However, Commissioner Nortz demanded a second meeting with Hitler, where he requested that the number of meetings remained at six instead of 12 and, more importantly, Hitler was to stage the consecration of the standards and flags inside the "Krone Circus" and not outside on the Marsfeld. Vaguely, Hitler indicated compliance with the request.

1ST NAZI PARTY DAY

The *Parteitage* was held between January 27 and 29, 1923, under the slogan *Deutschland Erwache*. Two brigades of men marched through the city of Munich and Hitler held all 12 mass meetings. He declared the swastika would be the national symbol of the future Germany. Furthermore, he stated: "The German spirit cannot be broken in these men, Germany is awakening, the German freedom movement

is on the march.' All the party members swore to be true to the party and the man who led and guided them, i.e. Hitler. It was proclaimed that the name of this movement was the NSDAP. The consecration of the first four *Deutschland Erwache* standards and NSDAP flags as originally planned on the Marsfeld amidst the typical January snowy weather took place on the third day of the *Parteitage* of the NSDAP.

BIRTH OF THE SS, MARCH 1923

Hitler realized the necessity of organizing a more dedicated élite personal guard. This guard should not be large, but it had to consist of men of proven calibre, of Nordic blood and of good character. They had to act as bodyguard and spearhead with an unequivocal allegiance to Hitler. They had to protect both Hitler and important members of his party while they travelled the breadth of Germany furthering the Nazi cause. The Brownshirts could be relied on to meet violence with violence, but they acted under Röhm's orders when they acted on orders at all. Many SA were ex-*Freikorps* members, and they were

▼ *A Nazi supporter in Bavaria in the early 1920s. Many Germans believed the Nazis could solve their nation's economic ills.*

accustomed to swearing loyalty to their immediate commander. They were too unreliable as far as Hitler was concerned; they fulfilled a short-term necessity, but for the future he needed a totally loyal Praetorian Guard. That guard would be later be the *Schutzstaffel* (Defence Squad), the SS.

In March 1923 the embryo SS consisted of just two men – Josef Berchtold and Julius Schreck – who called themselves the *Stabswache* (Staff Guard). Two months later a new unit, the *Stosstruppe Adolf Hitler* commanded by Josef Berchtold, was formed. In August 1923 Heinrich Himmler, its future leader, joined the NSDAP.

By the autumn of 1923 Hitler had made the Nazi Party a rallying point of opposition to the government in Berlin, but he now committed a major error in trying to seize power by force rather than constitutional means. He had seen Mussolini take power in Italy in October 1922 by marching on Rome, thus why could he not do the same?

Perhaps not as sole leader of right-wing forces, but certainly part of a small group that would include Ludendorff, a notable anti-republican and hero of the right.

Circumstances seemed to favour a coup against the Weimar government: Germany was almost bankrupt, a fact not helped by the world slump of 1921. She defaulted on reparations payments (one of the hated clauses of the Treaty of Versailles), which prompted the French to occupy the Ruhr, the centre of German industry, in January 1923, which acted as the catalyst for destroying the value of German currency. The fault was laid at the feet of the "November Criminals", those individuals who had signed the Treaty of Versailles, plus the communists, Jews, profiteers and social democrats who had betrayed the army during World War I – the "stab-in-the-back" theory – and who still worked for the downfall of Germany. All fanciful stuff, but very popular with ex-soldiers, serving

▲ Brownshirts in a Munich beer hall in the early 1920s. Battles with communists in beer halls became part of Nazi folklore.

▲ Hitler and senior Nazis stand before a huge swastika banner. The swastika (Hakenkreuz) became the most powerful political symbol of the twentieth century.

▶ Ulrich Graf, ex-soldier and butcher, was Hitler's personal bodyguard.

soldiers and the vast reservoir of anti-Semitism and anti-democratic resentment that existed in Germany at the time. To Hitler and the right, the time appeared right to take power by force of arms, and restore Germany's pride and place in the world.

Unfortunately for the Nazis, events conspired against them. A communist uprising in Hamburg was defeated on October 23, and by the end of that month the *Reichswehr* had defeated communists in the governments of the states of Saxony and Thuringia. This denied the Munich plotters the excuse of the threat of communism.

However, as far as Hitler was concerned the die was cast: the coup would go ahead. On the eve of the November 9 Munich *Putsch*, Gustav von Kahr, head of the Bavarian government, was to speak in the Bürgerbräukeller (Kahr was

sympathetic to the right and Hitler had tried to recruit him to his cause, but Kahr had prevaricated and withdrawn his support). Unnoticed, Hitler, Max Amann, Alfred Rosenberg and Ulrich Graf took up position in the hall. After Kahr had been speaking for about 20 minutes, 25 armed Brownshirts, accompanied by Hermann Göring – World War I air ace and now commander of the SA – burst into the hall. At this moment Hitler leapt upon a chair, fired a shot into the ceiling and shouted: "The National Revolution has begun. This hall is occupied by 600 armed men. No one may leave the hall. The Bavarian and Reich Governments have been removed and a provisional National Government formed. The army and police barracks have been occupied, troops and police are marching on the city under the swastika banner."

THE MUNICH *PUTSCH*

Most of what Hitler said was bluff, though the audience did not know it. Hitler ushered Kahr, General Otto von Lossow and Colonel Hans von Seisser into a side room and announced that they must join him in the new government with General Ludendorff. Hitler then rushed from the room and declared to the stunned audience that the three had agreed to join him in a new government. In a wild sense of

euphoria he returned to the three men as General Ludendorff arrived. The latter was in total ignorance of any of the proceedings and was furious that all of this was taking place using his name without his permission. But he supported the general principles of what was taking place and went along with Hitler. In apparent unity they all filed back into the hall. It was now that Hitler made the first of many mistakes, leaving the hall to attempt to settle a disagreement between army engineers and SA stormtroopers that had broken out. Everyone left the hall, including the generals. At the same time the *Reichskriegsflagge*, the Reich Flag of War, another right-wing organization, was holding a "social" in the Augustiner Beer Cellar, when Ernst Röhm, its commander, was ordered to seize the former *Reichswehr* ministry in the Leopoldstrasse.

KAHR WITHDRAWS

Lossow returned to his own headquarters and began to call up the troops from outlying garrisons. Kahr publicly denounced the whole episode, which should have signalled the collapse of the *Putsch*. Ludendorff, however, was now

heavily committed, and he persuaded Hitler to go ahead with the coup.

On what happened incidentally to be the 124th anniversary of Napoleon's *coup d'état* of Brumaire, Hitler had assembled over 2000 men to help him overthrow the Bavarian State government. At midmorning on November 9 they gathered into file and began to march towards the Ludwig Bridge leading to the centre of the city. At the head of the column marched Hitler between Ludendorff, Max Erwin von Scheubner-Richter and Ulrich Graf on one side, and Dr Christian Weber, Gottfried Feder and Colonel Kriebel on the other. Julius Streicher, Nazi rabble rouser, who had been ranting at the crowd in the Marienplatz, joined the second rank. Rosenberg and Albrecht von Graefe, representative of the North German Nationalists and who had come only at Ludendorff's summons, trudged resentfully along with the rest. Behind the leaders were three units marching abreast in columns of four. On the left was Hitler's 100-man bodyguard, steel helmeted and armed with carbines and "potato masher" grenades. On the right was the *Bund Oberland*, a paramilitary organization that had once been a

▲ *The SA marches to the War Memorial in Munich in 1923. A hatless Hitler reviews the parade from the pavement.*

Freikorps, and in the middle was the battle-seasoned Munich SA Regiment. Himmler, carrying the imperial war flag, led the *Reichskriegsflagge* column. Behind followed a motley collection of men, some in uniform or parts of tattered World War I uniforms, and some wearing work clothes or business suits. The cadets from Infantry School, smart and ultra military, were sandwiched between students, shop-keepers, middle-aged businessmen and hard-faced "Freebooters". The only common mark among them was a swastika brassard on the left arm.

FARCE

From the Marienplatz they turned down the Residenzstrasse towards the Odeonsplatz. Beyond was the old War Ministry where Ernst Röhm with other stormtroopers stood surrounded and impotent. At the end of the street the police were drawn up with carbines. There was only room enough in the street for eight abreast. Hitler locked arms with Scheubner-

Richter in preparation for trouble. Ludendorff touched no one, still supremely confident that no one would fire on him. Those who participated claimed the police shot first. Some said Streicher screamed: "Ludendorff! Don't shoot your General! Hitler and Ludendorff!" Others said it was Graf. At any rate the police fired. Ludendorff was unhurt and marched ahead. Scheubner-Richter dropped to the ground, fatally wounded, pulling Hitler to the ground with him, wrenching the latter's shoulder as he did so. Ulrich Graf, Hitler's bodyguard, covered Hitler with his body and received 11 bullets. Kurt Neubauer, Ludendorff's valet, who had sprung in front of the general to protect him, lay dead, shot in the head. As Hitler sprawled on the ground, thinking he had been shot in the left side, comrades tried to shield him. In all 18 men lay dead in the street, 14 followers of Hitler and four state police (all incidentally more or less sympathetic to National Socialism).

▼ *Hitler's attempt to seize political power by force: arms being distributed to his followers prior to the Munich Putsch.*

The crowd jammed up behind only heard firecracker explosions ahead, but then a rumour spread that both Hitler and Ludendorff had been killed. The *Putschists* scrambled to the rear; the crowd panicked and fled. Hitler, accompanied by a towering young local physician and chief of the Munich SA medical corps, Dr Walther Schultze (who would later become Reich Leader of Teachers), made good his escape. At Max Joseph Platz they finally reached Hitler's old grey Selve, and Dr Schultze bundled Hitler into it. After taking various routes of escape and increasing the pain in Hitler's dislocated shoulder, they took refuge 59km (37 miles) away at Uffing in the Hanfstaengl's villa (Ernst Hanfstaengl was the only literary member of Hitler's early inner circle; tall and a practical joker, he became a sort of court jester to the Führer before and after he came to power. He eventually fell out with Hitler and had to flee to the United States to save his life). Göring, also wounded, was carried into another car and driven by his wife Karin across the Austro-German frontier. Röhm surrendered at the War Ministry two hours

later. The *Putsch* ended in a fiasco: the rank and file surrendered their weapons, identified themselves to the police and returned home, while the leaders were arrested. Himmler returned to Landshut where he sold advertising space in the *Völkischer Beobachter* (*The Racial Observer*, the official newspaper of the Nazi Party).

THE *VÖLKISCHER BEOBACHTER*
The paper had originally been a weekly sheet devoted to spreading gossip, though immediately after World War I it became more anti-Semitic. In February 1923 Hitler, having raised money with the help of Hansfstaengl, made it a daily newspaper. The chief editor was Nazi racial "expert" Alfred Rosenberg, who filled its columns with anti-Jewish literature. He praised the Nordic race and launched scathing attacks on "coloured subhumanity". The treasurer of the *Völkischer Beobachter*, Max Amann, was Rosenberg's great rival, and they often fought with each other over editorial content. Rosenberg wanted to politicize readers by stressing the Nazi way of life, whereas Amann was only interested in making money for the party. Following the Munich Putsch, the paper ran a front-page headline proclaiming "Hitler's Triumph". The

issue was priced at eight billion Marks, a reflection of the state of Germany's currency at the time.

THE BANNING OF THE NSDAP

The Munich Beer Hall *Putsch* died with the men who fell in the streets. Though it was a failure, Hitler didn't consider it as such, but rather a success for what it ultimately achieved. It had created martyrs, and Hitler needed martyrs. The red flag blazoned with a black swastika on a white circular field that had been carried as the emblem and clarion call at the head of the march became another of those Nazi propaganda concepts which walked the fine line between the ridiculous and genuinely effective. The banner, made sacrosanct by the blood of the martyrs of the *Putsch*, was to become the icon of the party as well as the primary flag of the Nazi movement.

On the same date as the failed Putsch, the General State Commissar issued an order dissolving the NSDAP and stipulated heavy

▼ The Munich Putsch. *In this photograph are Rudolf Hess (second from left) and Heinrich Himmler (holding flag).*

penalties for anyone attempting to carry on the work of the party. The SA and the *Stosstruppe Adolf Hitler* were banned. Röhm was one of those put on trial; although found guilty of treasonable acts, he was released and dismissed from the army. Shortly afterwards he went to Bolivia to work as a military instructor. Berchtold, the *Stosstruppe Adolf Hitler* commander, managed to escape to Austria and remain in exile there. On the following day the police searched the headquarters of the NSDAP in the Corneliusstrasse and confiscated everything they could lay their hands on. It was during this difficult period for the Nazi movement that Julius Streicher tried his best to keep the banned NSDAP together as a unit. To evade the ban he set up a new party, the *Völkischer-Freiheits-Bewegung*. Streicher founded his own paper in 1923. Entitled *Der Stürmer* (The Stormer), he later claimed that it was the only paper that Hitler read from cover to cover. Among its more notable "achievements" was the discovery that Jesus was not a Jew. Following the *Putsch* Streicher worked as a teacher, though he clashed with his superiors on numerous occasions, not least

because he insisted that his pupils greet him each day with "*Heil Hitler!*". In many ways he was the archetypal Nazi: brutal, violent and sadistic, he advocated the use of force as the solution to any problem. Probably insane, after the war he was tried at Nuremberg, an event he denounced as "a triumph for world Jewry". Found guilty and condemned to death, his last words were "*Heil Hitler!*".

DEFEAT

The Nazi Party had been defeated and was in disarray, its leaders either arrested or having fled into exile. The Weimar government had seemingly triumphed. The party had 70,000 members in Bavaria before the *Putsch*, but by the middle of July 1925 this had fallen to 700. The original members had been mostly believers in *Völkish* ideas, which sought to promote Germanic culture and eliminate the influence of other peoples. The *Völkish* movement provided the ideological starting point of National Socialism. Hitler wrote in *Mein Kampf*: "The basic ideas of the National Socialist movement are *Völkish* and the *Völkish* ideas are National

deeds. And out of this time, which also included the period before 1923, came the *Alte Kämpfer* (the "old fighters"), the early members of the Nazi Party who were later revered for their role in the rise of National Socialism. When Hitler gained power the old fighters were given preference for jobs in the Nazi bureaucracy, and those who had been injured in street battles with communists were given the same benefits as the ones allowed to disabled World War I veterans.

Thus was the myth of the Munich *Putsch* created, which propelled Adolf Hitler onto the national stage. As Hitler was to state: "As though by an explosion, our ideas were

hurled over the whole of Germany." It had been a semi-farcical affair, and had stood little chance of success, even with the revered Ludendorff on board (he had walked right through the police lines on November 9, the policemen having turned their weapons away as a sign of respect). Hitler also learned a valuable lesson: that he would not achieve political power through direct action, especially without the support of the armed forces. He would have to achieve political victory by winning over the masses to his side, plus enlisting the support of wealthy industrialists. In this way he could gain power through legitimate channels.

▲ *The failed* **Putsch** *became a central part of Nazi myth. This Blood Order was later presented to those who took part.*

Socialist." However, he was keen to stress that the Nazis were different from the numerous discussion groups that existed to debate the finer points of what *Völkish* actually meant.

The Nazi Party's Programme, which contained 25 points, provides an example of these Völkish ideas. Point 1 advocated the union of all Germans within a Greater Germany; Point 8 called for the halting of all non-German immigration; Point 19 proposed the replacing of Roman Law, which was materialistic, with "German law"; and Point 23 stated that newspapers must be German-owned.

Though the party had been seemingly destroyed, many thousands still believed in its principles, hence it would be relatively easy to rebuild its power base. This is not to underestimate the task facing senior Nazis in the aftermath of the Putsch. Indeed, the period became known as the *Kampfzeit* (the "time of struggle"), which later was portrayed as a time of heroes and great

▶ *The shrine to the fallen of the Munich* **Putsch,** *the Feldherrnhalle in Munich, where the 16 martyrs were buried.*

1923-32

The failure of the Munich Putsch was the low point in the Nazi Party's fortunes. However, Hitler's lenient sentence meant he could rebuild the party relatively quickly. Though the party performed poorly at the elections in the 1920s, the world economic depression in 1929 gave Hitler and his followers a much-needed boost, as the German people saw their economy and standard of living nose-dive, and they began to listen to Hitler's rantings about Jews, communists and international conspiracies against Germany.

NOVEMBER 11, 1923

POLITICS, *BAVARIA*

A diffident young state police lieutenant, accompanied by two other officers, discovers Hitler at the Hanfstaengl Villa. Hitler shakes hands with the young man and says he is prepared to leave. Hitler arrives at the district office at about 21:45 hours and is formally arraigned, before being hustled to the prison at Landsberg. Throughout the tiring trip over winding, deserted roads, Hitler is depressed and sullen. At Landsberg Prison the chief warder is preparing for a possible attempt by *Putschists* to free him. An army detachment is on its way to stand guard but has not arrived by the time the great nail-studded iron entrance gate creaks open to admit him. He is brought to the fortress section of the prison and put into cell 7, the only one

▼ *General Erich Ludendorff, who took part in the Munich Putsch but was acquitted at the subsequent trial.*

▲ *The aftermath of the Putsch. Empty Munich streets as the Bavarian government rounds up Nazi participants.*

with an anteroom large enough for a military guard.

FEBRUARY 24, 1924

LEGAL, *MUNICH*

All Germany watches Munich this morning for the political significance of the treason charges against Hitler, Ludendorff and eight co-defendants, the ramifications of which go far beyond their personal fate. The new republic and democracy is as much on trial as one of Germany's most respected war heroes and a fanatic from Austria. Though they are on trial for treason, the odds are stacked in the defendants' favour. First, public opinion favours them; second, the minister of justice, Franz Gürtner, is openly sympathetic to the Nazi cause; and finally, the presiding judge, Georg Neithardt, is a fervent nationalist who regards Ludendorff as a national treasure. Hitler defends himself

brilliantly, though considering those who are judging him, he would have difficulty doing otherwise. In his closing remarks he portrays himself as a man of destiny: "Gentlemen, judgment will not be passed on us by you; judgment will be passed on us by the eternal court of history. This court will judge the accusations that have been made against us. The other court, however, will not ask: 'Did you or did you not commit high treason?' That court will pass judgment on us, on the General in command of the Quartermaster Corps of the old army, on his officers and soldiers, who as Germans wanted the best for their people and their country, who were willing to fight and die for it. Even if you find us guilty a thousand times over, the goddess of the eternal tribunal of history will smilingly tear apart the proposal of the Prosecutor and the sentence of the Court, because she will acquit us." The trial that only the *Putschists* wanted comes to an end on April 1, and although Hitler has won the battle of propaganda, he is back in prison and for all he knew would remain there four and a half years. However, he becomes a national hero in Germany, while Ludendorff is acquitted altogether. To a large segment of the German public and to the Western world in general, though, the sentence is ridiculously mild for treason and armed uprising. The whole affair has been a stunning defeat for the Weimar Republic, but a triumph for right-wing nationalism.

▶ *Kurt Daluege, who formed the* **Frontbann-Nord** *unit in Berlin following banning of the SA.*

APRIL 1924

NAZI PARTY, *REFORM OF THE SA*

Ernst Röhm is charged with the reconstruction of the officially still-illegal SA. In an attempt to get around the government law, Röhm founds an organization known as the *Frontbann*, basically the SA under another name. The *Frontbann*, meaning "Front Band", is formed as a substitute for the SA. Units are formed in various parts of Germany. *Frontbann-Nord* is founded in Berlin by Kurt Daluege, an ex-*Freikorps* member, and is destined later to be the basis of SA *Gruppe Berlin-Brandenburg*. In all the *Frontbann* numbers some 30,000 men.

MAY 1924

POLITICS, *ELECTIONS*

With the Nazi Party outlawed and Hitler in prison, some members stand as the National Socialist Freedom Movement. In the first election of 1924 this grouping win nearly two million votes and 32 of its 34 candidates – among them Strasser, Rohm and Ludendorff – enter the *Reichstag*, the German parliament. The second election in December 1924, however, sees the National Socialist vote more than halve as the National Socialist Freedom Party loses 18 seats (the *Reichstag* has a total of 472 seats).

DECEMBER 20, 1924

LEGAL, *LANDSBERG*

It is during his time in prison that Hitler dictates to Rudolf Hess, who has taken the position of his secretary, his book. Hitler initially titles it: *Four and a Half years of Struggle against Lies, Stupidity and Cowardice*. In it he attempts to set out his political dreams. However Amann, a rough, uncouth but shrewd and intuitive man, changes the title to *Mein Kampf – My Struggle*. He also arranges the publication of the book and organizes the royalties, which are to become Hitler's main source of income. He later supervises the dozens

▶ *Adolf Hitler photographed in 1926. He wears the Iron Cross and Wound Badge, both of which he won in World War I.*

▲ *Julius Schreck, who in 1925 formed the Stosstruppe Adolf Hitler to guard the leader of the Nazi Party.*

of editions published during Hitler's life, and with *Gleichschaltung* (the complete fusing of every element of German life into the Nazi social machine) of the press would become president of the Reich association of newspaper publishers and president of the Reich press chamber.

FEBUARY 1925

POLITICS, *NAZI PARTY*

It was not until January 1925 that the official ban was lifted on the NSDAP, and on February 27, 1925, in the Bürgerbräukeller in Munich, Hitler assembles the party faithful to re-establish the NSDAP. After re-establishment of the NSDAP the "interim" *Völkischer-Freiheits-Bewegung* is dissolved. Service time with the party is counted from February, with the time from that date to January 30, 1933 counting double in recognition of the *Kampfzeit* ("time of struggle") by members of the Old Guard. Himmler acts as General Secretary to Gregor Strasser who, in February 1925, agrees to disband his party and assimilate it into the reformed NSDAP.

APRIL 1925

NAZI PARTY, *REBIRTH OF THE SS*

Hitler orders the former member of the *Stosstruppe Adolf Hitler* and his chauffeur, Julius Schreck, to form a new guard unit. Two weeks later, Schreck forms a new headquarters guard and re-christens it the *Schutzstaffel* or SS Protection Squad,

▲ *After his release from Landsberg, Hitler worked hard to rebuild the Nazi Party. Here, he speaks in a Munich beer hall.*

though still called the *Stosstruppe Adolf Hitler*. Initially the new SS consists of only eight men, most of whom have previously been members of the *Stosstruppe Adolf Hitler*. Schreck, however, devises a plan to set up SS units throughout Germany.

A circular was sent out in September 1925 which called on party groups to set up *Schutzstaffeln*. These were to be small, élite squads of 10 men and one commander,

made up of respected young men in their communities and totally loyal to Hitler. By January 1926 Schreck's plan had worked and the SS had established itself on a national level. Josef Berchtold, the original commander of the Stosstruppe Adolf Hitler, returned to Germany from exile in Austria and in April 1926 took over command of the SS from Schreck.

JULY 1926

NAZI PARTY, *SECOND PARTY DAY*

It is at this rally, held in Weimar, that Adolf Hitler turns over the coveted "Blood Flag" to the SS and proclaims the SS to be his élite organization. As such, these small SS units have become the élite units of the SA. It is because of this that the SS is given the honour of bearing the *Deutschland Erwache* standards of the SA at party meetings and rallies.

SEPTEMBER 1926

NAZI PARTY, *INTERNAL POLITICS*

Gregor Strasser is appointed Reich propaganda leader of the NSDAP, and Himmler accompanies him to party headquarters as his secretary. Himmler now

◄ *Hitler at a meeting of the party hierarchy in the mid–1920s. To his left are Strasser, Himmler and Rosenberg.*

KEY MOMENTS

The Nazis in Decline?

A forecaster in 1928 would have predicted nothing but doom and gloom for the NSDAP. In fact the Nazi Party was in steep decline; it was going to "hell on a handcart". It suffered a significant humiliation in the polls that year. The political situation was dire, there was little to celebrate, and hence there was no Party Day in 1928 (at times the Nazis gave the appearance of being sulky children). The Weimar Republic, which Hitler had so bitterly criticized, was defeating the Nazis resoundingly in one political skirmish after another. Hitler had raved about the occupation of the Ruhr, which had been occupied by the French and Belgians in January 1923 following German failure to make timely reparations payments, when the French withdrew; the Weimar government reaped the reward. Hitler ranted about inflation; again the Weimar government stabilized the situation. Hitler's protestations on Law and Order were overlooked; when it was temporarily restored again the Weimar government received the applause. Politically, the Nazis were fading fast. The world economic depression of 1929, however, would see them become a force again in German politics, as Hitler blamed Jews and communists for Germany's economic troubles.

finds himself a local party official with command over the tiny SS in his district.

Strasser was de facto leader of the Nazi Party during Hitler's time in Landsberg. He established the National Socialist Freedom Movement with Ludendorff and Röhm, and also set up a newspaper, the Berlin Workers' Paper. He appointed Josef Goebbels to be editor.

Goebbels was born the son of a director of a small textile factory in Rheydt, a small industrial town in the Rhineland. His mother was a devout Catholic and he had two brothers and a sister. At four years old he contracted polio and the physician advised immediate surgery, but this could not prevent him having a crippled left leg and foot. This disability remained with him for the rest of his life, and gave rise to him having to wear special shoes, braces and bandages. Because of its visible effects he became a quiet boy who withdrew into himself, not being able to join in games with his brothers, sister or other children. Being physically inferior, the young Goebbels developed his intellectual powers. He would criticize at every

▼ *A Nazi Party rally in the 1920s. Military style parades were an important part of Nazi ritual for giving an image of strength.*

opportunity; his continual hateful remarks earned him the reputation of being arrogant and difficult to get along with. When World War I broke out he volunteered for the army, but inevitably was pronounced unfit for military service. He, as many German students of the time, attended no less than eight universities. He became superbly educated in philosophy, Greek and Latin. Slowly, feelings of nationalism began to grow in him, and as a result of this he was alienated from almost everything that surrounded him in these days: his family, hometown, leftist intellectuals, the leftist press and his communist friend of several years standing, Flisges. When he became a nationalist he betrayed everything he had formerly adhered to. His chauvinism was peppered with mysticism. He began to believe that Germany had a special mission to fulfil, and after some time came to the conclusion that non-Germans were by nature inferior and therefore of no importance. In consequence, he broke off all contact with Jews as, according to him they were not German. He once said later: "I treasure an ordinary prostitute above a married Jewess." In 1922, Goebbels returned to Munich where he studied, and soon became

a member of the NSDAP. He became Gregor Strasser's secretary, the man responsible for NSDAP activities in northern Germany. In 1925 important differences of opinion arose between the National Socialists in the north and those in the south. A meeting was held for all northern party officials. The discussion became so heated that at one point Goebbels cried out: "I propose that the insignificant bourgeois Adolf Hitler be thrown out of the party." The corruption and the confusing reports about the party in the south had undermined his faith in

▲ *The Nazi Party Day in Weimar in 1926, at which Hitler proclaimed the SS to be his élite organization.*

Hitler and had reached the point of no longer accepting Hitler's leadership. He led the *Gau* Ruhr from March 7 to June 20, 1926 with Kaufmann and Pfeffer. On November 9, 1926, he was appointed by Hitler *Gauleiter* (a *Gau* was a Nazi Party adminstrative region, each headed by a *Gauleiter*) for Berlin. Hitler knew only too well that the young intellectual would

▲ *Hitler consecrates Nazi standards while holding the "Blood Flag", the banner that was carried during the Munich Putsch.*

come into his own in the turbulent streets of the capital. On arriving there Goebbels found a corrupt and divided local NSDAP department. There were hardly any members and the communists and socialists were by far the larger movements. In early 1927, speaking to only 600 party members, he said: "We must break through the wall of anonymity. The Berliner can insult us, slander us, beat us, as long as they talk about us. Today we are 600 strong, but in six years time there will be 600,000 of us."

As for Gregor Strasser, he regarded himself as an intellectual, and he emphasized the socialist side of Nazism, and called for land nationalization and profit-sharing in industry. He began to wage a war of words with Hitler over this issue. However, at Bamberg in February 1926 Hitler spoke so strongly against the Strasserites that he won over Goebbels to his cause and ended Strasser's claim to ideological leadership of the party. His Berlin stronghold was put under Göbbels as *Gauleiter*, who at the same time was given full authority to write party propaganda. To an extent Strasser was

◄ *Hitler at the party Day held at Nuremberg in 1927. On the right is Franze Pfeffer von Salomon, SA commander.*

mollified by his new position, and giving him charge of party organization used his skills. Nevertheless, Hitler had defeated a major threat.

NOVEMBER 1, 1926

NAZI PARTY, *THE SA*

Hitler places *Hauptmann* Franz Pfeffer von Salomon as commander of the SA throughout Germany. A condition of Pfeffer von Salomon taking the position is that the SS also comes under the overall authority of the appointed SA leader. Hitler agrees to this because he needs Pfeffer's influence over the North German SA. Pfeffer von Solomon is unsentimental and a Prussian rather than Bavarian in outlook, and is not taken in by Hitler's image. "That flabby Austrian", the taut and austere Pfeffer von Solomon has reportedly called him.

▼ **Deutschland Erwache** *(Germany Awake)* *standards on parade. Hitler borrowed the phrase from one of Wagner's works.*

Under Pfeffer, recruitment to the SA continues, largely from the unemployed, bringing the strength from 2000 to over 60,000 by 1930. Many have joined it in the hope that in time it will be absorbed into the army. Röhm has encouraged this idea. As it grows, political elements in the SA begin to challenge the Nazi Party and demand a greater say in its running. In particular, they insist on nomination of SA men as party candidates in the Reichstag elections. Hitler views with alarm the increasing dissension of the Brownshirts, which appears to be encouraged by their leadership. The SS, meanwhile, remains totally obedient.

AUGUST 1927

NAZI PARTY, *THIRD PARTY DAY*

Hitler's speeches of the last few months have indicated that he is obsessed with his personal ideology, his *Weltanschauung* (World View). This states that the Aryan-Nordic race was the founder and is the maintainer of civilization, whereas the Jews are destroyers. Again and again he hammers at race and the fact that Germany's future lies in conquest of Eastern territories. Over and over he preaches his pseudo-Darwinist

Lebensraum was an integral part of Nazi ideology, which linked the twin concepts of space and race. Hitler believed that Germany needed more farmland to support itself – the need to be self-sufficient. Given the Nazi theory of race, it was only natural that she should take lands from the "inferior" Slav peoples of Poland and the Soviet Union.

JANUARY 9, 1928

NAZI PARTY, *INTERNAL POLITICS*
Hitler appoints Goebbels head of propaganda for the entire nation.

Goebbels later became Minister of Propaganda in Hitler's first cabinet. His ministry was situated in the heart of Berlin across from the Reich Chancellery. After an extensive renovation, he boasted that he was in charge of the smallest but most efficient ministry in the Reich. It consisted of 300 civil servants and 500 other employees. His heads of department were given a free hand and he expected a considerable amount of initiative from them. His top assistants were Otto Dietrich as press officer and Max Amann, head of *Eber Verlag*, the NSDAP Publishing

Company. All aspects of German artistic life came under the Reich Culture Chamber after September 22, 1933. The purpose of this institution was the furtherance of "German culture" and to bring together artists from all fields in a single organization under the control of the Reich. Any artist who had a reputation for being outspoken against the regime or critical of it was prohibited from carrying out their professional career. It was Goebbels who introduced national holidays, such as May Day and the *Erntedant*, the harvest celebration. These holidays, which became more and more inflated and extensive, offered excellent opportunities for speeches and for showing the people how fortunate they were to be living under National Socialism. With these holidays, Goebbels also created a Nazi tradition, and after a few years it seemed to most Germans that they had been celebrating them all their lives.

The outbreak of war in 1939 started a new chapter in Goebbel's propaganda programme. The people had to be prepared for war, and that war had to be justified. Therefore, in addition to domestic enemies

◀ *Hermann Göring (left), one of the first Nazis to be elected to the Reichstag, with Rudolf Hess, deputy party leader.*

▼ *Hitler in his supercharged Mercedes electioneering in the late 1920s. On the right is Kurt Daluege.*

sermon of nature's way: conquest of the weak by the strong. This programme is carried a step forward at the third Party Day. Almost 20,000 members, 8500 of them in uniform, flood into the ancient city of Nuremburg accompanied by the usual pageantry: marching with flags and standards to the strains of rousing military airs. It is on the last day of the celebrations, Sunday August 21, that Hitler connects the the central concept of *Lebensraum* (Living Space) with anti-Semitism, but few realize the significance of this misbegotten marriage, for the terms are too vague. He reiterates his demands for more living space for the German people, then points out that power and power alone is the basis for acquisition of new territory. But, he says, Germany has been robbed of her God-given power by three abominations: internationalism, democracy and pacifism. Hitler then links this evil trinity with racism. Are not internationalism, democracy and pacifism all creations of the Jew? Surely, if obscurely, Hitler has mated *Lebensraum* with anti-Semitism. His unsystematic search for *Weltanschuung* is close to realization.

▲ Hitler gives a speech to the party faithful in the late 1920s. By this time he had powerful industrial supporters.

mover. Hugenberg owned a huge propaganda empire, which included a chain of newspapers, news agencies and the leading film company in Germany, UFA. It was through this propaganda machine that Hitler managed to gain power (Hugenberg put the resources of his papers at Hitler's disposal). Following Hugenberg's lead were other important groups that added their weight to the Nazi cause. The *Stahlhelm* (Steel Helmet), for example, a militant right-wing nationalist ex-servicemen's association, had nearly one million members. The Pan-German League, Alberg Voegler, president of the United Steel Corporation and Hjalmar Schacht, president of the German Reichsbank (who was opposed to reparations payments), all lent their support to the Nazi cause. With this favourable climate, the Nazis deduced they

▼ Hitler Youth girls take part in gymnastics. The Nazis made great effort to recruit youngsters.

and the Jews, the injustice of the Treaty of Versailles was expounded, attention was directed towards the "cruel fate" of the pan-Germans in Czechoslovakia and Poland, and the "historical unity" of Austria and Germany was stressed. The propaganda had begun with "Germany Awake" and "The Jews are our Misfortune", but now the emphasis was placed on "Blood and Soil" and "People without Living Space" and "Guns for Butter".

Away from his work, Goebbels had a fancy for beautiful women, and he struck up a relationship with a young Czech actress, Linda Baarova. This blossomed into a serious love affair and when his wife Magda heard about it she considered divorce. She approached Hitler to seek his permission, whereupon he intervened. He summoned Goebbels and asked him for an update on the position. Goebbels informed him that he was in love and wanted to marry Baarova. Hitler became extremely agitated and demanded to know how could the German Minister of Propaganda get a divorce? Goebbels asked permission to resign, enabling him to seek a divorce and marry Baarova. He also sought to be made ambassador to Japan. Hitler flew into one of his manic rages: "Those who make history may not have a private life!" Goebbels was unmoved, so Hitler finally agreed on a

compromise. He might divorce Magda and remarry should he feel the same way a year later. But he was not allowed to see Baarova during the year. Goebbels gave his word of honour that he would obey. Goebbel's throne was shaky and many party leaders, among them Himmler, were convinced Goebbels would break his word. Göring and Ribbentrop also wished to usurp his position. As a result of these threats, Goebbels never saw Baarova again.

MAY 1928

POLITICS, *REICHSTAG ELECTIONS*

The Social Democrats increase their vote from 7.8 million to 9 million, whereas the extreme right-wing German National Party drop from 6.2 million to 4.3 million. The Nazis manage to win only 810,000 votes, giving them only 12 of the 491 seats in the *Reichstag*. Although a group of National Socialist deputies, among them Strasser and Goebbels, take their place in the House for the first time, closer analysis reveals that the right is suffering in German politics. Ironically, the elections were the best thing that could have happened to Hitler considering the circumstances. As right-wingers lose more and more positions and power through elections, they begin to search for another cause around which to rally. That cause is the Nazi Party.

1929 saw things moving in Hitler's favour. Germany's big industry began to support him. Alfred Hugenberg, a millionaire and right-wing politician, was to be a prime

could and should hold their rally, which was planned to be held at Nuremburg in August 1929. It was to upstage all spectacles held thus far. In 1927 Nuremburg had completed a war memorial in the form of a statue to commemorate the dead of World War I. Little did the city fathers know it would be used by the Nazis as the centrepiece of their rallies from this time on.

AUGUST 2-4, 1929

NAZI PARTY, *FOURTH PARTY DAY*

On August 2, the Nazi Party convenes its rally; there are 60,000 men and 2000 Hitler Youth present. At 11:00 hours in the Kulturvereinshaus, Gregor Strasser convenes the congress. Hitler sits passively

► *Hitler Youth members welcome their Führer to a Nuremberg rally. Boys found the militarized Hitler Youth very attractive.*

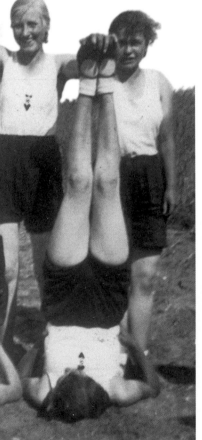

by as Julius Streicher welcomes the delegates and Adolf Wagner reads Hitler's opening statement. This rehashes all of the old dogmas: the injustice shown to German soldiers by the home front during World War I; those of the Treaty of Versailles; and finally a vitriolic attack on the communists and of course the Jews. Gottfried Feder speaks during the afternoon, discussing the Young Plan which required Germany to pay reparation for 59 years. Even though the reparations are less than those imposed

under the previous Dawes Plan (which proposed a rate of payment by Germany of 2000 million gold Marks a year), they are ammunition for the Nazis and employed with great advantage.

Nuremberg watches with amazement the pageantry that it would witness over the next years. The highlight of August 3 is a vast

▼ *Hitler said of his aims regarding German youth: "A violently active, dominating, brutal youth – that is what I am after."*

torchlight parade followed by a fireworks extravaganza. The most spectacular display takes place when five bands accompany the crowd in the singing of the national anthem. The centrepiece of the display is a swastika surrounded by a circle of green leaves and topped with a huge eagle.

A memorial celebration to commemorate the dead of World War I takes place in front of the new war memorial the following day. A stone coffin is topped by a helmet and covered with hundreds of wreaths. Hitler, escorted by dozens of flags, makes his entrance and General von Epp makes a short address. Then the highest leaders of the Nazi Party, accompanied by standard bearers, make their way onto the field while the band plays a march. There are 34 new standards, and as each new standard passes Hitler he touches it with one hand while holding the "Blood Flag" in the other. This part of the ceremony concludes with the massive crowd chanting *Deutchland Erwache* in unison; the party's rallying cry for the years to come.

Delegates have marched from the northern, middle and southern provinces of Germany to take part in this event, and it takes those from the south more than an hour just to march by. Many Hitler Youth also march. Delegates have even come from other countries: Austria, Sudentenland, Sweden, South Africa, and the Americas.

That evening in the Kulturvereinshaus, Alfred Rosenberg, Nazi ideological "expert"

and rabble-rouser, lashes out against his favourite foe – communism – in a vitriolic speech to the roar of the crowd.

One of the most prophetic speeches, though, comes from another delegate, Konstantin Hierl, who virtually proclaims that the Nazis, once they have achieved power, will prepare the state to be ready and willing to resort to war if necessary. These are strong words when the world is attempting to recover from the "War to End all Wars". Hierl leaves no one in doubt when he states: "As long as free nations exist that are willing to work towards their political goals, only war will be able to achieve the ultimate political aim."

Hitler closes the congress on the evening of August 5 with a final address on the

◀ The party created awards to inculcate a sense of belonging. This is the Germanic Proficiency Runes introduced by Himmler.

deterioration of German national power and says Germany's leaders to date have turned a great nation into nothing more than a state tourist country. As he calls his country to his version of greatness, which will banish the weak, the political opposition and the Jews from any role in society, and includes the resort to war if necessary to obtain what is "rightfully" Germany's, Hitler watches with pride as the audience roars its approval. In his own mind he has no doubts that he has taken the first step towards immortality, rather than his first leap towards infamy. However, he and his party are elated by their success. This was to be the last party day until the Nazis came to power in 1933.

JANUARY 6, 1929

PERSONALITIES, *HIMMLER*

Berchtold takes the new title of Reichsführer-SS as commander, although his power has been undermined by having his SS subordinate to the SA. Berchtold tries to keep the SS as independent as possible from the manoeuvring of the SA and also from party officials, but this becomes more difficult when the SA increases its numbers still further. Berchtold then resigns.

Erhard Heiden, Berchtold's deputy, was appointed Reichsführer-SS. Himmler's organizing ability had not gone unnoticed and he was appointed Deputy SS Leader.

▼ The "Adolf Hitler" cuff band worn by members of Hitler's bodyguard, which later became the Leibstandarte Division.

Heiden held the post until Hitler gave Himmler the appointment. Himmler retained his personal rank of *SS-Oberführer*, as *Reichsführer-SS* was not a personal rank at this time but rather a title as leader of the SS organization. He was born in Landshut on October 7, 1900, Bavaria, into a solid, respectable middle-class family. His father was a headmaster who was conservative in outlook and staunchly monarchist. Heinrich was named after his godfather, Prince Heinrich of Bavaria, to whom his father was tutor. As well as being a sickly child, he had to endure the discomfiture of attending his father's school. He welcomed the outbreak of war in 1914 enthusiastically, but it was not until January 1918 that he was able to report for duty as an officer cadet in the 11th Bavarian Infantry Regiment. But on December 17, 1918, after the war had ended, he was discharged and returned to school in Landshut. He attended the München Technical High School where he studied for a degree in agriculture. He became embroiled in right-wing politics, first joining the *Freikorps Oberland* and then the *Reichskriegsflagge*. He joined the NSDAP in August 1923 and during the Munich *Putsch* carried the imperial war flag and led the column as it marched through the streets of the city. The *Putsch* ended in a fiasco, the rank and file surrendered their weapons, identified

▲ *Hitler at Nuremberg in 1929. This would be a pivotal year for the Nazis, with the World Slump dealing Weimar a fatal blow.*

themselves to the police and returned home, while the leaders were arrested. He returned to Landshut where he sold advertising space in the *Völkischer Beobachter*. He acted as general secretary to Gregor Strasser who, in February 1925, agreed to disband his National Socialist Freedom Movement and assimilate it into the reformed NSDAP. Himmler now found himself a local party official with command over the tiny SS in his district. Strasser was appointed Reich propaganda leader of the NSDAP in September 1926, and Himmler accompanied him to party headquarters as his secretary. However his party career still allowed him time to run a chicken smallholding, where he carried out breeding experiments. He married Margarete Bodern, the daughter of a German landowner from Conerzewo, west Prussia, on the July 3, 1928. She was known as Marge and was eight years older than Himmler. She specialized in homeopathy and herbs, and when he met her in 1927 he became fascinated by her work and fell for her charms. It was in fact her money that enabled the setting up of the smallholding.

When the Nazis came to power Himmler had the power to indulge his fantasies. The

Himmler

Appointed Deputy SS Leader and then National Leader in January 1929 when he commanded approximately 1000 men, when the SS was still part of the SA. He gradually asserted the separation of the SS from the SA. Himmler became *Polizeipräsident* of Munich after Hitler became Chancellor in January 1933. This modest post enabled him to gradually gain control of the German police network except in Prussia, where Göring was Minister of the Interior. But he finally achieved complete control in 1936. Himmler devoted his life to the expansion of the SS, giving it many facets. These included the SS-financed research organization, the *Ahnenerbe*.

From the security point of view he took over the Gestapo and made it a Europe-wide organization. He controlled the concentration camp system, and in 1943 became Minister of the Interior as well. Himmler was appointed Chief of the Home Army in 1944, and a week before Hitler's suicide he made an effort to negotiate the surrender of Germany. Hitler, having heard of Himmler's treachery, dismissed him from all posts. Captured by the British in May 1945, he bit on a cyanide phial and was dead within seconds.

castle of Wewelsburg was rebuilt at immense expense as a shrine to a Germanic civilization. Here, the Hold Order of the SS was founded and from 1934 held ceremonies several times a year. Karl Wolff, Himmler's adjutant, ushered each SS leader into a monastic cell, where he steeped himself in Germanic mysticism surrounded by treasures from ancient Germany. Beneath their mock medieval coats of arms the leading 12 high SS officers were assigned places around an Arthurian table. Himmler started a ceramics works in Dachau concentration camp, which produced fine porcelain as well as earthenware. A Damascus smithy was also established. Himmler concerned himself with the perfecting of a future German élite through the SS. Not only would they be of guaranteed Aryan stock, but they would be encouraged to form the new race through the *Lebensborn* network of maternity homes (which ensured that the children of SS men and Aryan women were cared for).

The SS at the beginning of 1929 numbered 280 men, but it was still a part of the SA. Himmler began gradually to assert the separation of the SS from the SA, bringing in biological criteria and the concept of racial purity into new recruitment plans to trawl through the large number of applications from ex-*Freikorps* and unemployed bourgeois volunteers. The army, which perceived Röhm and his SA as a rival, took a favourable view to the SS as a force. This, combined with Himmler's considerable organizational skills, provided him with a personal power base.

SEPTEMBER 1929

PERSONALITIES, *HITLER*

Early in September Hitler moves from his monastic room to one of the most fashionable quarters of Munich. Here, he rents a luxurious nine-roomed apartment covering the entire second floor of 16 Prinzregentplatz. He brings along Frau Reichert, his landlady from the Thierschstrasse, and her mother Frau Dachs, together with his niece, Geli Raubal. He installs Geli in her own room while she

▲ *The streets of Meiningen are flooded with SA men in this 1931 photograph. By this time Röhm was in charge of the SA.*

pursues her medical studies in Munich. They are occasionally seen together in public at the theatre or at his favourite table in the garden of the Café Heck, where he often holds court late in the afternoon. There is vicious gossip in Munich that Hitler should stop cavorting with Geli or marry her. It is likely that Hitler's relationship with her at this time is platonic, for he obviously adores her and, according to many of his intimates, intends to marry her. Heinrick Hoffmann, however, holds a different view, especially after Hitler told him: "I love Geli and could marry her. But you know my views. I am determined to remain a bachelor."

JANUARY 14, 1930

NAZI PARTY, *HORST WESSEL*

Horst Wessel, the son of a Protestant clergyman from Bielefeld, was a songwriter who abandoned his law studies to live with a former prostitute in the slums of Berlin. He joined the party at 19 and became the leader of a troop of Brownshirts. He wrote the lyrics for the celebrated "Horst Wessel" song, originally titled by him "Raise High the Flag". A gang of communists that burst into his room murdered him. The supposed killer is Ali Höhler. The "official" Nazi Party version has it that Wessel was surprised by communists at his home at Grosse Fraankfurter Strasse 62 on January 14, 1930, and was shot in the mouth and died nine days later. Other more critical, but possibly more objective, reports go so far as to claim he was a procurer of prostitutes and was killed in a brawl over a girl. His untimely death has transformed him into a Nazi symbol, an idealist who has given his life for the Nazi cause.

Gobblels, never one to let an opportunity slip and in typically verbose language, calls him, "a Socialist Christ". The "Horst Wessel" song becomes the official anthem of the Nazis and takes second place only to the national anthem, "Deutschland, Deutschland". The tune is said to have been originally a Salvation Army hymn.

▲ Rudolf Hess (centre), Hitler's deputy, became increasingly overshadowed during the early 1930s by men such as Himmler.

▼ The massed ranks of the SA at a Nuremberg rally. Hitler described them affectionately as his "rough fighters".

▲ *Alfred Rosenberg, Nazi racial philosopher, giving an anti-Semitic speech. Many Nazis regarded him as a crank.*

Die Fahnen hoch, die Reihe dicht geschlossen!
SA marschiert mit ruhig festem Schritt.
Kam'raden, die Rotfront und Reaktion erschossen,
Marschiern im Geist in unsern Reihen mit.

The flags held high! The ranks stand tight together!
SA march on, with quiet, firm forward pace.
Comrades who, though shot by Red Front or Reaction,
Still march with us, their spirit in our ranks.

MARCH 27, 1930

POLITICS, *GERMANY*

The outside world is changing rapidly. The Muller coalition government resigns and Henrich Brüning, head of the Catholic Centre party, succeeds him and promises to cure Germany's economic problems of deflation and unemployment, but the Nazis and communists have voted against him in the *Reichstag*. Finally, on July 16, Brüning persuades President Hindenburg to use his emergency powers to put his decrees into effect. When his coalition partners refuse to vote for him, however, he dissolves the *Reichstag* and calls for new elections for September 14.

MAY 1930

NAZI PARTY, *ORGANIZATION*

With the money from the Ruhr magnates continuing to pour into the Nazi coffers, Hitler re-equipps and enlarge his SA. He purchases the Brown House in Munich on the Briennerstrasse, which he has re-designed as party headquarters. Originally built in 1828, it had by the 1920s fallen into some disrepair, which left it open for the internal changes that will be necessary for its use by the NSDAP. Contributions have been pouring in from many party members to help defray the costs. Professor Troost, Hitler's favourite architect, has been brought in to deal with the architectural and design features and is working closely with Hitler.

Inside the Brown House was stunningly impressive, at least by Nazi values. The conference room was garish red leather, and the black and red entrance hall was highlighted with swastikas, and there was a restaurant in the basement. The SA man from the country who visited his party headquarters left in awe, but possibly depressed, for many of the SA were in dire financial straits during this period.

SEPTEMBER 1930

SA, *STENNES MUTINY*

Many SA men, being unpaid and hungry, and exhausted from non-stop campaigning, are becoming disillusioned. So the districts under *Oberster SA-Führer Ost*, Walther Stennes, have gone on strike. Stennes a former *Freikorps* leader and follower of Strasser's radical Nazism, has become Pfeffer von Salomon's deputy and leader of the SA in eastern Germany. His men are for the most part unemployed and in poverty, and have heckled a speech by Goebbels, the *Gauleiter* of Berlin, and beat up his SS guard. Hitler's oratorical skills have not worked and he fears an SA revolt.

Hitler was in Munich at the time of the revolt. He raced to Berlin, because if the revolt continued or spread all would be lost in the coming elections. Hitler went from group to group, begging, pleading even sobbing. They were angry and frustrated. One SA-Führer actually grabbed Hitler by the tie and shook him.

Ernst Röhm, Hitler's long-time ally, is in Bolivia assisting that country in training its army. Hitler believes that Röhm is the one man who can control the uneasy SA. So he decides it is time to call Röhm back. In the meantime he quietly takes steps which assures his ultimate control of the SA. He names himself Oberster SA-Führer on September 2 with the second-in-command to be Stabschef answerable only to him.

Pfeffer von Solomon, following the SA mutiny and a dispute with Hitler over the nomination of SS rather than SA men to the *Reichstag*, was relieved of command of the SA. Hitler took it over personally and recalled Röhm from Bolivia to command it, demanding a personal loyalty oath from the men of the SA. For a time in 1930 it looked highly unlikely that there would be an SA rally in Braunschweig to pay homage to Hitler. During this period the Nazis took advantage of every opportunity provided to them.

During 1930 Strasser organized the party for the *Reichstag* elections, concentrating on key seats, making the party the second largest in the *Reichstag*. But again he quarrelled with Hitler over Nazi Party policy. His younger brother, Otto, was thrown out of a party meeting in Berlin and called for other radicals to form a new party with him. Gregor disowned him and remained at the centre of Nazi power, but his position was seriously weakened. It was further weakened when Otto Strasser and Stennes later fled to Prague and established the *Schwarze Front* (Black Front), an organization of dissident Nazis who represented "true National Socialist views".

SEPTEMBER 14, 1930

POLITICS, *REICHSTAG ELECTIONS*
In the elections, 30 million Germans have gone to the polls. The Nazis become the second-largest party in the *Reichstag* with 107 seats, second only to the Social Democrats with 143 seats. The communists are a poor third with 77 seats. A total of 6,409,000 votes have been cast for the

Nazis, and most of the men whose names would later become synonymous with National Socialism are now party deputies in the *Reichstag*.

While the Nazis are celebrating their gains, Heinrich Brüning, the Social Democrat Chancellor is faced with an appalling predicament. Not only does he not command an absolute majority but also there is obviously no way in view of the political mix that he can hope to get one.

All in all 1931 augured well for Hitler, save for the discontent in the SA. He had suddenly become a best-selling author. *Mein Kampf* had sold an average of a little more than 6000 annually until 1930, when the amount rose to 54,086. This got him a respectable personal income. Furthermore the Brown House, the new party headquarters, was opened on the first of the year. At the same time he was profoundly disturbed by a personal crisis. He learned that his chauffeur and companion Emile Maurice had become secretly enged to his niece Geli Raubal, who had been living a restricted life in the

▶ **Geli Raubal, Hitler's niece, who was driven to suicide by the Führer's jealousy.**

Prinzregentplatz apartment. Ironically it was the Führer himself, the perpetual matchmaker, who had given the idea to Maurice. "I'll come and have supper with you every evening when you are married," he urged the young man. "Following his advice," Maurice confided in a colleague, "I decided to become engaged to Geli, with whom I was madly in love, like everybody else. She gladly accepted my proposal." Finally he steeled himself to confess. Hitler flew into a rage, accused Maurice of disloyalty and dismissed him as chauffeur.

JANUARY 15, 1931

SA, *RÖHM RETURNS*
Röhm returns as chief of staff of the SA, answerable only to the Führer. Hitler is pursuing his personal goal with a vengeance, but the SA is venting its fury. It wants a bloody revolution to sweep away

the old order, not legal manoeuvrings, and it wants that revolution now.

APRIL 1931

LAW AND ORDER, *GERMANY*

Hitler submits to a government ban on public demonstrations. Stennes, meanwhile, is not placated and continues to fight for economic aid for the SA men in SA group *Ost*, but it is a losing battle. It is rumoured that Hitler is about to dismiss him. Stennes therefore holds a secret meeting of SA leaders which declares for him and against Hitler. But his men have no funds and cannot sustain a revolt. The party therefore expels them and Göring takes over the Berlin organization with SS men. Goebbels' role in the affair is not clear; it is possible that as a former radical himself he may have had some sympathy with the SA.

SEPTEMBER 18, 1931

PERSONALITIES, *GELI RAUBAL*

Hitler became increasingly possessive and jealous of his niece. So zealously did he guard her that in the end she was little more than a slave to his whims. That summer she announced to Hitler that she planned to continue her voice studies in Vienna. Hitler objected violently and the storm between the two intensified. On September 17, as Hitler boarded his car to drive to Hamburg, Geli called from the window: "Then you won't let me go to Vienna." Hitler retorted sharply: "No." Geli was found dead in her room the next morning, a bullet in her heart, having shot herself with Hitler's pistol. So great a loss has this been for him, that for two days and nights his friend Gregor Strasser has had to stay with him to prevent the Nazi Party leader from taking his own life.

SEPTEMBER 1931

NAZI PARTY, *ORGANIZATION*

Hitler spends the autumn consolidating the party and revamping the SA in light of the weakness made evident by the Stennes revolt. Hitler knows he needs Röhm, and Röhm knows he needs Hitler. Goebbels and Goring, meanwhile, feeling threatened by Röhm's position next to Hitler, cleverly acquire some "love letters" which the homosexual Röhm has written. These are then published in the newspapers. Röhm could have been destroyed by events, but he is not. Hitler comes to his rescue with a statement that includes these words; "the SA is not a moral institution for the education of well-to-do-daughters, but an association of rough fighters".

▲ *Josef Goebbels, propaganda supremo of the Nazi Party, was a philanderer who was nicknamed "the cripple" by his enemies.*

OCTOBER 17–18, 1931

SA, *RALLY AT BRUNSWICK*

On Saturday and Sunday October 17-18, *SA-Gruppe Nord*, under the leadership of *SA-Gruppenführer* Victor Lutze, hosts a rally at Brunswick, a town of 100,00 about 64km (40 miles) east of Hanover and about 240km (150 miles) west of Berlin. Some 104,000 members of the SA, SS, NSKK (*National Sozialistisches Kraftfahrer Korps* – National Socialist Motor Corps) and the Hitler Youth take part in a "token mobilization" of Nazi strength. Brunswick is the only state where the Nazis hold office and are allowed to wear uniform in public. There, just 10 months after Röhm's return, Hitler receives the salute. The parade takes six hours to pass the podium. He seems to sense that this is the "true beginning" of his awesome power.

It was at this assembly, which followed closely on the heels of the Stennes *Putsch*, that Hitler gained in public the assurance of the SA rank and file of its unqualified support for his leadership. Despite earlier revolts by certain elements in previous months, it never again wavered from that loyalty, the Röhm bloody weekend not withstanding. Hitler awarded the name *Horst Wessel* to *SA-Standarten* 5 Berlin, consecrated the SA *Deutschland Erwache* standard *Danzig*, and authorized the

creation of 23 other new standards, thus expanding the SA, and recognized the Motor-SA and NSKK. Lutze gained a reputation as a totally loyal party member and Hitler did not forget this act of loyalty in 1934, when he named Lutze to replace the executed Röhm.

In the disturbances that followed the rally two people were killed and some 50 or 60 more wounded.

NOVEMBER 1931

ESPIONAGE, *BOXHEIM PAPERS*

A Nazi group in Hesse under Werner Best, a Rhineland law student who was imprisoned by the French during their occupation of the Ruhr and who subsequently became a legal advisor to the Nazi Party, has drawn up plans to deal with the contingency of a communist revolution in Germany. The so-

▼ *By the early 1930s Hitler had created a cult of admiration around himself, which was particularly strong among the youth.*

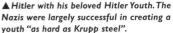

▲ *Hitler with his beloved Hitler Youth. The Nazis were largely successful in creating a youth "as hard as Krupp steel".*

called Boxheim Papers have been seized by the state and subsequently become known by the name of the house where the meetings were held: Boxheimer Hof. The plans contain a proclamation to be issued by the SA and emergency decrees which a provisional Nazi government would make, including the immediate execution of anyone resisting or failing to cooperate or found with weapons. Private property rights would be suspended, interest debts annulled, work made compulsory without reward, while people would be fed through public kitchens and issued with food ration cards. There would be courts martial under Nazi presidents. The discovery of the documents has resulted in a public scandal and Hitler has been forced to disavow the Boxheim Papers, assuring Rhineland industrialists that he would take power only by legal means.

This scandal did not do any lasting harm to the Nazis's election hopes. In 1932 there were four separate elections. The first two polls were for the presidency in which Hitler, though losing to Hindenburg, received 30.1 percent of the total vote in the first election and 36.8 percent in the second. The affair also did little to harm Best's rise: he was made Polie Commissioner of Hesse in 1933 and State Governor in July.

JUNE 1932

LAW AND ORDER, *SA BANNED*

Chancellor Brüning, feeling confident enough to take measures against the Nazis, orders the disbandment of the SA and SS under a decree which prohibits uniformed political organizations (when Brüning's decree came into effect, the SS had grown to 30,000 members or approximately 10 percent of the SA's strength). This is followed by police swoops to ensure the ban is respected. In some SA quarters there is an inclination to stand and fight, but Hitler immediately overrules this sentiment. People other than the Nazis are involved, however, and many Rightist and Nationalist groups had their own uniforms seized, including some like the *Stahlhelm* which were ostensibly veterans' organizations. Brüning may therefore have made a grave mistake, for the decree may be interpreted as an insult to those who have fought for Germany.

JULY 31, 1932

POLITICS, *REICHSTAG ELECTIONS*

The Nazi Party is very successful in the *Reichstag* elections of July 1932. Travelling by aeroplane, Hitler has appeared in the last two weeks of the campaign in almost 50 cities - "Hitler over Germany" - a ploy that has reaped dividends. In Berlin 120,000 people heard him in the Grünewald Stadium, while 100,000 more listened via loudspeakers outside. When the polls close, 13,732,779 Germans have voted for him, giving the NSDAP 230 *Reichstag* members. Hitler immediately demands the chancellorship and passage of an Enabling Act to run Germany by decree, in effect a dictatorship, but he is turned down on both counts by President Hindenburg.

▲ The SS Long Service Cross, awarded to SS members for 4, 8, 12 and 25 years of service (military service counted as double).

The last of the year's elections was held on November 6 and resulted in a setback. In it the party lost two million votes and was reduced to 196 seats, while the communists gained 750,000 votes and now had 100 seats. Even in alliance with the Nationalists, the Nazis could not command an overall majority.

NOVEMBER 17, 1932

POLITICS, *SCHLEICHER INTRIGUE*

General von Schleicher, chief military intriguer of the Weimar period and Minister of Defence, succeeds in organizing the downfall of Chancellor Papen's cabinet and thus his government. Informing Papen that the army and police would not defend his government, he stresses to Hindenburg that he should be chancellor. Hindenburg refuses, especially as he states he could obtain the support of Gregor Strasser and at least 60 Nazi *Reichstag* members to support his aims, and recalls Papen as chancellor. However, Hindenburg finally accepts that Schleicher has the support of the army and police forces, again dismisses Papen and now appoints Schleicher as chancellor.

He was to last as Chancellor for 57 days, and later stated that he was betrayed on each separate day.

▶ Honour Badge of the Technical Emergency Service, which under Hitler became a large emergency force.

DECEMBER 1932

POLITICS, *GERMANY*

The end of the year sees the political situation in Germany degenerate and take on the guise of near civil war. The socialists and the Communist Party field armed militia to battle the right-wing street fighters. The SA and SS reply with force and 10 SS men are killed with several hundred wounded during the violent street battles with the *Rötfrontkämpferbund*, or Red Front Fighters' Association. It suits the NSDAP's agenda to create the illusion that the country is on the slippery slope to all-out anarchy, especially with the crucial 1933 elections approaching, and that the party and its "valiant" street fighters hold the key to the political problems that grip Weimar Germany.

▶ *SS headquarters in Munich. Though the SS was smaller than the SA, it had a ruthless and determined head in Himmler.*

▼ *A Nazi Nuremberg rally in the early 1930s. The power of the party at this time can be judged by comparing this picture with the one on page 12.*

1933

The Nazis gained power via the ballot box, and some political dealings. But once in power Hitler quickly consolidated his control over the German state. New laws were introduced giving him dictatorial power, their passage made easier by the *Reichstag* fire in February. From then on, Nazi Germany became a centrally controlled totalitarian regime.

POLITICS, *GERMANY*

"The hour of the birth of the Third Reich"; Papen and Hitler agree on a coalition with Hitler as its head. Papen has pledged the support of the Rhineland industrialists in exchange for the vice-chancellorship, which Hitler has readily agreed to. Chancellor Schleicher fails to win over breakaway groups from the Nazis, such as that headed by Strasser, and is unable to keep control over the *Reichstag* parties. He resigns and President Hindenburg is persuaded to give Hitler the chancellorship, which is celebrated by Nazi parades in Berlin.

▼ *Chancellor Hitler and President Hindenburg. The latter had once vowed he would never make Hitler chancellor.*

40

Lubbe, but it is so convenient for the Nazis that they are suspected of complicity. On the eve of the arson attack on the Reichstag, for example, Rudolf Diels, Prussian State Police, reported to Hitler that the culprit, van der Lubbe was in custody and it was the work of a single demented pyromaniac. Hitler blamed the communists and burst out in fury: "This is a cunning plot! Every communist official must be shot. All communist deputies must be hanged this very night."

The police have quickly made some arrests: Göring, head of the Prussian State Police, has arrested 100 communist *Reichstag* deputies (the leader of the communists in the *Reichstag*, Ernst Torgler, has voluntarily surrendered himself to the police). Cynics are saying that it is a Nazi ploy to increase their popularity as defenders of the nation.

◀ The *Reichstag* burns in February 1933. This convenient event gave Hitler the excuse to strangle democracy in Germany.

JANUARY 30

NAZI PARTY, *BERLIN*

Hans E. Maikowski proudly heads his *Sturm* (Storm – an SA unit) during a parade at the Brandenburg Gate on this historic day. It isn't until the evening that *Sturm* 33 finally makes its way back to Charlottenburg. En route it is attacked by a mob of communists. During the bloody street-fighting Maikowski is severely wounded and taken to hospital. At midnight he dies, becoming the first martyr to the cause after the assumption of power by the NSDAP. Maikowski is given a lavish funeral, which takes place at the Charlottenburg Cathedral, and is buried in the Invaliden Friedhof.

FEBRUARY

GERMANY, *LEGAL*

Thirty-three decrees are published, including the banning of rival political meetings or publications and the dissolution of the Prussian parliament. Raids on Communist Party offices begin.

FEBRUARY 27

GERMANY, *ESPIONAGE*

The *Reichstag* Fire: the parliament building burns to the ground.

There are some mysteries concerning the Reichstag blaze. It was thought to be started by the Dutch ex-communist Marinus van der

▶ Ex-chancellor Franz von Papen, who persuaded Hindenburg to make Hitler chancellor in January 1933.

MARCH 1

GERMANY, *LEGAL*

Hitler is given emergency powers by presidential decree. Whereupon he issues a "Decree for the protection of people and State" which gives police powers to the SA and SS. Some 25,000 SA and 15,000 SS men have been issued with firearms and deployed as *Hilfspolizei* or auxiliary policemen. This also empowers the police presidents to take anyone into protective custody considered to be a political opponent in the broadest sense of the term. The *Reichstag* fire, the "affront to democracy perpetrated by communists", permits Hitler to flex his political muscle and the party's left-wing protagonists begin to be unceremoniously ushered into prisons and makeshift unofficial camps or "wild man camps", so-called due to the lack of supervision and the frightful stories of brutality which comes from them. By the end of July 1933, it is estimated that there are nearly 27,000 people being held in protective custody.

MARCH 3

NAZI PARTY, *INDIVIDUALS*

Göring assures a Frankfurt audience: "I don't have to worry about justice, my mission is only to destroy and exterminate, nothing else." On the same day Hitler is busy bending the law so that he can deal "legally" with any opponents. He is slowly

but surely increasing his iron grip over Germany and her people.

MARCH 5

GERMANY, *ELECTIONS*

Reichstag elections; the Nazis win a working majority. The Nazis poll 17,277,180 votes out of a total of 39,343,300. This is an increase of 5.5 million votes since the last election but still less than a majority. However, with the help of the Nationalists the Nazis can add an additional 52 seats to their own 288, giving them a majority of 17. The Nazis set about filling local and state government posts with their supporters, while Göring declares that there is no longer any need for individual state governments. Using the state of emergency decree, the Nazis slowly take control of Germany with "planned terror".

◀ *Baldur von Schirach, Reich Youth Leader. Once the Nazis came to power he sought to re-educate youth in the spirit of Nazism.*

The procedure was simple but effective: local SA and SS groups would start violent protests and unrest, which would be followed by the appointment of Nazi Reich commissioners who would take over local governments in order to restore order. During this period suspects were rounded up and herded into abandoned army and police barracks, where they were beaten and tortured. They were then sent to camps, which later would become infamous as concentration camps. Those rounded up were mostly social democrats and communists, and of course Jews. Most of the first concentration camps sprung up near Berlin, though the one at Dachau was near Munich in the south.

When Hitler came to power in 1933, the most pressing economic problem was high unemployment (it totalled over five million in 1933). Those on the socialist side of the Nazi Party pushed for nationalization and state control. Hitler, however, had no intention of dismantling large industrial

machine. This will have two consequences: first, the consolidation of his dictatorship; second, the eradication of organizations with differing political views.

MARCH 17

NAZI PARTY, *ORGANIZATION*

With Hitler's coming to power in January 1933, he decided that he was in need of a Praetorian Guard. The state protection rendered by the *Reichswehr* or police elements cannot, in his eyes, be entirely replied upon. Europe is a hotbed of plot and coup which he himself had been party to, so the Fatherland itself must be seen as suspect. Without delay Hitler decrees that there be formed a new full-time armed SS unit whose primary role would be exclusively to escort him wherever he was in Germany. "Sepp" Dietrich, one of Hitler's closest associates, is entrusted with the formation of the unit. Dietrich undertakes the task with zeal. By March 17, 1933, the embryo of a new Headquarters Guard named the SS *Stabswache Berlin* was founded. It comprised 120 hand-picked volunteers, of whom some were former

▼ *"Sepp" Dietrich (centre), the commander of the SS* **Stabswache Berlin***, Hitler's bodyguard.*

members of the *Stosstrupp Adolf Hitler* and whose loyalty to the Führer was unswerving. They were garrisoned in the Alexander Barracks on Friedrichstrasse and lightly armed with rifles, bayonets and pistols.

Two months later the unit was reformed as the *SS Sonderkommando Zossen* and enlarged with three training companies. The terms of engagement for the unit were expanded and the unit could now be employed for armed police and anti-terrorist activities, as well as the guard duties it already undertook. There was another metamorphosis during the proceeding months when a further three companies were formed as the *SS Sonderkommando Jüterbog*. This was the beginning of a unit that would become one of the greatest fighting formations in the German armed forces: the *Leibstandarte*.

MARCH 21

POLITICS, *GERMANY*

The new National Socialist *Reichstag* opens in the Kroll Opera House after the *Reichstag* building itself had been burnt down. To their eternal credit, the German people still did not give Hitler a majority in the elections, which took place in the first week of March. By then the Nazis were beyond any constitutional refinement and any communist

▲ *Hitler, Germany's new chancellor, photographed in Berlin in March 1933. To his right stands Papen, to his left, Goebbels.*

enterprises that would be useful for his war economy. To reassure big business, Hitler brought into his government a former president of the Reichsbank and a brilliant economist, Hjalmar Schacht, to run the economy. Nazi economic theory was slender and therefore Hitler turned to Schacht, who had resigned in 1930 in protest at reparation repayments and turned to the Nazis. "I desire a great and strong Germany and to achieve it I would enter an alliance with the Devil," Schacht exclaimed.

MARCH 12

NAZI PARTY, *IDEOLOGY*

Hitler speaks on *Gleichschaltung*, "the Co-ordination of the Political Will". Hitler is determined to fuse every element of German national life into the Nazi social

against malicious gossip. Finally, the setting up of a special court, the "People's Court", is approved. This is set up in Berlin to deliver quick verdicts for accused traitors of the Third Reich, though impartiality appears well down the list.

MARCH 22

GERMANY, *LEGAL*

Enabling Law is passed, giving special powers to Chancellor Hitler for four years. In essence the law provides the constitutional foundation for dictatorship. It gives the Nazis the right to pass laws without the consent of the *Reichstag*, to deviate from the constitution, to conclude treaties with foreign powers, and to place the right of issuing a law into the hands of the chancellor. Hitler said in 1932: "Once we have power, we will never surrender it unless we are carried out of our offices as corpses." It appears he means to honour his chilling pledge. The fact that the communists have already been eliminated from the *Reichstag* means the passing of the law is a mere formality.

MARCH 23

POLITICS, *REICHSTAG*

The surviving deputies to the *Reichstag* attend the Kroll Opera House to sanction an Enabling Bill to give Hitler supreme, untrammelled power. To make sure that all deputies have a rough grasp of the way they are expected to vote, the building has been surrounded and packed inside and out with ranks of SA and SS, who keep up a menacing chant demanding blood if the bill does not go through. With amazing courage, Otto Wels, leader of the Social Democratic Party, rises to oppose the bill, although he is alone and defenceless and the baying of the

and social democrat deputies who turned up for duty at the Kroll Opera House were simply arrested. Once they were out of the way, the Nazis and their allies had the necessary two-thirds majority to effect major constitutional change. Only one thing still commanded Hitler's respect: the German Army and its loyalty to Hindenburg.

Before opening the new *Reichstag* session Hitler lays on a service in the garrison church at Potsdam, shrine of the old Prussian Army, which is attended by the Brownshirts, Nazi deputies and high-ranking officers of the Kaiser's regime in a show of continuity between the old and new nationalist ideas. As a climax to this display Hitler makes an obsequious tribute to Hindenburg to keep the old

▲ *An early photograph of the inmates of Dachau concentration camp. The camp was filled with communists and Jews.*

soldier content. He then speeds back to Berlin to start the business of dealing with his remaining lesser opponents.

MARCH 21

POLITICS, *REICHSTAG*

The Nazi-controlled *Reichstag* opens. Decrees are passed on a general amnesty for all Nazis who committed offences during the so-called "struggle". On the other hand, punitive measures are introduced

▼ *Camp guards at Dachau. In 1933 there was little discipline among the guards, who committed many atrocities.*

stormtroopers could be clearly heard in the chamber. The last pretences are abandoned, as Hitler leaps to his feet and screams at Wels that his death-knell had sounded. The bill is then hurriedly passed by an enormous majority. From this moment on Germany is a dictatorship.

MARCH 29

GERMANY, *LEGAL*

Lex van der Lubbe gives retrospective sanction to execution by hanging for arson.

MARCH 31

GERMANY, *LEGAL*

First Coordination Law of States and Reich establishes new state and local assemblies, with membership in the same proportions as the *Reichstag* parties, i.e. a Nazi majority.

Thousands are rounded up and put into camps by police and the "auxiliary police", the SA. Dachau concentration camp is opened. SA troops in all states force state government resignations; the Bavarian state government is suppressed. Epp is appointed new Nazi Governor in Bavaria with Himmler as State Police President.

APRIL 1

GERMANY, *LEGAL*

Official boycott of Jewish shops and professional men begins. The attitude of the German population towards the Jews is curious. Though Nazi propaganda would have the world believe that every German hates the Jews, this is not the case. It is true that in places where National Socialism was able to attach itself to deeply rooted anti-Semitic traditions, the racially based anti-Semitism of the Nazis has found receptive ears. However, the mass of the population has not been induced into

▲ *Cuff band of the concentration camp guards. Hitler said of the camps: "Terror is the most effective instrument."*

actively supporting the persecution of the Jews. That said, the persecution of the Jews has not prompted any wide-scale popular criticism.

The Nazi Party has pledged to create a Germany in which Jews will be set apart from their fellow Germans and denied their place in German life and culture. Jews have been expelled from a number of smaller towns and forced to move to larger towns or cities, or emigrate. All but Nazi-controlled publications have been effectively suppressed.

The Law on the Reconstruction of the Professional Civil Services is introduced,

▼ *The Death's Head symbol, seen here on a concentration camp guard's sleeve insignia, became synonymous with Nazi terror.*

which makes no distinction between Reich, state or civil service cadres and giving transferability between each. All unqualified, disloyal or Jewish staff are to be dismissed (in the event, however, 90 percent of the civil service remained). Himmler is made Commander of the Bavarian Political Police.

APRIL 1

MILITARY, *NAVY*

The pocket battleships *Deutschland* was commissioned and the *Admiral Scheer* launched. *Deutschland* was one of three armoured ships - the so-called "pocket battleships" - laid down between 1928 and 1931. *Deutschland* was the first of the class, being launched in May 1931 and completed in April 1933. She was originally used as a seagoing training ship, to familiarize crews with her new technology. Designed as long-range commerce raiders, powerful enough to sink anything they could not outrun and fast enough to outrun anything they could not sink - except for the Royal Navy ships HMS *Hood*, *Renown* and *Repulse*. - and they often classed as "pocket battleships". Officially listed as *Panzerschiffe* ("armoured ships"), in reality they were raiding cruisers built to light cruiser standards and equipped with an exceptionally heavy main battery. They were built under a clause in the Treaty of Versailles that allowed Germany to build ships up to 10,605 tonnes (10,000 tons) with guns of up to 11in; this was intended to allow coast-defence battleships. Two further ships of this class were redesigned to become the "Scharnhorst" class in response to the French "Dunkerque" class. *Deutschland* varied in the style and arrangement of the superstructure. The Washington Treaty of 1921 left Germany quite limited in the amounts of ships that she could construct. Admiral Raeder had a vision of a fleet of ships that would tie up the Royal Navy and disrupt the sea line of communication for France and England, but this was not possible with the tonnage permitted by this treaty. There was only one solution to the problem – Germany would have to under-report the weights of her ships. Lying or not, in 1933 the *Deutschland*. was commissioned. She was underreported in her weight by at least 20 percent (reported at 12,294 tonnes [12,100 tons] but actually displacing 15,748 tonnes [15,500 tons]), but even this was a violation of the weights granted in the treaty. The French and British, the enforcers of this treaty, were not worried because they knew that the new French "Dunkerque" class and British ships like the HMS *Hood* could outgun and outrun this new class of German ship.

APRIL 7

GERMANY, *LEGAL*
Second Coordination Law appoints state governors.

APRIL 8

GERMANY, *LEGAL*
Law on the Reconstruction of the Professional Civil Service is introduced, making no distinction between Reich, state or local cadres, giving transferability between each.

APRIL 26

GERMANY, *POLICE*
A decree on the establishment of the *Geheime Staats Polizeiamt* (Gestapa), which was later renamed *Geheime Staats Polizei* (Gestapo), as a new department of the Prussian state police affiliated with the Minister of the Interior, to be headed by Diels. Göring is persuaded by his friend Diels that a secret police force was necessary to monitor the activities of the communists. The Gestapo becomes the political police of Nazi Germany.

The Gestapo ruthlessly eliminated opposition to the Nazis within Germany and its occupied territories and was responsible for the roundup of Jews throughout Europe for deportation to

extermination camps. Hermann Göring, Prussian minister of the interior, detached the political and espionage units from the regular Prussian police, filled their ranks with thousands of Nazis, and, on April 26, 1933, reorganized them under his personal command as the Gestapo. Simultaneously, Heinrich Himmler, head of the SS, together with his aide Reinhard Heydrich, similarly

reorganized the police of Bavaria and the remaining German states.

The Gestapo operated without restraints. It had the authority of "preventative arrest", and its actions were not subject to judicial appeal. Thousands of leftists, intellectuals, Jews, trade unionists, political clergy, and homosexuals simply disappeared into concentration camps after being arrested by the Gestapo. The political section could order prisoners to be murdered, tortured, or released. Together with the SS, the Gestapo managed the treatment of "inferior races," such as Jews and Gypsies. During World War II the Gestapo suppressed partisan activities in the occupied territories and carried out reprisals against civilians.

Gestapo members were included in the *Einsatzgruppen* (Special Action Squads), which were mobile death squads that followed the German army into Poland and Russia to kill Jews and other "undesirables." Bureau IV B4 of the Gestapo, under Adolf Eichmann, organized the deportation of millions of Jews from other occupied countries to death camps.

◀ *The badge of the German High Seas Fleet, which Hitler was determined to restore to its former greatness.*

MAY 2

GERMANY, *INDUSTRIAL RELATIONS*

All German Free Trade unions are dissolved, and their 5.5 million members incorporated into the newly formed German Labour Front, an affiliated organization of the NSDAP with virtually a parallel organizational structure. It is headed by Dr Robert Ley.

To weld German labour into a solid organization backing Hitler, Ley abolished the democratic trade unions and built up a powerful labour organization designed to facilitate German militarization and war preparations. He was also head of the *Bund der Auslanddeutsche* (Union of Germans Living Abroad).

MAY 6

NAZI PARTY, *IDEOLOGY*

Goebbels organizes a national "Burning of the Books". The Nazis begin an action against unwanted books. Many important literary works are also proscribed because their authors or subjects are considered subversive or "un-German".

Göebbels rationalizes the burnings by proclaiming: "Fellow students, German men and women! The age of extreme Jewish intellectualism has now ended, and the success of the German revolution has again given the German spirit the right of way.... You are doing the proper thing in

committing the evil spirit of the past to the flames.... This is a strong, great, symbolic act, an act that is to bear witness before all the world to the fact that the November Republic has disappeared. From these ashes there will arise a phoenix of a new spirit.... The past is lying in flames. The future will

▲ *The trappings of absolute power: the headquarters of Hermann Göring's air force, which was a secret in 1933.*

rise from the flames within our hearts ... Brightened by these flames our vow shall be: The Reich and the Nation and our Führer Adolf Hitler."

Hermann Göring summed up the Nazis' attitude to culture and art in his famous quip: "Whenever I hear the word 'culture', I reach for my revolver." Göring's attitude was echoed by most senior Nazis. Hitler hated the intelligentsia and all things intellectual, and seriously toyed with the idea of doing away with them once he was in power. After 1933, many German intellectuals saw the writing on the wall, especially those of Jewish descent, and emigrated. The list of those who fled says much for the strength of opposition to Nazism among German intellectuals, and this wave of emigration was a great loss for German culture: writers such as Thomas and Heinrich Mann, Arnold and Stefan Zweig, Franz Werfel and Jakob Wassermann; masters of the Bauhaus school such as Walter Gropius, Mies van der Rohe and Marcel Breuer; painters such as Max Beckmann, Oskar Kokoschka and Kurt Schwittens; film directors Fritz Sternberg and Fritz Lang; and actress Marlene

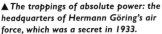

◀ *The pocket battleship* Deutschland. *The British and French were initially unconcerned about this class of ships.*

Dietrich. The loss of talented musicians and composers was particularly pronounced: Paul Hindemith, Otto Klemperer, Kurt Weill, Hanns Jelinek, Ernst Toch, Arnold Schönberg and Richard Tauber. Academics also left in their droves: Max Wertheimer, William Stern, Sigmund Freud, Paul Tillich, Ernst Bloch, Theodor Adorno, Ernst Cassirer, Kurt Goldstein, Erich Fromm, Fritz Reiche, Hans Bethe, Richard Courant, James Frank and Albert Einstein. Einstein's loss would be sorely felt when Germany embarked on its atomic weapons programme: it was Einstein's Theory of Relativity that was the basis of America's atom bomb dropped on Japan in August 1945. In total, some 2500 writers left Germany once the Nazis took power.

MAY 19

GERMANY, *INDUSTRIAL RELATIONS*
Establishment of Trustees of Labour. There are 13 departmental offices, each one headed by a Trustee of Labour. Their task is the "negotiation of work contracts between employer and labour".

MAY 20

GERMANY, *POLITICS*
Seizure of the assets of the Communist Party (KPD).

JUNE 1

GERMANY, *LEGAL*
First Law for the Reduction of Unemployment.

JUNE 9

GERMANY, *LEGAL*
Law on Payments Abroad.

JUNE 12

GERMANY, *LEGAL*
Law on Betraying the German Economy; notification of assets abroad.

JUNE 14

GERMANY, *LEGAL*
Law on the New Formation of the German Peasantry.

JUNE 22

GERMANY, *LEGAL*
Decree dissolving political parties: the Social Democrats.

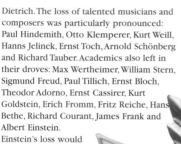

JUNE 27

GERMANY, *LEGAL*
Decrees dissolving political parties: DNVP.

JUNE 28

GERMANY, *LEGAL*
Decrees dissolving political parties: State Party. Theodor Eicke becomes Commandant of Dachau. He is brutal and dedicated to ensuring that the "enemies of Germany" are securely held in the camp.

JULY 4

GERMANY, *LEGAL*
Decrees dissolving political parties: DVP and Bavarian Party.

▶ *The leader of German women in Nazi Germany: Gertrud Scholtz-Klink. Women had little influence in the Third Reich.*

JULY 5

GERMANY, *LEGAL*
Decrees dissolving political parties: the Centre Party.

JULY 8

GERMANY, *TREATIES*
Concordat between Germany and the Vatican. Negotiated by the Catholic Franz von Papen, it conferred a

◀ *Part of the Nazis's drive to increase the birthrate – a badge awarded to mothers who produced babies.*

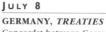

▲ Dr Robert Ley (seated in the front of the car next to the driver), the head of the German Labour Front.

◄ The reality of Nazi power: an SA man stands outside a Jewish shop in Berlin as the boycott of Jewish businesses begins.

certain legitimacy on the Nazi regime. Hitler sought to end Vatican support for the Catholic Centre Party while he proceeded to subordinate the churches and to corrupt Christianity into a state-centred form of neo-paganism. Pope Pius XI, like every other European statesmen after him, thought that he could appease and moderate the Nazis.

The Concordat gives Germans the right to practise religion and allows the church to administer itself. In return, Catholic priests are not to take part in politics. Some have charged that the Vatican, lured by guarantees for its schools and other institutions, has secured the Concordat by sacrificing the Centre Party, which had fought the *Kulturkampf* (Culture Battle). In fact, Pius XI does not believe that Catholic political action anywhere should serve as the primary means of defending church interests. Furthermore, it is clear from the

49

beginning of July that Hitler does not need the Concordat to remove the clergy from German politics.

JULY 14

GERMANY, *LEGAL*
Law against the Establishment of Parties is introduced.

JULY 15

GERMANY, *LEGAL*
Reich Regulations for the Corporate Reorganization of Agriculture. German agriculture is in dire straits, and under Minister of Agriculture Walter Darré the Nazis are making genuine efforts to improve the lot of German farmers.

AUGUST

NAZI PARTY, *INTERNAL POLITICS*
Röhm had always regarded the SA as his personal revolutionary army, but the power of the SA, conjoined with the ambitions of its leaders, were to consume it. Röhm's quest for personal power was not to Hitler's liking, and his concern over Röhm

was fuelled by the whisperings of Göring and Himmler. Himmler's objective was to eliminate the power of the SA, which had grown to be the largest of the Nazi formations, gathering considerable strength in the process. Hitler was looking to the future and decided to cast his lot with the generals of the army. Röhm had been aware of what was happening when he declared: "Anyone who thinks that the days of the SA are over must make up his mind that we are here and that we will remain."

AUGUST 31–SEPTEMBER 3

NAZI PARTY, *RALLIES*
A rally is held at Nuremberg which is called the *Parteitag des Siegers* or Victor's Party Rally. It marks the Nazi accession to power on January 31, 1933. At this rally Hitler formally recognizes the *Adolf Hitler SS Standart* and the dedication of the SS *Standarten* or regiments takes place. The *Adolf Hitler SS Standart* has been formed from *SS-Sonderkommando Zossen* and *SS-Sonderkommando Jüterbog*. A total of 785 men from these two units are present and

▲ *Young Germans take part in Goebbels' burning of literature considered by the Nazis to be "un-German".*

on the last day a salutary round is fired by a *Reichswehr* battery. *Grüppenführer* "Sepp" Dietrich receives the banner with the name *Adolf Hitler* on the box that surmounts it. The two *Sonderkommandos* have been granted the honour and right to wear the name *Adolf Hitler* on a cuff band on the left arm. The merged formation will later be renamed the *Leibstandarte-SS Adolf Hitler* or LSSAH.

SEPTEMBER

GERMANY, *RELIEF AGENCIES*
First *Winterhilfe* Campaign; the Help for the Winter campaign. It is an enormous charity for the better-off to help their poorer national and racial comrades. Collections are made by SA men on the streets, and though most people give voluntarily and a great deal of work is carried out, the threat of violence is used to back up donations.

SEPTEMBER 13

GERMANY, *LEGAL*

Law on Reich Food Costs. The Reich Food Estate will guarantee profitable prices for German farmers in an effort to make Germany self-sufficient in agricultural production.

SEPTEMBER 22

GERMANY, *CULTURE*

The tightening of control on the arts begins with a law that establishes a National Chamber of Culture, or *Reichskulturkammer*, which is a nationwide organization embracing all those whose professional remuneration comes from art, music, the theatre, press, radio, literature or the cinema. Its purpose is to act as a coordinating point for the various cultural and culturally related arts, with the ultimate control of the chamber vesting in the minister of propaganda, Dr Joseph Goebbels. The chamber consists of seven sub-elements: architecture and sculpting arts, music, theatre, literature, press, film and radio, with a president at the head of each element. Each chamber president has the power to regulate his respective field. Membership is compulsory for any person engaged in these fields.

OCTOBER

GERMANY, *TREATIES*

Hitler takes Germany out of the League of Nations. Germany has been a member of the league since 1925, but it has always been regarded by many nationalists as an agency of the Allied powers and an enforcer of the hated Treaty of Versailles.

OCTOBER 1

GERMANY, *LEGAL*

Reich Entailed Law stabilizes small firms.

OCTOBER 14

GERMANY, *PARLIAMENT*

The *Reichstag* is dissolved.

OCTOBER 27

GERMANY, *LEISURE*

On a visit to Italy in 1929 Dr Robert Ley had been impressed by the fascist *Dopolavoro* (After Work) Organization, and on his return plans for a German equivalent were formulated. It was launched at a joint Italian German ceremony at Koblenz, although a formal press announcement was not made until November 17, when it was referred to as *Nach der Arbeit*. Shortly thereafter the name was changed to "Strength through Joy". It was the opportunity to travel which caught the public imagination. To visit theatres, to own a car, or to holiday abroad were, before Hitler, a daydream for the average German worker. Ley was determined to make them a reality, and to a large extent he succeeded. Although principally associated with leisure and travel, the organization also included a "Beauty at Work" office under a then little-known architect called Albert Speer. The function of this office was to enhance the interiors and exteriors of workplaces, improve their amenities, ensure good ventilation and adequate light, and generally make the factory or workplace a more pleasant and agreeable place in which to work.

NOVEMBER 9

NAZI PARTY, *RALLIES*

The ceremonial consecration of the *Leibstandarte SS Adolf Hitler* is formalized in front of the Feldherrnhalle on the occasion of the Commemoration of the Munich *Putsch*. Here, the members of the *Leibstandarte* take a personal oath of allegiance to Hitler. This dispels any thoughts that these men are anything but his personal cohort. Himmler theoretically has control over the unit, however in reality the ultimate director of its function is Hitler, conjoined with the fact of his personal friendship with the Guard Commander, "Sepp" Dietrich, assumes an independence within the SS organization for the *Leibstandarte* that no other unit enjoys. This led Himmler to complain that it was "a complete law unto itself." Dietrich has scant regard for Himmler, addresses him on equal terms and is often engaged in arguments with him. The rivalry between the two men and the regard the officers of the *Leibstandarte* have for their commander can best be summed up by the gift he received on the occasion of his 50th birthday. A collection had been made among the officers so that an honour sword could be presented in the name of the entire officer corps. The gift was made by *Untersturmführers* Brohl and Peiper, and on the blade were the 105 names of the men. After wearing it during the Olympic Games in Berlin, Himmler forbade Dietrich from wearing the unofficial sword. The unruly Dietrich obviously upstaged the "Boss" and the officer corps had acted without obtaining Himmler's permission. This

amounted to insubordination that was too much to bear.

NOVEMBER 10

ARMED FORCES, *AIR FORCE*

When Hitler came to power in 1933 he introduced the *Deutscher Luftsport-Verband.* This organization is to stimulate air-minded young men. The club offers its members, most of whom have been in the armed forces, the active disciplined life for which they yearned, to such an extent that on November 10, 1933 Hitler introduces for the DLV a special uniform with rank and trade insignia. Under the direction of this organization the members will learn the three main aeronautical skills: ballooning, glider and powered flight.

Previously the *Reichswehr*, fearing that it was being left behind in its capacity to defend itself, secretly negotiated with the Red Army early in 1923 and finally signed

▼ *The* **Leibstandarte,** *Hitler's bodyguard, on parade in Berlin in 1933. They were the* **Führer's Praetorian Guard.**

▲ *Disgruntled SA men in 1933. Röhm's SA wanted more from the Nazi takeover of power than Hitler was prepared to give.*

an agreement in April 1925, which made the Lipezk Airfield in Russia available for German military training. In 1926, besides the fighter pilot training that was already underway, observer training began. Added to this, a special unit for testing new aircraft and weapons was also included. Between 1925 and 1933 approximately 120 officers returned from this flying school in Russia, being fully trained as fighter pilots.

Now Hitler has abandoned the school at Lipezk and relies on the DLV to train the new personnel of his clandestine *Luftwaffe* (Air Force).

NOVEMBER 12

GERMANY, *ELECTIONS*

A national referendum is held, in which 95 percent of the electorate approve Nazi policy. This vote is the culmination of the Nazis' work throughout the 1920s and early 1930s. Though the Nazis have undoubtedly

played on anti-Semitic feelings, scare-mongering and "stab-in-the-back" theories, they have also made expert use of newspapers, the radio and mass demonstrations of power. The *Kraft durch Freude* (Strength through Joy) movement is founded. Cardinal Faulhaber speaks out against Nazi anti-Christianity. Old *Freikorps* units are given a ceremonial dismissal parade by a grateful regime.

DECEMBER

GERMANY, *LEGAL*

Law to Secure Unity of Party and Reich. End of the *Reichstag* Fire trial. Only van der Lubbe is found guilty. This semi-blind, simple Dutch youth is sentenced to death by beheading to show the world that old German traditions were being brought back to the Third Reich.

In retrospect 1933 was one of the most successful years in the history of the Third Reich. The *Reichstag* fire of February 27 had provided Hitler with the pretext to begin consolidating the foundations of an authoritarian one-party state, and the "enabling laws" forced through the *Reichstag* legalized intimidatory tactics and suspended civil rights in Germany.

The extraordinary "achievement" of the Nazis compared with other fascist and authoritarian regimes of the period was the speed with which they eliminated opposition. Within 18 months of coming to power, for example, they had erased all forms of political opposition by successfully preventing their opponents from organizing collectively. Within six months political opponents had been rounded-up, incarcerated and outlawed.

However, the reality of Nazi rhetoric soon became apparent as political opponents disappeared into concentration camps, and the quality of life of Jews deteriorated rapidly. These things obviously did not concern Hitler and the Nazi leadership. What did concern them, however, was the attitude of Ernst Röhm and his SA. The two million Brownshirts represented a possible alternative power base, and this issue would have to be addressed. It would be, in 1934.

▼ *German agricultural workers. The Nazis made great effort to alleviate the poor state of German agriculture.*

1934

The tensions between the SA leadership and Hitler exploded in 1934. Ernst Röhm, believing that the Nazi revolution should be taken a step further, began to talk of the SA replacing the army. Hitler, however, now firmly in power, did not want to alienate the army or the conservative élites that were backing him. Egged on by other senior Nazis, the Führer decided to eradicate the SA threat. The result was the Night of the Long Knives, during which the senior leadership of the SA, including Röhm, was killed.

FEBRUARY 3

NAZI PARTY, SA

In a clear attempt to strengthen his hold on the veteran membership, Röhm issues an order authorizing all SA as well as SS leaders and subordinates who were members prior to December 31, 1931, and still members, to receive and wear a specially inscribed Honour Dagger. Röhm's dedication is inscribed on the reverse of the blade. The inscription *In herzlicher freundschaft Ernst Röhm*, "in cordial comradeship Ernst Röhm", was acid etched onto the blade from a template bearing Röhm's own handwriting. A total of 135,860 daggers are awarded, of which the SS receives 9900.

Röhm states "The SA and SS will not tolerate the German revolution going to sleep or betrayed at the halfway stage by

▼ *An imge of more harmonious times –*
Ernst Röhm, SA leader (left) with "Sepp"
Dietrich, SS Leibstandarte commander.

MARCH

GERMANY, *INDIVIDUALS*
Ex-Chancellor Brüning leaves Germany, for safety, settling in the USA. As a politician who opposed the Enabling Act, he has been at risk from arrest or violence from the Nazis for some time.

APRIL

NAZI PARTY, *SS*
Himmler becomes Inspector of the Prussian Gestapo and Heydrich heads the Gestapo.

JUNE 1

ARMED FORCES, *NAVY*
The pocket battleship *Admiral Graf Spee* is launched.

JUNE 5

NAZI PARTY, *SA*
Röhm is summoned to a private conference with Hitler which results in a month-long leave for the whole of the SA in July.

▼ *Hitler with the bullet-scarred Röhm. The Führer was quite fond of the SA leader, and went ahead with the purge reluctantly.*

▲ *SS supremo Heinrich Himmler, who was outraged by the SA's sedition and disgusted by Röhm's homosexuality.*

non-combatants." He further assures his SA: "You won't make a revolutionary army out of the old Prussian NCOs ...You only get the opportunity once to make something new and big and that'll help us lift the world off its hinges."

Röhm once again begins to make plans to merge the SA with the *Reichswehr* to form a "people's army" and also continues talking about a second National Socialist revolution. The party leadership clearly does not approve of these ideas, not least due to the fact that Hitler needs the support of the *Reichswehr*.

FEBRUARY 20

NAZI PARTY, *SA*
Röhm gives a speech in which he claims that the SA is the true army of National Socialism, that the regular army should be relegated to a training organization and that the Ministry of Defence should be reorganized. The inferences are unequivocal; this is a treasonable statement aimed at the Nazi Party and the German Army. Röhm holds the allegiance of over three million SA members. Things are moving to a head between Röhm and the Nazi hierarchy.

KEY MOMENTS

Night of the Long Knives

The killing of Röhm and the emasculation of the SA was prompted by such senior Nazis as Himmler, Göring and Goebbels, who were united in their dislike of Röhm. Hitler to the end tried to reach an accommodation with the SA leader, but to no avail. The army was also delighted that the SA would no longer be a threat to its position as sole bearer of the nation's arms, and was grateful to Hitler for dealing with the SA. However, just over a month later the army had a new master, when Hitler, following Hindenburg's death, became supreme commander of the armed forces. All German soldiers henceforth had to swear an oath of allegiance to him: "I swear before God this sacred oath: I will render unconditional obedience to Adolf Hitler, the Führer of the German nation and people, Supreme Commander of the armed forces, and will be ready as a brave soldier to risk my life at any time for this oath." In this way the army had been outman-oeuvred by Hitler, who had deftly taken advantage of the vacuum left by the death of Hindenburg and the army's gratitude over the Röhm Purge.

JUNE 14

GERMANY, *INTERNATIONAL RELATIONS*

German diplomats arrange a meeting between Hitler and Italian dictator Mussolini in Venice. Hitler stated in his writings from *Mein Kampf* "that it would be an advantage for Germany to improve relations with Italy in the future". The pursuit of this policy has not been possible after his coming to power due to one major stumbling block: Hitler's own birthplace, Austria.

The peacemakers of 1919 had granted this small country which was the last fragment of the Hapsburg Empire to Italy to be her guarantee of security – it served as a buffer zone. For this reason Italy could not allow Austria to be absorbed into Germany or fall under German control. In 1934, civil war broke out between the Austrian Clericals and the Austrian Socialists. These hostilities in turn stirred up the Austrian Nazis. German diplomats hope that Hitler will not actively push the Austrian question at this meeting between him and Mussolini. They believe that by meeting Mussolini face to face Hitler can be pushed into concessions. At this meeting

▼ *Röhm at an SA rally. The man mounted next to him is his lover, who was also shot during the Night of the Long Knives.*

military intelligence organization, claims to have secret SA orders to stage a *coup d'état*. The army has cancelled all leave.

JUNE 26

NAZI PARTY, *SA*

Himmler warns senior SS and SD (*Sicher-heitsdienst* – the party's intelligence and security body) officers of an impending SA revolt.

JUNE 27

NAZI PARTY, *SA*

"Sepp" Dietrich, commanding the SS Guard in Berlin, goes to army headquarters and is given extra weapons and transport for his men. A rumour spreads that the SA plans to kill the army old guard.

JUNE 28

NAZI PARTY, *SA*

Hitler travels from Berlin to Essen to attend the wedding of the local *Gauleiter* Terboven.

JUNE 29

NAZI PARTY, *SA*

The *Völkischer Beobachter* prints an article by Minister of Defence Blomberg pledging loyalty to Hitler and asking for curbs on the

▲ *Minister of Defence General Werner von Blomberg, who ordered that the army take an oath of allegiance to Hitler.*

Hitler and Mussolini pronounce their mutual dislike of France and the Soviet Union and Hitler renounces any desire to annex Austria. The *Duce* requests that the Austrian Nazis drop their campaign, and in return Dollfuss, the Clerical Chancellor, will treat them more sympathetically.

JUNE 20

NAZI PARTY, *SA*

The meeting between Hitler and Röhm seems to have done little to ease tensions. A shot fired at Hitler wounds Himmler; it is thought to have been fired by an SA escort.

JUNE 25

NAZI PARTY, *SA*

The "League of German Officers" disowns Röhm and expels him. The *Abwehr*, the

▶ *Hermann Göring directed operations from Berlin during the Röhm Purge. Like other Nazis, he disliked Röhm intensely.*

JUNE 30

SA. Hitler visits Labour Camps and goes on
to Bad Godesberg near Bonn, on the Rhine,
where he is joined by Goebbels. Göring,
meanwhile, mobilizes his Berlin police and
SS units. The SA in Munich have been
ordered out aimlessly on the streets by
anonymous notes – the local *Gauleiter*
tells Hitler this is proof of the SA's
disloyalty.

JUNE 30

NAZI PARTY, *RÖHM PURGE*
Hitler accepts an invitation to attend a
conference of SA high leaders at the
Vierjahreszeiten Hotel in Bad Weissee,
hosted by Röhm. Hitler drives to Bad
Weissee where Röhm and other SA men
are staying at the hotel. But then Hitler
flies at dawn to Munich with Goebbels,
Dietrich and Lutze of the SA. The Führer is
in a highly volatile state, ranting and
making threats. He orders Schmidt and
Schneidhubber, leading SA officers, to be
sent to Stadelheim jail. The Munich
Gauleiter is given lists of SA men and
others in Bavaria to arrest. He orders them
all to Stadelheim, some 200 of them,
except for Heines, the SA commander of
Silesia, who is found in bed with a man and
is shot immediately. Goebbels now sends a
codeword *Colibri* to Berlin for action. SA
leaders in Berlin are taken to the army
cadet school at Licherfelde and shot
immediately. Murders of hundreds thought
to be dangerous to the Nazis take place,
including ex-Chancellor von Schleicher.
Hitler prepares announcements from the
Brown House in Munich and flies back to
Berlin. Röhm is still alive, but the Night of
the Long Knives is over.

JULY 2

NAZI PARTY, *RÖHM PURGE*
Röhm is shot after refusing to take his own
life. In recognition of the part Eicke played

▲ *Italian Fascist dictator Mussolini moved troops towards the Austrian border to halt German designs on Austria.*

▼ *The cuff band of one of Theodor Eicke's newly created **SS-Totenkopfverbände** battalions – Thüringen.*

in the Night of the Long Knives, Himmler appoints him Inspector of Concentration Camps and head of the *SS-Totenkopf-verbände*. As a direct result of the Röhm *Putsch* most of the unofficial camps or "wild man camps" are closed. The remaining SA camps are removed from the jurisdiction of the civil authorities and taken over by the SS. The first full-time SS *Konzentrationslager*, concentration camp, unit was recruited from members of the *Allgemeine-SS* (General SS – the overall SS body) and is placed entirely under the overall command of the SS district south, who makes it a depository for its unwanted personnel in its ranks. The conditions that the guards live under are little better than the inmates.

Eicke improved conditions, lifted the morale and discipline of his men and formulated service regulations for both guards and prisoners which remained virtually unchanged until the end of the war. With his new inspectorate firmly established at Oranienburg, near Berlin, Eicke reorganized and enlarged the *SS-Totenkopfverbände* into five numbered *Sturmbanne* or battalions: I *Oberbayern*, II *Elbe*, III *Sachsen*, IV *Ostfriesland* and V *Thüringen*.

JULY 4

NAZI PARTY, *SS*
Three days after the SS has successfully carried out the purge of Röhm and his supporters, Himmler personally presents specially dedicated SS Honour daggers to 200 of the major participants in the action. The dagger follows the same pattern as the dagger given out by Röhm, but with Himmler's name replacing Röhm's and the inscription being in Himmler's hand writing. This was his final stamp of authority on the proceedings.

JULY 14

GERMANY, *LEGAL*
A law is issued legitimizing all the killings that took place during the Night of the Long Knives. Hitler makes a speech in the *Reichstag* explaining and justifying the affair, claiming that only 19 senior and 42 other SA men had been shot, while 13 had been shot resisting arrest and three had committed suicide (other estimates put the number of dead at 1000). The SS is now formally separated from the SA.

▶ *General Werner Freiherr von Fritsch was appointed the commander of the Germany Army in 1934.*

JULY 25

AUSTRIA, *POLITICS*
Hitler has done nothing to fulfil Mussolini's demands. The Nazis of Vienna occupy the Chancellery, murder Dollfuss and attempt to seize power, all with Hitler's support. At this critical moment Mussolini makes his first major bid as an international leader. He mobilizes Italy's crack mountain regiments in the mountain gorges leading to the Brenner Pass, threatening to beat any German force into Austria if necessary. This gesture is sufficient to halt the German plans for the absorption of Austria into the Reich. It should be noted that Mussolini is very disappointed that the Western Powers have stood aside and failed to support Italy. He later remarked to his wife: "I expected more from our Western friends, Rachele. They've let me down. Their apathy could have been disastrous." Hitler can do nothing to help his Austrian adherents and stands helplessly by while Schuschnigg, successor to Dollfuss, restores order under Mussolini's protection.

AUGUST 2

GERMANY, *PERSONALITIES*
Field Marshal Paul von Hindenburg dies at Neudeck; the only barrier between Hitler

Heydrich

He was born in Halle, Saxony, on March 7, 1904, the son of the founder of the Halle Conservatory. He was a rounded individual, possessing exceptional intellectual ability, as well as being an accomplished sportsman. In 1922 he joined the navy as a cadet and was under the orders and tutelage of Canaris, but in April 1931, due to allegations of dishonourable conduct towards a young lady who declared that he had impregnated her, he was brought before an honour court, presided over by Canaris, which found him guilty and dismissed him from the service. He became engaged to Lina von Osten and it was she who was to convert him to Nazism, and he joined the NSDAP in 1931. Lina enlisted the help of Frederick Karl von Eberstein to bring him to Himmler's notice, which he did on the June 14, 1931. Himmler found him appealing; the interview was short and he came straight to the point: "I want to set up a security and information service within the SS and I need a specialist. If you think you can do this management job, will you please write down on paper how you think you would tackle it, I'll give you 20 minutes."

His considerable organizational abilities, his total ruthlessness, the intensity of anti-Semitism and his Nordic appearance were self-evident. Himmler perhaps perceived the perverse view that Heydrich's fear of being considered Jewish, or partly Jewish, would be a means of controlling his talented associate. Whatever the truth in this, Heydrich rose quickly within the SS and became Protector of Bohemia and Moravia in September 1941. Tipped to be a future leader of the Third Reich, he was assassinated in 1942.

and unrestrained power disappears with Hindenburg's demise. Within three hours Goebbels announces that the office of president is abolished, and the fusing of the two roles of chancellor and president. The Führer of the NSDAP is now the Führer of Germany. Hitler also becomes commander of the armed forces.

SEPTEMBER

ARMED FORCES, *HIGH COMMAND*
General Werner Freiherr von Fritsch becomes chief of the High Command of the German Army.

SEPTEMBER 5–10

NAZI PARTY, *PARTY DAY*
Party Rally of Unity is held in Nuremberg. It is the first rally to last for over a week. The event is recorded by the film-maker Leni Riefenstahl, who makes a three-hour film entitled *Triumph of the Will.*

SEPTEMBER 24

NAZI PARTY, *WAFFEN-SS*
The chief of the three branches of the *Wehrmacht* (armed forces) are officially advised of the creation of the *SS-*

▲ *Hitler at Hindenburg's Memorial Chamber at Tannenberg in late 1934. Hitler now had absolute power.*

Verfügungstruppe (SS Militarized Troops) by means of a circular letter. It states that the *SS-Verfügungstruppe* is to be formed on a basis of three regiments modelled on infantry regiments of the army, each to contain three battalions, a mortar company and a motorcycle company, as well as being supported by a signals battalion. It also provides for three officer cadet schools. The formation will be under the personal command of the *Reichsführer-SS* except in time of war, when it will come under the control of the army.

OCTOBER 24

GERMANY, *LEGAL*
Hitler issues a decree establishing the scope and aims of the DAF, "The German Labour Front is the organization of all German professional and manual workers. It includes, in particular, the members of the former labour unions, of the unions of employees, and of the former associations of employers, which are united in the

▶ *Party Day at Nuremberg, 1934. Beside Hitler stand Himmler (left) and Victor Lutze (right), the new SA commander.*

Labour Front on a footing of complete equality. The aim of the Labour Front is the formation of a real national community of all Germans. The Labour Front has the duty of adjusting the legitimate interest of all parties in a manner conforming with National Socialist principles. Attached to the Labour Front is the organization 'Strength through Joy'. The Labour Front has the further duty of looking after the professional education of its adherents." Thus Dr Ley is given responsibility for the social, educational and political well-being of the entire German working population. Membership in the DAF is of two kinds, individual and corporate. Hitler charges *Reichsleiter* Dr Robert Ley, leader of the DAF and all affiliated labour organizations, with leading the German labour effort. The term *Reichsleiter* is the official designation for Hitler's position as leaders of the Third Reich. However, it is also applied to departmental heads, and is highly regarded by senior Nazis.

NOVEMBER 12

ARMED FORCES, *NAVY*

The pocket battleship *Admiral Scheer* is commissioned.

DECEMBER 14

SS, *WAFFEN-SS*

The *Leibstandarte*'s "first blooding" was over when the Röhm *Putsch* shooting finally ended on July 2. As a reward for their loyalty and involvement, Dietrich was promised by Hitler that he would see that the *Leibstandarte* became a fully equipped regiment. A rare honour was conferred on

the *Leibstandarte* in early October 1934 when it was decided that it should be fully motorized. At this time the *Reichswehr* in the main is still horse-drawn and this decision leads to whispers of discontent in military circles. The Political Readiness Detachments were to be reorganized into battalions and then amalgamated within the *Leibstandarte* under Himmler's orders. The *Leibstandarte* now consists of: one Staff, three motorized infantry battalions, one motorcycle company, one motor company, one signals platoon, one armoured car platoon, one regimental band.

1935

This year was a pivotal period for the Third Reich's relations with the rest of the world. Adolf Hitler announced he was reintroducing universal conscription, which was a repudiation of the hated Treaty of Versailles, and was warmly welcomed at home. In addition, as German troops marched into the Saar, he was determined to reintegrate those ethnic Germans who were living outside Germany back into the Reich. On the domestic front, more laws were introduced against Jews, who were becoming second-class citizens in their own country.

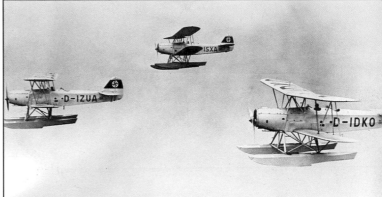

◀ *German troops march into the Saar in March following the plebiscite. It had been under League of Nations control.*

▲ *Heinkel He 42 floatplanes fly over the Fatherland, part of Hitler's new Luftwaffe and a breach of the Treaty of Versailles.*

JANUARY 13

GERMANY, *ELECTIONS*

The inhabitants of the Saar overwhelmingly vote to return to the Reich, which in 1919 was placed under League of Nations control for 15 years under the terms of the Treaty of Versailles. The Saar plebiscite is the instrument upon which Hitler founds his "return of the Saar to Germany" campaign.

JANUARY 20

NAZI PARTY, *SS*

The great SS Leaders' conference is held in Breslau. An interesting illustration of the British policy of appeasement has been given in a British newspaper report: "Germany's secret police are not always the sinister beings they are supposed to be", and goes on to note "the happy faces of the SS chief and his men as they arrive at the meeting".

FEBRUARY 26

ARMED FORCES, *AIR FORCE*

As the NSDAP begins to feel its political might, Hitler becomes more confident and announces the official formation of the new *Luftwaffe* (German Air Force). All the secrecy that has surrounded it is blown away, as if as a prelude to events that were to come, by the winds of war. The DLV is

◀ *Counting the votes in the Saar plebiscite, which overwhelmingly favoured returning to the Reich.*

disbanded and all its former members are encouraged to join the new *Nationalsozialistisches Fliegerkorps* (NSFK) that has been introduced in its place. In this manner the party brings together under its control all of the country's flying clubs into one organization, which in fact is paramilitary. The NSFK can thus operate with the fledgling *Luftwaffe* and both can grow and gather strength together.

MARCH 1

GERMANY, *THE SAAR*

The German Army, accompanied by armed SS units, marches into Saarbrücken.

MARCH 16

GERMANY, *TREATIES*

Adolf Hitler renounces the Treaty of Versailles' disarmament clauses. He makes his famous proclamation in which he repudiates the Treaty of Versailles and reintroduces military conscription, announcing this to the German parliament as a political statement, in direct contravention to the Treaty of Versailles, which expressly forbids a standing army of over 100,000 men. Parts of the speech are word-for-word those written seven years earlier by Defence Minister Groner. Hitler appears to have been the first frontline politician prepared to stand up and present it. He certainly expects some repercussions

from the Allies, but they are too engrossed with their own internal affairs and actually take very little no notice.

MARCH 16

SS, *WAFFEN-SS*

Hitler officially establishes the *SS-Verfügungstruppe*, although at this time it

▶ *Aircraft of the new **Luftwaffe** entertain the crowd at a mass Nazi rally, while antiaircraft guns let loose salvos of blanks.*

already consists of 11 battalions. The intention was always that the *SS-Verfügungstruppe* would benefit from the highest possible standards of training available. To facilitate this, two highly regarded former army officers, Paul Hausser and Felix Steiner, have been recruited to supervise training. Both were ultimately to become among the finest field commanders of the Waffen-SS.

APRIL

ARMED FORCES, *AIR FORCE*
The *Luftwaffe*'s existence is formally declared. The first German fighter squadron emerges under the command of Major Ritter von Greim, which bears the title *Jagdgeschwader Richthofen 2*.

The first Luftwaffe fighter school was established at the *Deutsche Verkehrsfliegeschule* (German Commercial Pilots School) at Schlelssheim, thus completing the formation of the new Luftwaffe and the *Nationasozialistische Flieger Korps*. Hitler's conjuring trick had worked; through skilful propaganda and deception an astonished world was convinced that he had been able to produce a force as technically involved as the *Luftwaffe* virtually out of a hat. This feat added to Hitler's international diplomatic aura and as the *Luftwaffe* gained experience in Spain later in the Civil War, the fear of this "terror machine", which was interlaced with the chivalry of

those knights of the air from the former days, often settled a diplomatic disagreement.

APRIL 10

NAZI PARTY, *PERSONALITIES*
Göring finally asks the actress Emmy Sonnemann to marry him. Emmy, in her youth, was a provincial actress who developed into a beautiful and gracious lady who captivated Göring. Congratulatory telegrams and presents pour in from all over the world, which includes jewels, oriental rugs and two paintings by Cranach. This is a union that meets with Hitler's approval. Their wedding is one of the "grandest social occasions" of the Third Reich that rivals any Hollywood spectacular. The ceremony is held in Berlin, where more than 30,000 members of the paramilitary organizations line the streets. Bells sound, and a formation of the latest German aircraft fly overhead as Hermann and Emmy drive in an open-topped

▼ *SS soldiers are inspected by Hitler. Paul Hausser and Felix Steiner were appointed as SS military instructors in March.*

▲ Joachim von Ribbentrop, the head of the Ribbentrop Bureau, which was set up as a rival to the German Foreign Office.

▲ Erich Raeder inspects men of his newly titled Kriegsmarine. The building of surface ships and submarines was increased in 1935.

Mercedes to the cathedral. Here, Hitler greets the bridal couple on the steps in front of the cathedral. The Reich Bishop, and armed forces chaplain, Ludwig Müller conducts the service, while Hitler undertakes the duties of best man. In all its riotous details, the proceedings are reported live on radio. The couple left the cathedral accompanied by an enormous band, which played the celebrated march from Lohengrin. The Görings saluted the large crowd that had gathered to view their marriage pageant.

MAY 21

ARMED FORCES, *NAVY*
The German Navy, formerly the *Reichsmarine*, is renamed *Kriegsmarine*.

▶ A prime example of garish vulgarity at its worst – the marriage of Hermann Göring to Emmy Sonnemann.

JUNE 18

NAZI PARTY, *RIBBENTROP BUREAU*
Under Hess' secretariat the Ribbentrop Bureau is established in the Wilhelm Strasse, provocatively across the street from the foreign office. This is in direct opposition to the ministry, with the avowed objective of proving Nazi methods are more effective than the foreign ministry's traditional policies. Careerists and journalists of dubious qualifications staff it.

Joachim von Ribbentrop, having served in 1934 as special commissioner for disarmament, seized his big chance when he was able to conclude the Anglo-German naval treaty in May 1935, unaided by foreign ministry officials, let alone having informed the ministry. The German object was to trap the British Government into an agreement to flout the naval restrictions of the Versailles Treaty. The British Government, with Anthony Eden the main negotiator, with what now seems a mixture of credulity and arrogance, fell into Ribbentrop's trap.

▲ *Hitler attacks the Treaty of Versailles, which he described as a "shame and an outrage" designed to destroy Germany.*

▲ *The Submariner's Badge, one of the awards given to the members of Hitler's new U-boat service.*

Neither the League of Nations nor Italy and France were consulted. The Anglo-German Naval Agreement was signed by Sir Samuel Hoare for Britain and by Special Envoy Joachim von Ribbentrop for Germany. His reputation, especially with Hitler, had now been definitely established. From *Reichsführer-SS* Himmler he received the honourary rank of *SS-Gruppenführer*. Hitler told Admiral Erich Raeder, Commander-in-Chief of the German Navy, that the day the agreement was signed was the happiest of his life. Raeder himself told his officers they could not have hoped for better conditions during the coming decade. He went on to say that the Agreement ruled out the possibility of Germany having to fight another war against Britain.

With this agreement, Hitler hoped to show that he had no desire to conduct war against Britain. Germany volunteered to restrict her maritime strength to 35 percent of that of the Royal Navy. However, submarines were considered as a separate case, and a 45 percent ratio was agreed. Parity in submarines was also agreed in principle, but in that event Germany would have to sacrifice tonnage in other categories, and Britain would have to approve the move.

JUNE 29

ARMED FORCES, *NAVY*
The first of the new submarines, *U-1*, is commissioned.

JULY 30

NAZI PARTY, *SS*
The *SS-Hauptamt*, or Main Office, is established to organize all branches of Himmler's SS.

SEPTEMBER 10–16

GERMANY, *LEGAL*
Party Rally of Freedom takes place. It is at the seventh Party Congress that the new Reich Citizen's Law, and Law for the Protection of German Blood and German Honour, which were known thereafter as the Nuremberg laws, are proclaimed. The laws define two degrees of humanity: the *Reichbürger*, the Citizen of Pure German Blood, and the *Staatsangehörige*, the subject of the state, i.e. Jews. Intermarriage between the two groups is strictly forbidden. The lot of Jews living in Germany is getting progressively worse, and many are leaving the country.

The Nazi swastika banner is made the official national flag.

SEPTEMBER 27

ARMED FORCES, *NAVY*
Karl Dönitz, who had previously been the commander of the light cruiser *Emden*, commissions the 1st U-boat Flotilla, called Flotilla *Weddigen*.

NOVEMBER

GERMANY, *LEGAL*
National Law of Citizenship comes into effect, which provides the definition of who is a Jew and *Mischling*, or mixed race. To be Aryan is a precondition for public appointments. First Decree of the Law for the Protection of German Blood and Honour (see above); marriages between Aryan and Jew or *Mischling* are forbidden.

NOVEMBER 2

ARMED FORCES, NAVY
The light cruiser *Nürnberg* is commissioned.

▶ *Berlin Jews who, by the National Law of Citizenship, became second-class citizens in their own country.*

NOVEMBER 15

GERMANY, *CULTURE*
Dr Goebbels has long controlled communications and the media, but the establishment of the National Senate of Culture offers him the opportunity to extend his control still further, and utilize various art forms to convey his National Socialist propaganda themes to a wider audience. The chamber is composed of individuals connected with the various arts or those who have assisted in the advancement of German culture and it is from these members that the Senate appointments are chosen.

It is doubtful that the membership of the Senate underwent very many changes during the proceeding years, which would have limited the membership to probably less than 300.

1936

JANUARY 6

ARMED FORCES, *NAVY*
The pocket battleship *Admiral Graf Spee* is commissioned.

FEBRUARY

SS, *GESTAPO*
The Gestapo is given national status with Heydrich as its head.

The Olympic Games gave Nazi Germany a chance to show the world that the Third Reich was a well-ordered, powerful society. For propaganda purposes measures against Jews were relaxed, and Berlin became the home of fraternal international friendship, albeit temporarily. However, away from the Olympics the Germans re-occupied the demilitarized Rhineland and began to channel military aid to the Franco's Nationalists fighting a civil war in Spain. As they did so, Great Britain and France, the major powers of Europe, did nothing but watch idly.

On October 5, 1931, Heydrich became a member of the SS and after a short spell at the Brown House, decided to set up the SD out of the view of enquiring eyes. Certainly from this time on Heydrich experienced a meteoric rise, becoming the second most powerful man in the RSHA. Heydrich's ancestry was in SS terms questionable, however; his father had been listed in the *Lexicon of Music and Musicians* under Heydrich's real name Süss, a clear

▼ *German troops move into the Rhineland in March 1936. They had orders to withdraw if opposed by the French.*

GERMANY, *TREATIES*

The Locarno Treaty is renounced. This was a non-aggression treaty signed in 1925 between Germany, France and Belgium. It recognized the demilitarization of the Rhineland as being permanent, with the post-Versailles Treaty borders of the three signatories being mutually accepted.

MARCH 7

GERMANY, *THE RHINELAND*

It had been another specification of the hated Treaty of Versailles that the Rhineland should be demilitarized. This turned the Rhineland into an unoccupied buffer zone between Germany and France. It comprised all German territory west of the Rhine and a 48km (30-mile) strip east of the river which included Köln, Düsseldorf and Bonn.

Hitler has been burning to send troops marching back into the Rhineland, both in order to assert that it is an indivisible part of his new Germany and to show his contempt for the Treaty of Versailles. His chance came in February 1936 when the nervous French ratified a treaty with the Soviet Union, a power which Hitler

indication that he was Jewish. However, investigations carried out into this later tended to indicate that Süss was in fact not Jewish. It is said that Heydrich had erased the name Sarah from his mother's gravestone because of its Jewish connotations.

FEBRUARY 4

SWITZERLAND, *NAZI PARTY*

Wilhelm Gustloff was born in Schwerin and went to live in Davos, Switzerland. He joined the *Ausland* Organization of the NSDAP in 1929 and went on to found his

▲ *Potsdam Naval Academy, which in 1936 was producing personnel to crew such ships as the new* **Admiral Graf Spee.**

own group in Davos in 1931. On this day David Frankfurter, a Jewish student, murders him in a Davos Hotel.

The body of Wilhelm Gustloff was brought back to his home town of Schwerin for burial. Gustloff is declared a martyr of the Nazi movement.

Frankfurter was found guilty and imprisoned, since there was no capital punishment in Switzerland.

▼ *Images to fool the world: well-fed concentration camp inmates receive their cigarette rations from the SS.*

GERMANY, *RAD*

The Labour Service, *Reichsarbeitsdienst* (RAD) is created. Its began in 1931 when Chancellor Heinrich Brüning authorized the formation of state-sponsored labour camps to help ease unemployment, the *Freiwillige Arbeitsdienst* (FAD). These camps were controlled by individual states and their use varied greatly across the country. When Hitler became chancellor he soon appointed Konstantin Hierl as Secretary of State for the Labour Service, the control of which was transferred from the states to the central government. The RAD was used for various tasks, mainly for reclaiming land for farming, helping with the harvests and construction roads, but also for various emergence relief projects.

claimed, at the time, was particularly detestable to his Nazi State because it is Asiatic and Bolshevik. In response to this threat, and against the advice of his more cautious associates, he orders his army to march into the Rhineland in an operation codenamed Winter Exercise on the morning of March 7. The new *Luftwaffe* fighters make their first public display, while the *Leibstandarte* provides the advance guard in the retaking of the Rhineland demilitary zone. Orders to the *Wehrmacht* are to retreat immediately should French forces move to oppose the occupation. That evening the Führer makes a gloating speech in the packed *Reichstag*.

The occupation of the Rhineland has been an enormous risk, which only a man as determined as Hitler would have taken. The German Army had only mustered one division to make the march into the Rhineland, and of that only three battalions had crossed the Rhine. If the worst had come to the worst, these puny forces could only have been strengthened by a few brigades, while the French, with their Polish and Czech allies, could have immediately mobilized 90 divisions and brought up reserves of 100 more.

To make the situation even more dangerous, the re-occupation of the Rhineland is not a mundane breach of the Treaty, but a *casus foederis*; that is to say that it virtually obliges France to declare war. However, despite the terrifying prospect of a humiliating climb-

▲ *General Francisco Franco (centre, waving), leader of Spain's Nationalists whom Hitler supported from 1936.*

down, Hitler was confident that the French would make no move against him and he has been proved right.

After this success Hitler's diplomacy began to take on a new edge. This operation was achieved without the predicted political and military consequences. In the ensuing crisis Hitler's resolute position split Great Britain and France diplomatically, ensuring the international acceptance of his fait accompli and giving him confidence to undertake his other expansionist desires.

MAY 8

SS, *CONCENTRATION CAMPS*

Reichsführer-SS Himmler conducts a group of Nazi Party officials around Dachau concentration camp. He is extremely proud of this new institution. The SS camp guards have formed as *Totenkopfverbände*, and currently number 3000 men.

JUNE 20

GERMANY, *SS*

By decree of the Führer the party post of *Reichsführer-SS*, held by Himmler, is formally combined with the newly established government post of Chief of the German Police. Himmler is steadily increasing his powers.

JULY 2

SS, *IDEOLOGY*

Himmler lays a wreath on the empty tomb of the Saxon King Heinrich I, who was nicknamed Henry the Fowler, on the occasion of the thousandth anniversary of his death. Himmler also participated in a solemn ceremony in the crypt of Quedlinburg Cathedral. He regards himself as the embodiment of this warrior king, who had defeated the Slavs and was founder of the German Reich.

JULY 17

SPAIN, *CIVIL WAR*

The Spanish Civil War begins. A revolt against the Spanish Republic breaks out in

▲ *Nationalist troops in Spain during the Civil War. Assistance given by Nazi aircraft was crucial to the Nationalist cause.*

▼ *One of the Junkers Ju 52 transport aircraft used to ferry Franco's men to the Spanish mainland in 1936.*

many of the military garrisons in Spanish Morocco. The revolt is led by General Mola and General Francisco Franco Bahamonde, who has been the governor of the Canary Islands until his dismissal from his post by the Popular Front Government. The revolt spreads rapidly throughout Spain, resulting in serious fighting between government troops and anti-government forces. For several years Spanish generals and other Nationalists agents had been in contact with, and successfully seeking support from, both Hitler and Mussolini. Hitler, who is wholly committed to oppose what he sees as the communist threat in Western Europe, makes the decision within a few days of the Nationalist rebellion to stand by General Franco and actively to support him in his "fight against Bolshevism". It will also be an excellent testing ground for Germany's new tanks and aircraft.

▼ *A model of the grand Berlin Olympic Stadium, plus the swimming pool, is shown to foreign and German guests.*

JULY 11

GERMAN, *TREATIES*

The "Gentleman's Agreement" between Hitler and Schuschnigg of Austria, in which Hitler recognizes the full sovereignty of Austria and in return Schuschnigg acknowledges that Austria is an "German State", agrees to admit members of the so-called "National Opposition" into his government and give amnesty to Nazi political prisoners in Austria. The final stumbling block regarding close German-Italian relations has eliminated by this agreement.

JULY 31

SPAIN, *GERMAN AID*

The first detachment of 85 German air and ground crew volunteers drawn from Sonderstab W, and travelling as a party of tourists, leaves Hamburg for Cadiz in the Woermann liner *Usamoro*. They take with them six Heinkel He 51 fighters. Simultaneously, 20 Junkers Ju 52 transport planes piloted by German airmen are

▲ *A clearly bored Führer watches an ice hockey game between Great Britain and Hungary at the Olympic Games.*

flown from Berlin to Morocco. It has been recognized that the most valuable service Germany can render General Franco at this stage is to help him ferry his Moorish troops into Spain. Under the command of Hauptmann Henke, 42 Luftwaffe pilots began to ferry Franco's Moroccan troops of the Spanish Foreign Legion from Tetuan to the aerodrome of Tablada at Seville. The first flight is made with 22 soldiers and their equipment on board each plane. On subsequent flights the number of passengers carried on each plane was increased to 30. Untiring, Henke and his pilots flew to and fro sometimes four or five times a day. By the beginning of September this small unit had transported from Africa to the mainland the astonishing number, for its time, of 8899 soldiers, 44 field guns, 90 machine guns and 137 tons of ammunition and equipment.

AUGUST

BERLIN, *OLYMPIC GAMES*

The Olympic Games open in Berlin. The occasion is used by the Nazis to present the success of National Socialism to the world.

▶ *Black athletes winning gold medals was not part of the Nazi plan. This is Mitte Woodruff, winner of the 800 metres.*

As such, it has resulted in a quietening of the anti-Semitic campaign. The opening ceremony is conducted by 40,000 SA men and a choir of 3000 sings *Deutschland* and the *Horst Wessel* song. On the first day of the games Hitler presents medals to the winners. German athletes do well in the games, winning the most gold, silver and bronze medals. However, Hitler declines to award any more medals when black American athletes start winning

▲ *The games were an ideal opportunity to show off Nazi militarism. Here, 2000 military musicians entertain the crowd.*

competitions, especially Jesse Owens, who wins four gold medals.

AUGUST 11

GREAT BRITAIN, *DIPLOMACY*

Joachim von Ribbentrop is appointed German Ambassador to the court of St

▲ *Great Britain's King George V, whom Ribbentrop greeted with a "Heil Hitler!" salute whilst Ambassador to Great Britain.*

James in London. He accepts his appointment as ambassador grudgingly, and shows his reluctance by taking up his post three months after his appointment. Once there he travels back and forth between London and Berlin so often that the British satirical magazine *Punch* calls him "the roving Aryan", while a highly placed official in the German Foreign Office suggests the possibility that von Ribbentrop regards his appointment to the Court of St James's as a part-time job. He is convinced, not without justification, that Foreign Minister Neurath is trying to get him out of the way with this position. It now becomes Ribbentrop's ambition to replace Neurath as Minister of Foreign Affairs.

Ribbentrop made the unforgivable mistake of greeting George V, King of England with "Heil Hitler" at a court reception in 1937. He was rejected by British society as a result, which deeply offended him. After this episode he had a deeply ingrained

hatred for everything British, a hatred that certainly played a role in the turbulent developments leading up to the outbreak of World War II.

SEPTEMBER

SPAIN, *GERMAN AID*

In September a further flight of fighters, a flight of reconnaissance aircraft, a heavy battery of antiaircraft guns and two tank companies are sent to Franco from Germany through Portugal. The pocket battleship *Deutschland* appears off Ceuta. The German submarines *U-33* and *U-34* have been in Spanish waters since the outbreak of the civil war, having been sent there to represent German interests. Also in September, *Oberstleutnant* Walter Warlimont, a general staff officer from the

army general staff, is appointed Plenipotentiary delegate of the *Wehrmacht* in Spain. The German Minister of Justice, Hans Frank, conveys to the *Duce*: "The Führer desires to receive you in Germany at the earliest possible moment, not only in your capacity as head of the government but also as founder and *Duce* of a party with affinities to National Socialism." Mussolini expresses his wishes to undertake the trip: "It must, however, be well prepared so as to produce concrete results. It will cause a great stir and must therefore be historically important in its results." The *Duce* was anxious to prove that he could excite a Berlin crowd to the same heights of enthusiasm as he had done in Rome. Count Ciano personally makes the plans for the state visit, scheduled for September 25-29, 1937. He also emphasizes the importance of uniforms during the visit: "We must appear more Prussian than the Prussians."

SEPTEMBER 8–14

NAZI PARTY, *RALLIES*
Party Rally of Honour, Nuremberg.

OCTOBER

GERMANY, *ECONOMICS*
Göring initiates the Four-Year Plan, which is designed to make Germany industrially independent.

Despite the grand promises, there was no coherent national programme to ensure Germany's military spending was pegged to economic capacity. Göring was a hopeless administrator, with the result that each of the services pursued its own rapid expansion, setting ludicrous targets and then competing for the necessary

▼ *The pocket battleship* **Deutschland** *was active in supporting the Nationalists in Spain in 1936.*

allocations of capital investment and raw materials. The truth was that Germany did not have the money or raw materials to meet the demands of the armed services. The *Luftwaffe*, for example, had plans to build 19,000 frontline and reserve aircraft by 1942. Even if this target had been met, fuel needs to keep such an air fleet flying would have required 85 percent of the world's oil production. To make matters worse, Germany required vast amounts of iron ore, copper, bauxite, nickel, petrol and rubber, and these had to be imported as Germany was rich only in coal. Though the Four-Year Plan encouraged the development and production of synthetic substitutes, none of these products could balance the demands made by the arms buildup. In fact, the armaments industry was constantly in crisis, with stocks of raw materials being exhausted and no money for fresh supplies.

▶ *Hans Frank, Reich Leader of the NSDAP.*

▲ *Ribbentrop, Ciano, Italian foreign minister, and Hitler develop the Rome-Berlin axis in November 1936.*

OCTOBER 1

SS, *WAFFEN-SS*

A special Inspectorate of the *SS-Verfügungstruppe* has been created to supervise administration and military training. The new inspectorate has the objective of moulding the mainly ill-trained and far flung units of the *SS-Verfügungstruppe* into an efficient fighting force. *SS-Oberstgruppenführer und Generaloberst der Waffen-SS* Paul Hausser, who was to become known affectionately as "Papa" Hausser to his men, is chosen as inspector of the *SS-Verfügungstruppe*, although he has only just been appointed inspector of the *SS-Junkerschule* (Officer Schools) at Bad Tölz and Brunswick.

OCTOBER 3

ARMED FORCES, *NAVY*

The battlecruiser *Scharnhorst* is launched. Based on a World War I design, she is a fast battlecruiser that is designed to be faster than any enemy she will encounter on the seas. She will need this speed because she is terribly undergunned for her size, being armed with 11in guns. Part of Raeder's Plan-Z, she is designed to be a stopgap. She will eventually compliment the larger *Bismarck* and *Tirpitz* in the new German fleet.

NOVEMBER

SPAIN, *GERMAN AID*

With the realization that the Civil War is likely to last a long time, the German Government decides to increase its economic and military commitment to the Nationalists. Hermann Göring, as the Commander in Chief of the German Air Force, is eager to advertise the power of his *Luftwaffe* and to test its new aircraft under combat conditions. Because the German Army is reluctant to commit any substantial numbers of regular troops, German participation in the Spanish Civil War becomes primarily a *Luftwaffe* affair. This force, the Condor Legion, is sent to Spain to fight the communists.

NOVEMBER 1

ITALY, *TREATIES*

Mussolini publicly announces a German-Italian agreement, which constitutes an "Axis" around which the other European powers might work together. In the shaping of the Axis, Galeazzo Ciano goes to Germany where he meets Hitler and Joachim von Ribbentrop, the Führer's special advisor on foreign policy. The birth of the Rome-Berlin Axis is now imminent. Italy's relations with England and France have been severely strained by the opposing interests brought about by the Abyssinian conflict. The advisability of standing with Germany and confronting the Western powers is clear. At this and subsequent meetings at Berchtesgaden, Hitler's retreat in the Bavarian Alps, five points are worked out in collaboration between the two countries, and the viewpoints of both dictators are carefully examined. Ciano's report of the meetings was found satisfactory and Mussolini publicly announces the agreement.

Despite the Axis and the repeated mutual professions of friendship, the relations between the two leaders remain strained with certain suspicions. They watch each other's diplomatic activities with Great Britain closely, and also the pressures each exert over Austria, the piece of territory sandwiched between the two.

NOVEMBER 2

NAZI PARTY, *AWARDS*

Hitler introduces an order that formalizes the awards of the party and forbids the wearing on party uniforms badges that have, by tradition, become considered genuine party commemorative or honourary awards. Badges and awards are an important part of Nazism. The order

reads as follows:

"They may be worn on the civilian overcoat or jacket by all party members on the left lapel. All party members who were permitted to wear their party badge or the national emblem badges which now not be worn at all, except that issued in the year 1929, but the ones which will be issued in future at such gatherings may only be worn for the duration of the

gathering. The wearing of club medals on duty or party uniform is herewith forbidden or any of the party's associated branches."

NOVEMBER 3

SPAIN, *GERMAN AID*
Warlimont returns to Germany and

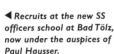

◄ Recruits at the new SS officers school at Bad Tölz, now under the auspices of Paul Hausser.

Generalmajor Hugo Sperrle is appointed by Göring to command the Condor Legion, which at the outset comprises, in addition to those German forces already in Spain, the following assets:
1 bomber group with 3 squadrons of Junkers Ju 52s
1 fighter group with three squadrons of Heinkel He 51s
1 reconnaissance squadron with 12 Heinkel He 70 aircraft
4 batteries of 88mm antiaircraft guns
2 batteries of light antiaircraft guns
1 air signals unit with a wireless, telephone, a communication and an air security company
1 Air Park with machine shops
1 leadership staff

NOVEMBER 6

GERMANY, *TREATIES*
Germany joins the London Submarine Protocol. This international treaty was originally signed by the major naval powers in 1930, and seeks to impose rules on submarine warfare. Surprise submerged attacks on merchant vessels are not permitted. Instead, the submarine should surface, stop the vessel and inspect its papers. It can only be sunk if its cargo comes under a specified list of contraband and the safety of the crew can be ensured. As lifeboats are not

▲ Eagle's Nest at Bertchesgaden, Hitler's retreat in the Bavarian Alps, where he often entertained cronies and guests.

▶ The head of the Inspectorate of the SS-Verfügungstruppe, Paul "Papa" Hausser.

considered suitable accommodation on the high seas, the ship's crew are supposed to be taken aboard the submarine.

NOVEMBER 9

SS, WAFFEN-SS

Felix Steiner is the luminary when it comes to the actual training programme of the *SS-Verfügungstruppe*. In 1935, he joined the *SS-Verfügungstruppe* and helped to

▲ A Heinkel He 111 of the Condor Legion. Early operations were not a success: in one raid the Legion bombed Nationalists.

▲ Hermann Göring, the head of the Luftwaffe, whose Condor Legion aided the Nationalists in Spain.

develop the 3rd battalion of the *SS-Standarte Deutschland*, stationed in Munich and the SS training camp at Dachau concentration camp. He applied his military training to the men, instituting rigorous training schedules in application of his motto "sweat saves blood".

One recruit in three fails basic training the first time round. However, for the successful candidates there is a passing-out parade where they take the SS oath, which is taken separately from members of the other SS branches. At 22:00 hours on the occasion of the November 9 anniversary celebrations of the Munich *Putsch*, the ceremony takes

▶ Hugo Sperrle (right), appointed by Göring to be commander of the Condor Legion in 1936.

place. They have been described as a "uniquely holy event on which the venerated cadre of the survivors of the Munich *Putsch* silently re-enacted their march through the crowd-lined streets of the Bavarian capital in a bombastic travesty of the Passion Play". The finale is the torch-lit oath-taking ceremony for candidates of the *SS-Verfügungstruppe*, which takes place in Hitler's presence before the Feldherrnhalle and the 16 smoking obelisks, each of which bear the name of the first

▶ *The battlecruiser* Gneisenau *was launched in December 1936. She was sister to the* Scharnhorst.

fallen party faithful. The oath is a major ingredient in the SS mystique, binding each successful candidate in unswerving loyalty to Adolf Hitler. During the ceremony a voice intones the 16 names, and after each one a thousand voices chant "Hier".

NOVEMBER 25

GERMANY, *TREATIES*
The Anti-Comintern Pact is signed with Japan. The agreement was concluded first between Germany and Japan and then between Italy, Germany, and Japan (November 6, 1937). Ostensibly it was directed against the Communist International (Comintern), but

▶ *The annual ceremony held at the Feldherrnhalle in Munich to commemorate the fallen of the 1923* Putsch.

by implication, specifically against the Bolshevik Soviet Union.

The treaties were sought by Adolf Hitler, who at the time was publicly inveighing against Bolshevism and who was interested in Japan's successes in the opening war against China. The Japanese were angered by a Soviet-Chinese non-aggression treaty of August 1936 and by the subsequent sale of Soviet military aircraft and munitions to China. For propaganda purposes, Hitler and Benito Mussolini were able to present

themselves as defenders of Western values against the threat of Soviet communism.

DECEMBER 8

ARMED FORCES, *NAVY*
The battlecruiser *Gneisenau* is launched. She is a small battleship, with smaller guns and armour on the battleship scale. Designed to allow replacement of triple 11in guns with dual 15in, she and her sister *Scharnhorst* is a reply to the French "Dunkerque" class.

1937

Germany and Italy had not always been close allies; indeed, during the early 1930s Mussolini had moved troops up to the Austrian border to deter Hitler from influencing events in Austria. However, Hitler had supported Mussolini's war in Ethiopia and both dictators found themselves supporting the anti-communist cause in Spain. It was, therefore, perhaps logistical that they should ultimately become allies. That process was cemented by the *Duce*'s historic trip to Germany in 1937, when the Nazis pulled out all the stops to win over Italy's leader.

FEBRUARY 6

ARMED FORCES, *NAVY*

The heavy cruiser *Admiral Hipper* is launched. This ship is part of Germany's Plan-Z, a plan to build a navy that will be able to meet the British Royal Navy on their own terms.

Admiral Raeder was told by Hitler to develop a plan for a major fleet rebuilding that would be able to defeat the British merchant navy shipping in the Atlantic and be able to suppress the naval forces that would be there to protect them. Raeder planned on doing this by having a well-balanced fleet and dividing his ships in battle groups to strike when and where he needed to. This reflected Raeder's experience with the Kaiser's Navy, where German raiders were able to disrupt the seas in favour of Germany. It was a long-

▼ *Hjalmar Schacht (left), the Minister of Economics and Plenipotentiary General for the War Economy, resigned in 1937.*

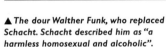

▲ *The dour Walther Funk, who replaced Schacht. Schacht described him as "a harmless homosexual and alcoholic".*

decree further empowers the Minister of the Interior, Dr Frick, to take the necessary measures to prevent the departure or transit through Germany of volunteers, German or foreign. It should be noted that this decree has been promulgated over three months after the formation of the Legion Condor. Few are deceived by this decree.

▲ *The heavy cruiser Admiral Hipper, part of Germany's Plan-Z to build a fleet to match those of Great Britain and France.*

▶ *Minister of the Interior Wilhelm Frick, who carried out a cosmetic exercise to prevent aid to Franco.*

term plan that was to be complete by 1948. The following ships were planned:

6 battleships of 50,800 tonnes (50,000 tons), plus the *Bismarck* and the *Tirpitz*.
8 Heavy Cruisers of 20,329 tonnes (20,000 tons), later increased to 12.
4 aircraft carriers of 20,329 tonnes (20,000 tons).
A large number of light cruisers.
233 U-boats.

FEBRUARY 20

SPAIN, *GERMAN AID*

Despite the setting up of a European non-intervention committee, of which Germany is a member, intended to prevent the possibility of international participation in the Spanish Civil War, Germany very swiftly, and secretly, sets about organizing a powerful, semi-autonomous air component for collaboration with General Franco. An example of the lengths to which the German Government is prepared to go in order to deny to the world the existence of the Condor Legion and its commitment of arms and men to Franco can be seen from the decree published in Germany on February 20, 1937. This forbids German nationals to enter Spain or Spanish possessions, including Spanish Morocco, in order to take part in the Civil War. The

KEY MOMENTS

Deutschland Incident

The importance of the attack on the *Deutschland*, both militarly and politicaly, to the Nazi government cannot be under-estimated. It was therefore of the highest importance to Hitler to see that this outrage was fully recognized. The *Deutschland* was in the Ibiza harbour and this was a declared war zone. On the evening of May 29, she was lying in a roadstead of Ibiza along with the tanker *Neptune* and the torpedo boat *Leopard*. Although assigned to international sea control and off duty, the *Deutschland* was attacked by two unidentified aircraft, which dropped two bombs. The attack was carried out by two Soviet pilots flying SB-2 Katiuskas who thought they were bombing Franco's flagship, the *Canarias*.

For political reasons, the Republican government in Spain attributed the attack to two Spanish pilots, José Arcega and Leocadio Mendiola. The first bomb fell on the crewmen's mess, resulting in 22 killed and 83 wounded. The second fell on the side deck which caused little damage. The *Deutschland* then sailed to Gibraltar where it disembarked the dead and wounded. The wounded were attended to by the British at the British Military Hospital. Nine more soldiers died, bringing the death toll to 31 with 74 wounded. This led to a number of awards to British medical personnel of the German Red Cross Decoration 1937–1939 in varying grades. A temporary funeral was conducted in Gibraltar, where the cortege with the coffins draped in the German battle flag was escorted by Royal Marines. The coffins were disinterred and returned on board the *Deutschland*, which then sailed to the port of Kiel.

MARCH

GERMANY, *RELIGION*

Pope Pius XI issues *Mit brennende Sorge* (*With Burning Anxiety*), a paper listing violations of the Concordat and Nazi persecution of the Catholic church.

APRIL

GERMANY, *LOCAL GOVERNMENT*

Carl Gördeler resigns as Mayor of Leipzig. Formally a Nazi supporter, he has become disillusioned by rearmament and growing anti-Semitism.

APRIL 20

NAZI PARTY, *PERSONALITIES*

On the occasion of his 48th birthday, Hitler receives the good wishes and an expensive hand-crafted SS sword bearing the inscription: "In good times and bad, we will always be the same", from the leadership corps of the SS.

APRIL 26

SPAIN, *GERMAN AID*

The bombers of the German *Luftwaffe* are sent to help Franco destroy Guernica, the cultural and spiritual home of the Basques. It is market day and the square is crowded

when the bombers, Heinkel He 111s and Junker Ju 52s, escorted by fighters, appear and pound Guernica with high explosives. They then set the town alight with incendiary bombs and strafe it with machine-gun fire. Eyewitnesses later tell of the death that rained down on them. The bombing has shocked the world.

There were military targets in Guernica: it was a communications centre and it had a

▼ The Deutschland, *seen here behind the* Admiral Scheer, *was badly damaged in a Republic air attack in Ibiza in May.*

▲ *Nazi Party Day in 1937. The figure on the extreme right is Martin Bormann, who at the time was a* Gauleiter.

▶ *Another shot of the 1937 Party Day. Here, Hitler talks with Rudolf Hess, whose influence was beginning to wane.*

munitions factory. But there is no evidence that the German bombers aimed for them. They simply unloaded their bombs indiscriminately on this undefended town.

MAY 5

ARMED FORCES, *NAVY*
In the presence of Hitler, a new "Strength through Joy" ship was named *Wilhelm Gustloff* is launched by Gustloff's widow

JUNE

NAZI PARTY, *GESTAPO*
Secret orders are issued from Heydrich ordering "protective custody", meaning concentration camp, for those jailed for "racial offences" after release from jail, i.e. Jewish liaisons with Aryans. Heydrich now heads both the SD and Gestapo under the structure of the Reich Security Administration.

By this time the Gestapo was joined with the *Kriminalpolizei* (Kripo – Criminal Police) under the umbrella of a new organization, the *Sicherheitspolizei* (Sipo – Security Police)

JUNE 8

ARMED FORCES, *NAVY*
The heavy cruiser *Blücher* is launched.

JUNE 17

ARMED FORCES, *NAVY*
A state funeral, attended by Hitler, is held at Kiel for the 31 dead of the *Deutschland.*

Their names are:

Lobitz, Martens, Schmitz, Martin, Zimmermann, Busche, Sehm, Denno, Gerbardt, Männing, Oelrich, Schübert, Inglen, Bochem, Faltin, Wille, Gallus, Brüchner, Mies, Manja, Röbers, Schöslkopf, Bismark, Eckart, Schubert, Holzwarth, Meyer, Woftweber, Fischer, Steiger and Dürr.

AUGUST

GERMANY, *ECONOMICS*

Hjalmar Schacht resigns as Minister of Economics. Though he had stated that he would support Hitler and the Third Reich as long as he had breath in his body, he has become disillusioned by the regime's anti-Semitism and also the Night of the Long Knives. He has played an important part if Germany's rearmament programme, but has found it difficult to battle inflation. After reading *Mein Kampf* he decided that Hitler was a genius who could restore Germany's greatness. Walther Funk replaces him.

SEPTEMBER 6–13

NAZI PARTY, *RALLIES*

Party Rally of Labour.

SEPTEMBER 24

GERMANY, *DIPLOMACY*

As Mussolini boards the train in Rome for his visit to Germany, he wears a splendid uniform specially designed for the occasion: a grey-blue Corporal of Honour uniform with a cornflower blue sash across his chest and a black militia cap adorned with a red cord. His staff, which consists of Ciano, Alfieri, the minister of press and propaganda, Storace, the party secretary, and about 100 officials, journalists and subordinates, are also bedecked in finery. From Rome Mussolini's train stops at Forli where he pauses for family kisses and well-wishes. His special nine-coach armoured train then progresses on its historic journey, which will be one of the pivotal moments in the history of the Third Reich and Fascist Italy.

When the train pulled into the Alps, it stopped for five hours during the night to give the *Duce* an opportunity for a rest.

SEPTEMBER 25

GERMANY, *DIPLOMACY*

The following morning the train enters Austria. There, Chancellor Dr Kurt von Schuschnigg's cabinet is deeply concerned at the possibility of the *Duce's* assassination. This trip not only exposes him to the usual danger of anti-Fascist attacks, but also the bitter hatred of the Tyrolese as a result of Italy's annexation of South Tyrol. Some 4300 Austrian soldiers have been stationed along the 160km (100 miles) of railway line, their backs to the "Mussolini Special" with orders to shoot to kill without question anyone suspected of bombing, shooting at or stoning the train.

▼ *A beaming Mussolini arrives in Germany on September 25 to begin his historic trip to the Third Reich.*

of Staff; Dr Robert Ley, Leader of the German Labour Front; Victor Lutze, commander of the SA; General Franz Ritter von Epp, Governor of Bavaria; Adolf Wagner, Gauleiter of Munich; Ernst Wilhelm Bohle, leader of Germans living abroad; Konstantin Hierl, Labour Corps leader; and a number of less known dignitaries. They exchange the Fascist salute with their Italian guest, then Hitler and Mussolini shake hands, who subsequently introduces the members of his immediate party. The Duce and the Führer march side by side through the station on a crimson carpet and emerge to the roar of heavy German guns crashing 21 times in salute. As they come in sight of the decorated Bahnhofplatz, a wide square in front of the station, they are met by the glitter of steel and standards from the army and Nazi honour detachments. Massed bands

◀ **Hitler shows off his bodyguard to the Duce. Mussolini was visibly impressed by Germany's military strength.**

When Mussolini arrives in Innsbruck, the *Duce* openly admires the scenic beauty of the country.

At 08:52 hours Mussolini's train stops at the German boarder town of Kiefersfelden. There, Reichsminister Rudolf Hess and the Italian Ambassador Attolico meet the Duce and board his special carriage. The trip from the German border to Munich is lined with *Bund Deutscher Mädel* (BDM – League of German Girls) and *Jungvolk* (Young People – junior division of the Hitler Youth) members, who muster on the platforms of every station to wave their welcome. As the train slowly enters the outskirts of Munich, the city seems aflame with masses of red, white and black swastika flags fluttering beside the warmer Italian combination of red, white and green. At 10:00 hours the train arrives at the station, and a smile lights Mussolini's face. Everywhere he sees tall pillars surmounted

▶ **Constantin Freiherr von Neurath, senior diplomat, was one of those wheeled out to meet Mussolini.**

by Roman Eagles and a spectacular scarlet and gold Caesarean festoons set off by Nordic fir and laurel. When the train halts he is the first to step off. Adolf Hitler and his group of diplomats, which comprise Dr Josef Goebbels, Minister of Propaganda; Heinrich Himmler, head of the German Police and commander of the SS; Dr Alfred Rosenberg, in charge of party ideological schooling; Baldur von Schirach, Reich Youth leader; Colonel-General Werner von Fritsch, Chief

▲ The Brown House welcomes Mussolini. There was a restaurant in the basement of the party's Munich headquarters.

spontaneously break into "Giovinezza", the Fascist hymn, and cheering squads set up rounds of "Heil Hitler" and "Duce, Duce!"

After an inspection of the guard of honour, which was comprised of one company each from the army, navy, air force, SS, Labour Corps and the SA, the dictators entered an open Mercedes. They were slowly driven through the Munich streets where double-lined SS troops stood shoulder to shoulder. Mussolini and his retinue were taken to Prince Karl Place where they would stay while in Munich. A short time later, Hess called on the *Duce* and escorted him to the Fuhrerhaus at 6 Prinzregentstrasse. At 11:32 hours the two leaders met for an extended conversation. Count Galeazzo Ciano and Baron Constantin von Neurath, the German Foreign Minister, also participated in these talks. The discussions were general rather than particular and all that emerged was a firm agreement on a friendly attitude towards Japan and the greatest possible support to Franco in Spain. At this time the *Duce* presented Hitler with a commission as a Corporal of Honour in the Fascist

Militia, which had been created for himself alone. In turn the Führer bestowed upon the *Duce* one of Germany's highest awards, the Eagle Order, Grand Cross in Gold with Diamonds, which was not to be repeated for any future holder.

The early part of the afternoon was spent touring the carnival-decked streets and palaces and laying wreaths on various Nazi monuments in the Bavarian capital. Among these was the Feldherrnhalle in Königsplatz, which held the bodies of 16 Nazi heroes killed in the 1923 Munich *Putsch*. The two leaders later attended a lunch at the Führerhaus with members of the *Alt Kämpfer* of the Party. The Königsplatz resounded to the stomp of boots as Mussolini looked on in admiration from his saluting base. He later commented to Hitler: "It was wonderful!", as they stood side by side on the small reviewing stand in front of the Temples of Honour: "It couldn't have been better in Italy." This massive

demonstration left an indelible impression on the *Duce*.

An afternoon reception was held in their honour at the Museum of German Art. Fräulein Leni Riefenstahl, feminine arbiter of the Nazi film world, gathered more than 100 of Germany's most beautiful stage and cinema actresses for the occasion. Hitler proudly toured Mussolini through the new museum, pointing out favourite specimens and explaining at length his elaborate plans for beautifying Berlin, Munich and other cities. After the tour, the two dictators attended a tea in the museum's restaurant. It is interesting to note, however, that at the tea the female glances were towards boxer Max Schmeling who was also a guest. At this time, Mussolini spoke of an impending visit to Rome by Hitler. "It will be an occasion for wearing my new uniform," replied Hitler, commenting on his newly acquired rank of Corporal of Honour.

That evening Hitler and Mussolini boarded separate trains, lest perchance one wreck killed them both, which sped across Germany to the Baltic province of Mecklenburg-Schwerin.

SEPTEMBER 26

GERMANY, *DIPLOMACY*

Hitler and Mussolini arrive in the morning at the little village of Lalendorf, near the centre of the manoeuvre area, to witness the final stages of post-World War I Germany's greatest military manoeuvres. Hitler and Mussolini's entourage are met at the station by high officials of the German defence forces, which are led by War Minister Werner von Blomberg, Air Minister Hermann Göring, the Army Chief of Staff, Colonel General Werner von Fritsch, and Naval Chief of Staff Admiral Erich Raeder. In an open touring car, Hitler and Mussolini dash from area to area observing the latest in artillery, infantry and armoured

▶ *As the two dictators were driven through the streets of Munich, 36,000 guards lined their route.*

▼ *Then came a display of Nazi standard bearers, rank upon rank of Brownshirts marching in perfect unison.*

techniques. Throughout the lightning tour, they are cheered by German soldiers who are of the class of 1935. These troops are the first to have been called up when Hitler restored universal conscription to the German way of life.

At the conclusion of the manoeuvres, Hitler and Mussolini boarded a special train to Kröpelin, in the northwestern corner of Mecklenburg-Schwerin. There they inspected the new flying field at Wustrow, examined several new types of military aircraft and later observed air exercises. The famous slow-flying "Storch" was demonstrated by Major-General Udet, with Air General Milch as passenger. Flying the versatile aircraft at minimal speeds of 19-24km/h (12-15 mph), once again the *Duce* was visibly impressed. Up until now Mussolini had seen German art, laid wreaths on monuments, inspected honour guards and observed war games. He now wanted to inspect one of Germany's most closely guarded secrets, the mighty Krupp munitions works at Essen. The German schedule had called for a short trip to Berlin from the Baltic for a triumphant welcome, but Mussolini's insistence now called for the dictators to travel across

▲ *Then came a parade of NSKK vehicles. This was a paramilitary unit that oversaw the training of the army's motorized units.*

▶ *Among the dignitaries present was air ace Ernst Udet, who at this time was Technical Officer of the Air Ministry.*

Germany to Essen and then cross it once more, back to Berlin. Immediately German Minister of Propaganda and Public Enlightenment Dr Josef Goebbels broadcast to the astonished citizens of Essen that they were to deck their city with green branches and flags in honour of the Italian leader, who would arrive the next day. To ensure that all arrangements would be in readiness, he and several assistants rushed by special train to Essen.

SEPTEMBER 27

GERMANY, *DIPLOMACY*

After travelling across Germany in separate trains, the Hitler and Mussolini specials rumble into Essen at 08:07 hours. Essen and Krupp have done themselves proud; all is in readiness. Due to security precautions, correspondents are not allowed to join in the tour while the *Duce* and Hitler inspect the hush-hush realm of munitioneer Dr Gustav Krupp von Bohlen und Halbach. At the company's offices, the dictators are received by the director of Krupp, who presents the members of his family. He then explains the growth and organization of his gigantic concern. The party was then escorted to the main plant by car. There they see the production of artillery, tanks and every conceivable weapon of war. Mussolini is highly impressed by the discipline of the workers, scale of operation and tremendous output of weaponry. The Krupp inspection ends at 10:45 hours. Once again the leaders travel in separate trains from Essen.

Elaborate measures were taken with true German thoroughness to ensure that for the last 24km (15 miles) of the journey to Berlin, the two trains would run side by side, signifying the equality of the two revolutions. Before arriving at the station, Hitler sped ahead, enabling him to be on the platform to properly greet his guest. The arrival in the German capital was, as Count Ciano stated in his diary, "Triumphal".

The first three days of the state visit had been for indoctrination, but the culmination was the welcoming in Berlin. Never before in German history had Berlin witnessed such a display. This spectacle dwarfed the Munich pageantry to the dimensions of a country fair. With the aid of professional stage designer Benno von Arendt, Berlin's central sections were transformed into a prop fairyland. The city was decorated with thousands of German and Italian flags from the station at the Heerstrasse to the Presidential Palace in the centre of the city. A 38.4m (126ft) flag tower erected in Adolf Hitler Platz, midway between the railway station and the Brandenburg Gate, was bedecked with German and Italian flags 36.5m (120ft) long. The Pariserplatz before the Brandenburg Gate had two coloured water fountains and four massive towers covered alternately with Italian and German flags. Dusk fell as the leaders drove through the floodlit Brandenburg Gate onto the famous Unter den Linden. There, four rows of white, illuminated pylons, 10m (33ft) high bearing golden eagles and Nazi and Fascist emblems, glowed in the night. Banners in the German and Italian colours hung from rooftops to the pavements and in the Wilhelmstrasse. It is estimated that approximately 50,00 square metres (55,000 square yards) of bunting had been woven for the decoration of these two streets. As the crowds roared a welcome to the Italian dictator, Mussolini stood up to let himself

be seen, obviously delighted with his reception. The Führer remained seated at his left, allowing his guest to enjoy the full glory of the moment. Work had ceased in Berlin at 16:00 hours on the day of the arrival, enabling the total population to be present. Hitler took personal precautions in the security measures to protect the *Duce*. Approximately 60,000 troops lined the route of travel. In some places they stood

▲ *Colonel-General Erhard Milch (right), Luftwaffe commander, laid on a flying display for the Italian dictator.*

three and four deep. The city's police was reinforced by detachments from Saxony. Plainclothes men mixed in the crowd while armed launches patrolled the River Spree. That evening a state banquet was held in Mussolini's honour. Members of the government and all leading members of the party were present at the Berlin reception. Hitler, a strict vegetarian and teetotaller, nibbled throughout the banquet and toasted his guests with sweet German champagne.

SEPTEMBER 28

GERMANY, *DIPLOMACY*

This day has been given as a national holiday. Mussolini visits the Arsenal Museum on Unter den Linden where he views mementos from previous wars.

He stood reverently for a few minutes before President von Hindenburg's death mask. He and his party then motored to Potsdam near Berlin and inspected Sanssouci, Frederick the Great's palace. After walking to the famous Garrison Church, Mussolini placed a wreath on the tomb of Frederick the Great. The *Duce* then returned to Berlin and called on the Italian Embassy and the headquarters of *Fascio*. There he was saluted by 25,000 Italian Fascists now resident in Germany and 3500 members of the Fascist youth organization. At noon he drove with Ciano and Bernardo Attolico, his new ambassador to Berlin, to Schorfheide 64km (40 miles) from Berlin. He then attended a luncheon given by Göring and his wife at their beautiful hunting lodge Waldhof Karinhall. It was at this time that he was presented with the Luftwaffe's highest award, the Pilot-Observer Badge in gold with diamonds. Later he took afternoon tea with Dr Goebbels and then retired to the Presidential Palace where he dined privately that evening.

Simultaneously that day a mammoth demonstration was being organized on the Maifeld, the polo ground adjoining the Olympic Stadium. Since early that morning a crowd of approximately 650,000 had gone to the city's outskirts and gathered before the official tribune. At 18:00 hours the Olympic Bell began to ring, signifying that Hitler and Mussolini were en route. Their arrival was announced by trumpets, while the large personal standards of the *Duce* and the Führer were hoisted on either side of the tribune. Despite threatening rain clouds, the crowd was good natured. Dr Goebbels mounted the speakers tribune and stated: "Three million people have taken part in this historic demonstration of the National Socialist movement, either along the route, on the Maifeld or in the stadium." All of Germany's radio stations were connected to the

▲ Once proceedings had finished in Munich the tour moved on to Berlin. Here, a torchlit display entertains Mussolini.

▼ Mussolini was treated to seeing Hitler's Berlin at its zenith. This is the Bismarckdenkmal und Siegessäule.

Maifeld speaker system. Twenty countries in Europe and North and South America were also united in the gigantic hook-up, which the Propaganda Ministry had arranged for this occasion. Great Britain did not accept the broadcast, however, and Russia was not invited to do so. As Dr Goebbels, the man who had supervised this engineering wonder, told the two dictators in presenting them to the audience: "The whole world is listening to you."

Hitler was the first to speak to the German nation by wireless. He introduced the *Duce*: "What moves us most at the moment is the deep-rooted joy to see in our midst a guest who is one of the lonely men in history. These two men are not put

stress on the 115 million Germans and Italians and the need for them to unite "in one single, unshakable determination".

After the speeches, Hitler and Mussolini walked across the field to the Olympic Stadium. There, in the huge green and brown Olympic arena, marched the massed bands of three army corps. There were 4000 musicians in all, 33 brass bands, 25 fife and drum corps and 10 trumpet bands. They goose-stepped in perfect precision to the tune of "Preussens Gloria", a favourite military march, and wheeled into three

◀ *Panzer II tanks in a side street in Berlin wait to move out to parade past Hitler and Mussolini.*

to trial by historic events but determine the history of their country themselves." Mussolini then stood up and climbed the podium to speak. Before him thousands of Germans arms rose in the Roman salute. Mussolini delivered his carefully prepared speech in fluent German, but with an Italian accent. In the midst of the *Duce*'s speech a darkening sky suddenly opened and a torrential rain fell on the Maifeld. Unfortunately, he became overcome by the excitement generated by the dynamic spectacle before him and spoke faster and faster. This, plus the sounds of the downpour, caused his words to be almost inaudible. His script was soon a sodden

▲ *The memorial to the unknown soldier in Berlin, where Mussolini laid a wreath to commemorate the dead of World War I.*

mass but he continued as the patient crowd became soaked to the skin. In the course of his speech the *Duce* pronounced: "Fascism has its ethical principles, to which it intends to be faithful, and they are also my morals; to speak clearly and openly, and, if we are friends, to march together to the end." He also spoke of the awakening of Germany through the Nazi revolution, Bolshevism, the common enemy, and Germany's friendly stand during the Ethiopian War. The speech ended with a

columns in the centre of the arena. The trumpet bands came from the cavalry and artillery and the rest of the units from the army, navy and air force. As the floodlights shone on them, the massed musicians sent forth strains of the great marches from Verdi's "Aida", for the Italians' benefit, Wagner's "Rienzi" for the Germans. Then the "Bavarian March Past" was struck up and from under an arch at the side of the Stadium, a battalion of torchbearing *Schultzstaffeln* appeared. They flowed into the arena like a living flame, wheeling halfway around, dividing and moving to each side in columns of four. These again divided and became streamlets of twos, which in turn divided, countermarched and passed each other in single file just as a second torchbearing battalion came from under the arch. The first battalion marched in single file around the arena and took rigid stations at its edges, approximately 3m (9ft) apart. The second battalion divided, subdivided and moved through the massed musicians forming with them a huge "M" with its base towards the dais on which Hitler and Mussolini stood. After this complicated manoeuvre, the musicians began a march to Beethoven. Simultaneously, three "honour companies" from the army, navy and air force entered. They goosestepped halfway around the arena, then wheeled to the front and came to attention. Their mounted commander came forward, faced the dais, and reported to Hitler: "1600 of your defence forces, Mein Führer."

Outside the stadium, 50 concealed searchlights threw up long beams of light, forming "the tent of light" which was now a feature at German pageants. The troops came to present arms and the massed bands very softly played the German Army

hymn, followed by the Italian national anthem, "Giovinezza," "Deutschland uber Alles" and the "Horst Wessel Lied".

As the spectacle came to an end, the rain began to fall once more. Standing equally unprotected, side-by-side, Mussolini made a remark to Hitler. Hitler made a gesture to a nearby SS officer, who threw rain capes around the shoulders of both leaders. The end of this massive pageant came when the huge swastika and Fascist standards, above the host and guest, were lowered as they departed from the stadium.

SEPTEMBER 29

GERMANY, *DIPLOMACY*

The mornings activities are confined to placing a magnificent wreath at the German War Memorial on Unter den Linden by Mussolini, Count Ciano and Marshal Badoglio. After reviewing the guard of honour at the War Memorial, Mussolini marches past about 100 war invalids in self-

propelled wheelchairs and salutes them. He then joins Hitler in a salute to 14,000 men of the army, navy and air force on Charlottenburger Chaussee. The parade, which is led by General Witzleben, commander of the Third Army Group, takes one hour and 20 minutes. Some 591 officers, 13,000 rank and file, 2000 horses, 600 motorized vehicles and 144 motorcycle

▼ *Nazi supporters the Duke and Duchess of Windsor arrive in Berlin to ingratiate themselves with Germany's leaders.*

▲ *One of Berlin's most famous landmarks, the Brandenburg Gate, which was riddled with shells by the Red Army in 1945.*

units, all drawn from Berlin and neighbouring garrisons, pass by.

The army contingent was comprised of five infantry regiments, four artillery, one cavalry, besides pioneer, armoured, signal and machine-gun battalions. The air force contributed three motorized antiaircraft regiments, while the navy contributed two

companies of cadets. During the parade an incident occurred that Mussolini later recalled: "During the military review the mace bearer was too quick and struck a soldier behind him on the head, and an artillery horse kicked over the traces and bolted right in front of the box. Hitler laughed and so did I. Then he turned to me and remarked confidentially, 'I don't like to think what'll happen to the wretched private. Our perfect German organization will set in motion. The general will go for the colonel; the colonel will go for the major; the major will go for the captain; the captain will go for the lieutenant; the lieutenant will go for the sergeant-major; the sergeant-major for the sergeant; the sergeant for the corporal; and finally poor private!'" After the impressive review, Mussolini was taken to the Reich Chancellery for a farewell luncheon. He was then escorted to the Lehrter Station in Berlin. There, he and Hitler shook hands heartily and continued an animated conversation from his window after the *Duce* had boarded the train. Personal gifts accompanied him: three crates of geese presented by the curator of the Berlin Zoological Gardens. Hess, Hitler's deputy, travelled with the Italian party as far as the German frontier. The Rome-Berlin axis had been pronounced for all the world to see.

OCTOBER 22

GERMANY, *DIPLOMACY*
Nazi leaders, including Hitler's adjutant, *SA-Obergruppenführer* Wilhelm Brückner, are among the party who wait on the platform

▼ *Leading from the Brandenburg Gate, stone pillars surmounted by swastikas reminded visitors who ruled Germany.*

to meet the Duke and Duchess of Windsor as they arrive in Berlin. Flowers and cries of "Heil Edward" greet the couple from the large crowds that throng the station to watch. Dr Robert Ley, leader of Hitler's Labour Front, hands the Duchess a bouquet of pink and yellow roses. The Duke and Duchess of Windsor later meet the Führer. They are ostensibly in Berlin to "study social conditions and housing problems". They visit the first "National Socialist model factory", where they lunch with the workers before attending a concert given by the Nazi district orchestra.

NOVEMBER 1

GERMANY, *LEGAL*
The Enabling Law is renewed, ensuring Germany remains a National Socialist dictatorship. Confiscation of Jewish businesses without legal justification continues.

NOVEMBER 1

ARMED FORCES, *AIR FORCE*
Generalleutnant Hellmuth Volkmann is appointed commander of the Condor Legion. He will hold the command from November 1, 1937 until November 1, 1938. Volkmann won promotion to *General der Fliege* and on his return to Germany was appointed Commandant of the *Luftkriegsakademie* in Berlin.

1938

Though the early years of World War II saw a string of German military triumphs, 1938 was probably the most successful year for Adolf Hitler. The removal of Blomberg and Fritsch ensured the total loyalty of the army, which *de facto* became an unthinking tool of Hitler's will. On the international front the union of Austria and the Sudetenland with the Third Reich was a stunning coup, and one achieved without firing a shot. At home Hitler was viewed as a genius, a leader who could do no wrong and who had kept his promise to bring ethnic Germans back into the Reich.

JANUARY

ARMED FORCES, *POLITICS*

Minister of War Blomberg is dismissed after a scandal, and Fritsch, commander-in-chief of the army, is forced to resign on false charges of homosexuality.

The slight irritation which Hitler felt towards Blomberg and Fritsch (the former had opposed the march into the Rhineland and the latter was hostile to the Nazis, especially the SS), was increased by the events which followed his decision to reoccupy the Rhineland. The generals were only too aware that the operation carried a grave military risk as insignificant forces could only carry it out – Germany's rearmament had not by then advanced far. Hitler was contemptuous of their fears and later compared them with his own aplomb in bluffing his way through the crisis. This was the beginning of the constantly reiterated claim that the Führer was always right and his timid generals often wrong. In November 1937, Hitler warned the army to prepare for action against Austria and Czechoslovakia and stated that he was prepared to risk war with the Western powers. Blomberg and Fritsch were anxious about this

▲ *General Freiherr Werner von Fritsch, army commander-in-chief, disliked Nazism. He was removed following a sex scandal.*

▶ *Field Marshal Werner von Blomberg. He opposed Hitler's plans to march into the Rhineland and the Sudetenland, and was therefore removed.*

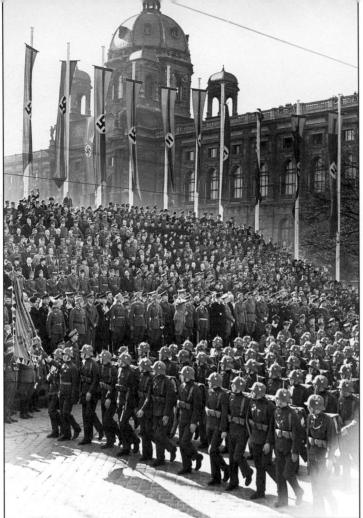

▲ *Wilhelm Keitel, Hitler's new chief of staff. His total subservience to Hitler earned him the nickname "lackey".*

▲ *Nazi troops march in Vienna following the Anschluss with Germany. Chancellor Schuschnigg was sent to Dachau.*

▶ *Ribbentrop, the new ambassador to Great Britain, had a wretched time in his new post. He was disliked by the British.*

and Fritsch even had the temerity to warn the Führer against such a suicidal course. While these two senior soldiers were low in Hitler's esteem as a result of such faint-heartedness, they were framed and disgraced in a conspiracy which was probably organized by Göring and Himmler. Blomberg was a widower who was considering marriage to his secretary. This would have been a slight misalliance by the strict standards of the officer corps, but Göring encouraged the wretched "rubber lion" and even shipped off a rival for the young lady's affections to South America. The 60-year-old field marshal married his secretary Fraulein Gruhn on January 12,

1938. On January 25, 1938, Göring brought the Führer startling evidence that Blomberg's new wife was a prostitute with an extensive history with the German police. There were even salacious photographs of the new Frau Blomberg in pornographic poses. Blomberg was forced to resign, but before he left for an extended honeymoon on Capri to console himself with the arts which his new wife had learned in a Berlin massage parlour, he was given a word of encouragement by Hitler. As far as is known, Hitler told Blomberg that he would be recalled to the supreme command in the event of war. This promise was never fulfilled.

95

At that moment Himmler's Gestapo was also moving against Fritsch. It produced a dossier which allegedly proved that Fritsch was a homosexual susceptible to blackmail. When Fritsch protested his innocence, the Gestapo produced a degenerate called Hans Schmidt who claimed to have seen the army chief committing an unnatural act with a certain "Bavarian Joe" in a dark corner near Potsdam railway station.

▼ *General Walter von Brauchitsch (right) became the new army commander-in-chief following the removal of Fritsch.*

Although Fritsch was later found innocent of this ludicrously clumsy frame-up, he was relieved of his command "for health reasons" on February 4, 1938.

FEBRUARY

ARMED FORCES, *HIGH COMMAND*
Hitler becomes Minister of War and Commander-in-Chief of the armed forces with Keitel his chief of staff and Brauchitsch succeeding Fritsch. Ribbentrop is appointed Foreign Minister. Austrian Chancellor Schuschnigg is called to Berchtesgaden and given an ultimatum to allow the Nazis in Austria a free hand.

MARCH 12

AUSTRIA, *POLITICS*
The *Anschluss* (Union) with Austria. Seyss-Inquart becomes

Reich Governor of *Ostmark*. All laws of Germany, including racial laws, are now in operation in Austria.

In July 1934, Austrian and German Nazis together attempted a coup but were unsuccessful. An authoritarian right-wing government then took power in Austria and kept perhaps half the population from voicing legitimate dissent; that cleavage prevented concerted resistance to the developments of 1938. In February 1938 Hitler invited the Austrian Chancellor Kurt von Schuschnigg to Germany and forced him to agree to give the Austrian Nazis virtually a free hand. Schuschnigg later repudiated the agreement and announced a plebiscite on the *Anschluss* question. He was bullied into cancelling the plebiscite, and he obediently resigned, ordering the Austrian Army not to resist the Germans. President Wilhelm Miklas of Austria refused to appoint the Austrian Nazi leader Arthur

▲ *The cuff band of the SS-Polizei Division, one of the Waffen-SS units created from the SS-Verfügungstruppe.*

▶ *The Dresden Hotel at Bad Godesberg, where Hitler and Chamberlain met to discuss the Czech problem in September.*

Seyss-Inquart as chancellor. The German Nazi minister Hermann Göring ordered Seyss-Inquart to send a telegram requesting German military aid, but he refused, and the telegram was sent by a German agent in Vienna. On March 12 Germany invaded, and the enthusiasm that followed persuaded Hitler to annex Austria outright on March 13. A controlled plebiscite of April 10 gave a 99.7 percent approval.

APRIL

GERMANY, *LEGAL*
All Jewish wealth is to be registered.

MAY 21

ARMED FORCES, *NAVY*
The battlecruiser *Gneisenau* is commissioned.

JUNE

GERMANY, *ANTI-SEMITISM*
Destruction of Munich synagogue by Nazi thugs. A new decree demands registration of all Jewish businesses.

JULY

GERMANY, *RESISTANCE*
Carl Gördeler, ex-Mayor of Leipzig, goes to London but fails to convince the British of the strength of anti-Hitler resistance. Chamberlain visits Hitler at Berchtesgaden to consult with him on Czechoslovakia.

JULY 11

SPORTS, *GREAT BRITAIN*
The International Motorcycle Six Day Trials is held at Donnington Park in England. It is

▲ *A destroyed synagogue following Crystal Night, the anti-Jewish pogrom organized by Reinhard Heydrich.*

forces already in existence. Therefore, it is able to be legitimately trained by the *Reichsführer-SS* in Nazi theories of race and also to be manned by volunteers who have completed their commitment in the *Reichsarbeitsdienst*, the Reich Labour Service. The Führer decree also states that in time of war, elements of the *Totenkopfverbände* will reinforce the *SS-Verfügungstruppe*. If mobilized, it will be used firstly by the commander-in-chief of the army under the jurisdiction of the army, making it subject only to military law and order, but still remaining a branch of the NSDAP and owing its allegiance ultimately to that organization. Secondly, in the event of an emergency within Germany, the *SS-Verfügungstruppe* will be under Hitler's control through Himmler.

The army had always been suspicious of the SS. As the supposed sole arms bearers of the state, it regarded the creation of armed units within the SS as a betrayal by Hitler. It

▼ *German troops receive a rapturous welcome as they march into the Sudetenland in September.*

won by the SS motorcycle team made up of Mundhenke, Patina, Knees and Zimmermann.

When the SS-emblazoned green leather-clad team marched up to receive the Adolf Hühnlein Trophy and gave the Hitler salute, a loud raspberry was blown by the director of the British team.

AUGUST

GERMANY, *RESISTANCE*
General Ludwig Beck, Chief of the General Staff, having sent Ewald von Kleist-Schmenzin to London to try and warn the British of Hitler's plans, submits a paper on the danger of going to war to Brauchitsch, who informs Hitler. Beck is forced to resign.

GERMANY, *ANTI-SEMITISM*
The destruction of the Nuremberg synagogue. A decree is issued requiring all Jews to carry the first name of either "Israel" or "Sarah" from 1939.

AUGUST 17

NAZI PARTY, *WAFFEN-SS*
Hitler defines the *raison d'être* of the *SS-Verfügungstruppe* as being an armed force at his personal disposal, stating that it is not a part of the armed forces nor of the police

had been hypothesized that Hitler was playing a double game and allowing the expansion of the *SS-Verfügungstruppe* as a counter to any possible coup by the army.

In the early stages of his regime this was extremely unlikely, and Hitler bent over backwards in his efforts to appease the army. From these provisions emerged the first four of what were to become known in 1940 as the *Waffen-SS* divisions: the *Leibstandarte Adolf Hitler*, *Das Reich*, *Totenkopf* and *Polizei*, plus the nucleus of a fifth, *Wiking*.

AUGUST 22

ARMED FORCES, *NAVY*
The heavy cruiser *Prinz Eugen* is launched.

SEPTEMBER

GERMANY, *DIPLOMACY*
British prime minister Chamberlain meets first with Hitler at Godesberg, then with Daladier and Mussolini at Munich, where they agree that the Sudetenland should go to Germany (see box right). This signals the collapse of the army generals' plot against Hitler's regime.

KEY MOMENTS

The Munich Agreement

After his success in absorbing Austria into Germany proper in March 1938, Adolf Hitler looked covetously at Czechoslovakia, where about three million people in the Sudeten area were of German origin. It became known in May 1938 that Hitler and his generals were drawing up a plan for the occupation of Czechoslovakia.

The Czechs were relying on military assistance from France, with which they had an alliance. As Hitler continued to make inflammatory speeches demanding that Germans in Czechoslovakia be reunited with their homeland, war seemed imminent. Neither France nor Britain felt prepared to defend Czechoslovakia, however. In mid-September, Hitler agreed to take no military action without further discussion, and Chamberlain agreed to try to persuade his Cabinet and the French to accept the results of a plebiscite in the Sudetenland. The French premier, Édouard Daladier, and his foreign minister, Georges Bonnet, then went to London, where a joint proposal was prepared stipulating that all areas with a population that was more than 50 percent Sudeten German be returned to Germany. The Czechs were not consulted. The Czech government initially rejected the proposal but reluctantly accepted it on September 21.

On September 22 Chamberlain again flew to Germany and met Hitler, where he learned he now wanted the Sudetenland occupied by the German Army and the Czechoslovaks evacuated from the area by September 28. The Czechs rejected this, as did the British Cabinet and the French. On the 24th the French ordered a partial mobilization: the Czechoslovaks had ordered a general mobilization one day earlier.

In a last-minute effort to avoid war, Chamberlain then proposed that a four-power conference be convened immediately to settle the dispute. Hitler agreed, and on September 29, Hitler, Chamberlain, Daladier, and Mussolini met in Munich, where Mussolini introduced a written plan that was accepted by all as the Munich Agreement: the German Army was to complete the occupation of the Sudetenland by October 10, and an international commission would decide the future of other disputed areas. Czechoslovakia was informed by Britain and France that it could either resist Germany alone or submit to the prescribed annexations. The Czechs capitulated.

Before leaving Munich, Chamberlain and Hitler signed a paper declaring their mutual desire to resolve differences through consultation to assure peace. Chamberlain returned home a hero.

SEPTEMBER 5–12

NAZI PARTY, *RALLIES*
Party Rally of Greater Germany.

SEPTEMBER 27

SS, *WAFFEN-SS*
SS *Totenkopf* units are moved into the Sudetenland to reinforce the frontier guards and provide the cadre for the Sudeten Free Corps, whose overt mission was the protection of the German minority and covert mission the maintenance of disturbances and clashes with the Czechs.

OCTOBER

GERMANY, *ANTI-SEMITISM*
Passports for Jews are to be stamped "J" henceforth. The expulsion of 17,000 former Polish Jews from Germany takes place.

OCTOBER 1

CZECHOSLOVAKIA, *SUDETENLAND*
Germany occupies the Sudetenland in accordance with the terms of the Munich Agreement reached in September (see box on page 99).

▲ *The heavy cruiser* **Prinz Eugen**, *which was launched in August as part of the Kriegsmarine's rearmament policy.*

▼ *The army parades its standards in salute of Hitler in 1938. The army was delighted that he had restored its pride.*

NOVEMBER 9

GERMANY, *ANTI-SEMITISM*

Ernst von Rath was a young diplomat holding a secretarial position in the German Embassy in Paris. A Jew named Herschel Grynszpan had the idea of assassinating the German Ambassador, Count Johannes von Welczek. Grynszpan went to the embassy and asked the receptionist for an interview with the ambassador. The receptionist inquired as to the nature of his business, to which he gave no reply and began to act suspiciously. The

NOVEMBER 1

SPAIN, *GERMAN AID*

The last commander of the Legion, *Generalmajor* Wolfram Freiherr von Richthofen, has served as Chief of Staff to both Sperrle and Volkmann. He now takes over the command of the unit and retains it throughout the remaining months of the Spanish Civil War. Though many of the aircraft are in a poor state of repair, many pilots have gained valuable combat experience. Richthofen would lead the Condor Legion back on its triumphant return to Germany in 1939.

▲ *The cutting edge of Hitler's army: panzers. German propaganda always exaggerated their number.*

▼ *The map of Europe in 1938. Within months, Austria and the whole of Czechoslovakia would be German.*

▲ *Tanks and armoured cars (shown here) spearheaded the takeover of Austria and the Sudetenland to show German strength.*

[Map of Europe in 1938 showing: FINLAND, NORWAY, SWEDEN, ESTONIA, USSR, LATVIA, DENMARK, LITHUANIA, EAST PRUSSIA, UK, NETHERLANDS, POLAND, GERMANY, BELGIUM, CZECHOSLOVAKIA, FRANCE, AUSTRIA, SWITZERLAND, HUNGARY, ROMANIA, ITALY, YUGOSLAVIA, PORTUGAL, BULGARIA, SPAIN, ALBANIA, TURKEY, GREECE]

receptionist rang for assistance from the inner office. Ernst von Rath answered the call and proceeded to the entrance hall to assist the receptionist. Grynszpan, thinking Ernst von Rath was the ambassador, pulled out a revolver and shot at him six times. Only three of the rounds found their mark, one hitting him in the foot, another in the shoulder and the third in the stomach. He was rushed to hospital, but died later.

In response, Heydrich organizes "Crystal Night", a pogrom against the Jews. More than 20,000 Jews are imprisoned, 74 killed, decrees eliminate Jews from the economy and demand a collective fine of 12,500 million Marks to pay for the destruction caused by the Nazi mob. The expulsion of all Jews from schools follows. Roosevelt, US president, recalls his ambassador.

DECEMBER

GERMANY, *LEGAL*

Compulsory Aryanization of all Jewish shops and firms.

1939

Despite the appeasement of Great Britain and France, Hitler's territorial ambitions could only be satisfied by the conquest of Poland. Great Britain and France finally realized that Hitler was determined to absorb Poland just as he had the Austrians and Czechs. They therefore signed treaties with the Poles guaranteeing to declare war on Germany should Hitler invade. But the world was stunned by the Russo-German Non-Aggression Treaty, which sealed the fate of Poland. On September 1 German forces attacked Poland. World War II had begun.

JANUARY 12

NAZI PARTY, *PERSONALITIES*
The SS leadership pay their respects to Göring on his 46h birthday. Present are Heissmeyer, Daluege, Himmler, Heydrich, Nebe, Wolff, Besr, Darré, Backe and Greifelt.
GERMANY, *MEDIA*
Members of the SS show-jumping team are interviewed on German television. The team comprises Hermann Fegelein (who would later marry Eva Braun's sister) and his brothers Waldemar and Temme.

FEBRUARY 14

ARMED FORCES, *NAVY*
The battleship *Bismarck* is launched. The ship was ordered to be built by the shipbuilding firm Blohm & Voss. The keel was laid down on July 1, 1936 at the Blohm & Voss shipyard facilities in Hamburg. By September 1938, the hull was already complete to the level of the upper deck. The launching ceremony is attended by thousands of people, military personalities, government officials, and yard workers. Adolf Hitler delivers the pre-launch speech and the hull is then christened by Frau Dorothea von Loewenfeld, granddaughter of the German chancellor Otto von Bismarck, after whom the ship was named. Moments afterwards, at 13:30 hours, *Bismarck*'s hull slipped into the water.

▶ *The pride of the German fleet, the battleship* **Bismarck** *glides into the water on the day of her launch.*

After launching, the ship was moored to the equipping pier where the boilers, turrets and all other parts of the superstructure began to be installed. In addition, the original straight stem was replaced with a new "Atlantic" bow that offered better sea-keeping capabilities and a different arrangement for the anchors. The war started in September 1939, but despite this and the hard winter that came after, the construction work continued as scheduled to produce a potent warship.

MARCH

GERMANY, *AGGRESSION*
Germany occupies Bohemia and Moravia as "Protectorates" – Czechoslovakia has disappeared from the map of Europe. Memel is also annexed from Lithuania. The

▲ The Germany Army rolls into Bohemia in March as Hitler declares it and Moravia German "Protectorates".

Free City of Danzig and the "Polish Corridor" is also demanded. German nationalists were outraged when Poland was given the narrow strip of land that divided Prussia from the rest of Germany. At this time, Nazis within Danzig are agitating for union with Germany.

▲ The waterfront in Danzig, The Free City that Hitler wanted back. Note the Nazi flags; there were many Nazis in the city.

◄ Another German conquest on the Baltic. These smiling troops are the new rulers of Memel.

▼ Grand-Admiral Erich Raeder, commander of the Kriegsmarine, which grew dramatically under the Nazis.

APRIL

GERMANY, *LEGAL*

Confiscation of all Jewish valuables. A law on Tenancies is passed, foreseeing all Jews living together in "Jewish houses".

APRIL 1

ARMED FORCES, *NAVY*

The battleship *Tirpitz* is launched. Erich Raeder is promoted from General-Admiral to Grand-Admiral, a rank unused since World War I.

SS, *TOTENKOPFVERBÄNDE*

The organization of the *SS-Totenkopfverbände* was fixed at: four *Standarten* of three *Sturmbanne* with three infantry companies, comprising 148 men each, one machine-gun company comprising 150 men, and medical, transport

midnight on this day. It states:

Today the Red Army is captive and disarmed and the Nationalist troops have achieved their final military objective. The war is over.

APRIL 14

NAZI PARTY, *AWARDS*

Hitler, in response to the last Nationalist military communiqué from Spain, announces the institution of an award for the bravery of the members of the Condor Legion, which is also to serve as a campaign medal. It is worthy of note that the title bestowed on the entire series of this new award at the time of request for design approval was that of the Spanish Cross of the Legion Condor.

APRIL 27

GERMANY, *DIPLOMACY*

Hitler repudiates the Anglo-German Naval Treaty, which had been signed four years earlier.

and communications units. By the end of 1938 Eicke's men had all received some basic military training. The *SS-Totenkopfverbände* made no tactical contribution to the German campaign in Poland, but was extensively employed in the Führer's social plan for that country where the *SS-Totenkopfverbände* received its initiation in blood, being employed in terrorizing the civilian population.

APRIL 2

SPAIN, *GERMAN AID*

The end of the Spanish Civil War is officially announced in the last Nationalist military communiqué, issued in Madrid at

▲ *The Roman Triumph laid on in Berlin for the returning Condor Legion.*

▶ *Wolfram Richthofen (far right), the last commander of the Condor Legion.*

▼ *Veterans of the Condor Legion march past Hitler during the parade in Berlin.*

APRIL 29

ARMED FORCES, *NAVY*

The heavy cruiser *Admiral Hipper* is commissioned.

MAY 12

SPAIN, *GERMAN AID*

Barajas Field, some 13km (eight miles) from Madrid, serves on as the venue for Generalissimo Franco to bestow 15 German and eight Italian flyers with Spain's second-highest military decoration, the Military Medal. As each man is decorated, a Spanish aviation staff officer pronounces: "In the name of Spain this is given in recognition of your technical service and bravery in the anti-Bolshevist crusade."

of Generalissimo Franco. Franco then addresses the men of the Condor Legion drawn up for their final inspection. In his speech to the Legion he states that it was with the feeling of great pride that he has under his orders German leaders, officers and men. He asks them to take back with them to Germany "the imperishable gratitude of Spain".

MAY 24

NAZI PARTY, *PERSONALITIES*

Hitler attends the funeral of Friedrich Graf von der Schulenburg, the former Prussian general, and one of the most eminent names to hold honourary SS rank. Honourary members of the SS were allowed to wear uniform but had no duties or powers.

MAY 19

SPAIN, *GERMAN AID*

The victory parade celebrating the Nationalists triumph in the Civil War is held in Madrid. Over 42,000 troops representing all units of the Nationalist forces march past General Franco, who takes the salute. The parade is headed by 10,000 Italians under the command of General Gambara, leader of the Italian Legionnaires; the rear of the parade is brought up by 3500 men of the German Legion Condor under Richthofen. Apart from Spanish, Moorish, Italian and German infantry units, there is a prominent display of artillery, tanks and antiaircraft guns, while 880 aircraft fly past overhead.

▲ *A final roll call for German troops serving with the Nationalists in Spain, who will return to Germany in triumph.*

The parade, which lasts several hours, concludes with a short speech by a jubilant General Franco.

MAY 23

SPAIN, *GERMAN AID*

A final farewell parade is held for the Condor Legion at Leon in northwest Spain. On the aerodrome of "Our Lady of Travellers" *Generalmajor* von Richthofen presents his troops with Spanish decorations of varying grades in the name

MAY 25

SPAIN, *GERMAN AID*

The German troops begin to embark on six "Strength through Joy" ships that have arrived at Vigo, and shortly afterwards they set sail for Germany. Before leaving Spain, the German and the Italian Legionnaires hand over their arms and war materials to the Spanish Government.

▼ *Franco shows his gratitude: honours are showered on the Condor Legion by Spain's new ruler.*

▲ *The Soviet dictator Stalin (left) and his foreign secretary Molotov, who negotiated the Non-Aggression Treaty with Germany.*

MAY 30

ARMED FORCES, *RALLIES*

The Condor Legion lands at Hamburg where it receives an official welcome from *Generalfeldmarschall* Göring. Göring announces that Hitler has instituted a new decoration, The Spanish Cross, in four classes of Bronze, Silver, Gold and Gold with Brilliants. All volunteers from the Civil War are to receive one of the four classes. It is further announced that the Condor Legion is to be officially disolved within a few days, and that in proud memory of the Legion's battle against international communism, the name "Condor" has been bestowed by Hitler himself on a *Luftwaffe* aircraft wing, an antiaircraft regiment and a signals battalion.

A few days after their arrival in Hamburg, the troops of the Legion proceeded to Döberitz, the military centre near Berlin.

JUNE 4

ARMED FORCES, *RALLIES*

At Döberitz, the Legion is visited by Grand-Admiral Raeder, the commander-in-chief of the German Navy. The Grand-Admiral distributes decorations to the naval contingent and *Generalfeldmarschall* Göring presents decorations to the *Luftwaffe* members of the Legion.

JUNE 6

ARMED FORCES, *RALLIES*

The Condor Legion undertakes its last public appearance. At a special military parade held in the Reich capital, over 14,000 troops from the Legion, which includes 3000 sailors and 1000 men from the army, march past Hitler in review order. The Legion is led by *Generalmajor* von Richthofen and the three previous commanders: Volkmann, Sperrle and Warlimont. The population of Berlin give them a reception worthy of a victorious army. The Marble Gallery of the new Reich Chancellery is the venue for a special ceremony where Hitler, accompanied by Göring, presents the Spanish Cross in Gold to air force officers of the Condor Legion and naval officers from the pocket battleship *Deutschland*.

It would appear that there was no prerequisite for having a higher award, and the grade of the cross tended to be related to the rank of the person to whom it was

▲ *The British ambassador to Berlin, Sir Neville Henderson (left), who at first believed that Hitler would not go to war.*

▼ *Preparations for world war – the pocket battleship* Admiral Graf Spee *slips out of Wilhelmshaven.*

awarded. Who received which grade was dependant upon the highest Spanish decoration a German volunteer received.

JULY

GERMANY, *DIPLOMACY*

Hitler's foreign minister, Ribbentrop, starts trade talks between the Soviet Union and Germany, which include secret talks on improving political relations and mutual spheres of influence.

AUGUST 18

ARMED FORCES, *NAVY*

The German Naval High Command orders the previously planned "Three Front War Programme" to come into effect as an emergency measure.

AUGUST 19

ARMED FORCES, *NAVY*

14 submarines leave Germany and sail to their war stations in the North Atlantic.

AUGUST 21

ARMED FORCES, *NAVY*

The pocket battleship *Admiral Graf Spee* sails from Wilhelmshaven.

AUGUST 23

GERMANY, *TREATIES*

Ribbentrop and his Soviet counterpart, Molotov sign the Russo-German Non-aggression Treaty, by which neither party would attack the other and spheres of influence were agreed regarding the Baltic states and Poland.

▲ *Cuff band of the SS-Heimwehr Danzig, an SS unit set up in the city to assist the German invaders.*

In order to avoid a two-front war Hitler decided that the Soviet Union would have to be neutralized; to which end Hitler directed Ribbentrop to open negotiations with the Soviets. His first diplomatic overtures in Moscow were not successful. The Soviets were stalling for time as they were already negotiating with Great Britain and France. Hitler, desperate to conclude an agreement, decided to intervene personally and on August 20 sent a telegram to Stalin asking him to receive his foreign minister immediately and adding: "The conclusion of a non-aggression pact for me means the fulfilment of a long-standing German policy.

▲ *Members of the SS-Heimwehr Danzig in action against Polish troops in Danzig at the beginning of September.*

◄ *German motorized infantry tackle one of Poland's dirt roads during the Blitzkrieg (Lightning War) campaign.*

Germany now resumes a political course that was beneficial to both states in past centuries. In view of the intention of both states to enter into a new relationship to each other it seems to me best not to lose any time. I therefore propose that you receive my Foreign Minister on Tuesday, August 22, or at the latest Wednesday August 23. The Reich Minister has the fullest power to draw up and sign the non-aggression pact as well as the protocol. In view of the international situation a longer stay by the minister in Moscow is impossible. A crisis may arise any day. Germany is determined to use all measures at her disposal to protect the interests of the Reich. I should be glad to receive your early answer."

On the evening of August 21, Hitler was handed a telegram from Stalin. The Führer was overcome with uncontrollable excitement. "To the Chancellor of the German Reich, A. Hitler. I thank you for your letter. I hope that the German-Soviet non-aggression pact will bring about an important improvement in the political relations between our countries. The people of our countries need to live in peace with each other. The Soviet government have instructed me to inform you that they agree to receiving your Herr von Ribbentrop on the August 23 in Moscow."

Hitler was apprehensive about the meeting and its outcome, feeling that his good fortune may not hold. During the negotiations Stalin made claims on the Baltic states of Estonia, Latvia and Lithuania. Ribbentrop telephoned Hitler who authorized him to accept the Soviet proposals. The protocol reached now achieved the aims of both dictators, as all of Eastern Europe had been divided up into spheres of influence between the two countries. Hitler's attitude – that he could confidently localize any Polish conflict – was reinforced with the conclusion of the pact with the Soviet Union.

Despite British guarantees, the situation for Poland had become intolerable. Not withstanding the many assurances she received, speedy assistance from the West was most improbable. Powerful enemies,

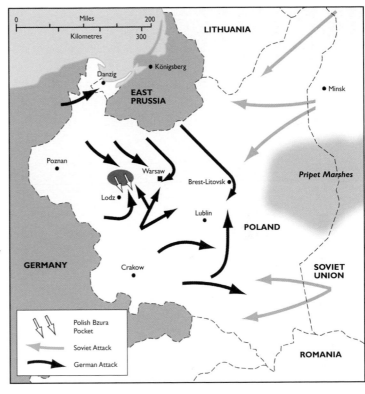

▲ *Poland's strategic situation was hopeless. She had German armies on three sides and the Soviets in the rear.*

who had just become reconciled to each other and were hungry to devour her, now hounded her on both sides. Hitler for his part counted on a Western renunciation of military intervention similar to those which had taken place in 1936, 1938 and again in the spring of 1939.

AUGUST 24

ARMED FORCES, *NAVY*
Two more U-boats depart to their war stations. The pocket battleship *Deutschland* (Hitler does want to risk a ship named after the Fatherland being sunk in any hostilities), now renamed *Lützow*, leaves Wilhelmshaven.

AUGUST 25

GERMANY, *AGGRESSION*
Hitler orders the attack against Poland in the afternoon, and about two hours later the German Army in the East leaves its position of readiness for the fateful march over the Polish frontier between the Carpathian Mountains and Lithuania. Later that afternoon Hitler has a change of heart when he receives a letter from the British

▼ *Danzig, assaulted by the German Army externally and riddled with Nazi sympathizers, fell almost at once.*

GERMANY, *MERCHANT MARINE*
German merchant ships are instructed to
return home to Germany or to make for the
nearest neutral port. The threat of war
hangs over Europe like a black cloud.

GERMANY, *ARMED FORCES*
In German military circles there is little

◄ *Warsaw burns following a Luftwaffe raid on September 25, carried out on Hitler's personel orders.*

government that reaffirms the British
intention to help Poland if Germany
invades that country, and that a mutual
assistance programme between England
and Poland has been worked out in detail.
Hitler orders Keitel: "Stop everything at
once, I need time for negotiations."

The Anglo-Polish treaty was signed on the
same day at 17:40 hours and, following the
advice of his commander-in-chief who was
seeking to preserve the peace, Hitler
decided to call off the attack. Despite the
imposed radio silence, the order to halt was
passed right up to the frontline, a masterly
achievement in communication techniques.
The army generally regarded the halt as a
psychological and diplomatic weapon in the
political war of nerves; similar to that used
in the previous autumn before entering
Czechoslovakia. But since the Poles had
observed the advance and had secretly
begun to mobilize, the Germans lost their
planned operational surprise and with it all
the advantages which might have ensued.
On the other hand, they too were able to
use the time for further mobilization.

◄ *Germans in Poland. Having achieved complete air superiority on the first day of the campaign, victory was certain.*

enthusiasm for war, leading to rumblings of
disquiet. Most of the officers are well aware
of the possible military and political
difficulties which its armed forces might
encounter. These objections, which Hitler
regards as defeatist, he overrides, believing
in his own intuition.

The Polish mobilization on the March 25,
1939, caused Hitler to decide that the
German-Polish question could now only be
resolved by force, even at the risk of a
probable outbreak of war. Hitler was
confident he could localize any such
conflict, grossly underestimating both his
opponents and his influence on world

opinion. War on two fronts was Hitler's great fear, stemming from the bitter experience gained by Germany in World War I, one which, as yet, he was not ready to risk.

AUGUST 28

GREAT BRITAIN, *DIPLOMACY*

At 22:00 hours at the Chancellery in Berlin, Sir Neville Henderson, the British ambassador, meets Hitler to deliver another letter from the British Government stating it intends to stand by Poland. Henderson's observation was that "Hitler was once again friendly and reasonable and appeared to be not dissatisfied with the answer which I

▲ *The bombing of Warsaw broke the back of Polish resistance in the capital. The Luftwaffe had established its reputation.*

arrival, then effusive greetings at the door by Chief of the Chancellery, Otto Meissner. However, it was another matter once inside the Chancellery. Henderson's recollections were vivid: "I immediately sensed a more uncompromising attitude than the previous evening on Hitler's part." The British Government's letter received a reply from

Hitler that was starkly uncompromising, stating that the Danzig problem must be settled peacefully on German terms by the following day or he would use force. Henderson left the Chancellery noticing that the anteroom was filled with German Army officers. The die was cast.

AUGUST 30

POLAND, *ARMED FORCES*

The Polish mobilization is officially announced. Hitler can wait no longer and

▲ *Little thought was given to the vanquished. These Polish refugees have had their homes destroyed by bombing.*

▶ *Though the campaign in Poland was quick and decisive, over 10,000 German soldiers were killed fighting for the Führer.*

had brought him. Our conversation lasted for well over an hour."

AUGUST 29

GREAT BRITAIN, *DIPLOMACY*

At 21:15 hours, Henderson again goes to the Chancellery, this time to receive Hitler's reply to the British Government's letter. His reception outside the building was the same as usual: SS guard of honour at the main door, roll of drums announcing his

on the next day he gives the order to invade Poland at 04:45 hours.

The time has come to undertake the deception Hitler perceived was necessary to legitimize the invasion. *SS-Sturmbannführer* Alfred Naujocks was chosen by *SS-Obergruppenführer* Heydrich to lead a simulated attack on the Gleiwitz radio stations. Formerly an engineering student at Kiel University; *SS-Sturmbannführer* Naujocks became an official of the *Amt* (Office) VI of the SS security service and was one of the most audacious commanders in the SD. He wasn't an intelligent leader and lacked the mental capacity for creating plans such as those which *SS-Obergruppenführer* Heydrich conceived. However, he was an expert at carrying out an operation once it was explained. He helped Heydrich with some bombings in Slovakia, which were blamed on Slovak nationalists. At 16:00 hours on August 31, *SS-Obergruppenführer* Heydrich alerted *SS-Sturmbannführer* Naujocks in Gleiwitz and ordered him to be at the radio station at 21:45 hours that evening.

The Dachau concentration camp corpses loaded on Müller's lorries were expected to arrive at approximately 21:25 hours. The dead "Polish soldiers" could then be scattered "convincingly" around the station. The deception party arrived on time at the station, finding a 1.8m- (6ft-) high wire

fence surrounding it, but the two attached buildings which were used for living quarters were unguarded. The German operational staff of the station were not privy to Heydrich's plan, so when Foitzik, an engineer, encountered *SS-Sturmbannführer* Naujocks and his companions entering the station, he mentally questioned what they were doing. As they ascended the steps leading to the broadcasting studios, he called out to them – where did they think they were going? He was silenced by the muzzle of a pistol being pointed at a spot between his eyes

On reaching the broadcasting studios, *SS-Sturmbannführer* Naujocks and his men began making as much noise as possible, hoping to give the impression that the station was under attack by a large Polish insurgent force. The ceiling of the studio received several shots, adding to the bedlam and petrifying the radio personnel. The staff of the station, who had by this time decided that resistance to the strangers was futile, surrendered, were handcuffed and taken to the basement of the building. Meanwhile, a flaw was discovered in the plan: Naujocks and his SS men did not know how to operate the

▼ *A beaming Hitler inspects men of the* **Leibstandarte** *as he tours newly conquered Poland.*

radio equipment. The SS men were frantically turning dials and flipping switches until they finally found the storm switch. This permitted them to interrupt the programme in progress, allowing Naujocks' Polish-speaking announcers to broadcast anti-German statements, to the background accompaniment of shots fired by other SS men for the next five minutes. Having decided they had convinced the listeners that the radio station was under attack by armed Poles, *SS-Sturmbannführer* Naujocks and his men withdrew.

A successful mock attack on the German customs station at Hochlinden was also made by Heydrich's SS detachment. Additional concentration camp corpses were dressed in Polish uniforms. The fact that the dead inmates' bodies were rigid due to the time of their death many hours earlier was of little importance to the SS leaders. The Polish military forces and police would not be able to investigate the bodies at Gleiwitz or Hochlinden. Hitler now had his justification for invading Poland. In fact, his soldiers and tanks were on the move before the SS men had returned to their bases.

SEPTEMBER 1

POLAND, *GERMAN AGGRESSION*

The incident at Gleiwitz is reported by the *Völkischer Beobachter* as being "clearly the signal for a general attack on German

▲ *Swastikas fly in Danzig following the end of the Polish campaign. The city was once more part of the Reich.*

territory by Polish guerrillas". Feigning outraged indignation regarding the attack on the radio station, Hitler sends a message to the German armed forces the same day: "The Polish Government, unwilling to establish good neighbourly relations as aimed at by me, wants to force the issue by way of arms The Germans in Poland arc being persecuted with bloody terror and driven from their homes. Several acts of frontier violations which cannot be tolerated by a great power shows that Poland is no longer prepared to respect the Reich's frontiers. To put an end to these mad acts, I can see no other way but from now onwards to meet force with force."

Hitler solemnly mounts the rostrum in the Kroll Opera House that morning and announces to a hushed *Reichstag* that Germany is at war with Poland, declaring towards the end of his speech: "From now on I am just the first soldier of the German Reich. I have once more put on the coat that was the most sacred and dear to me. I will not take it off again until victory is secured, or I will not survive the outcome." Those in the audience noticed that Hitler

▶ *Some of the 750,000 Poles captured by the Germans in a campaign that was characterized by speed and ruthlessness.*

had discarded his customary brown party jacket for a field-grey uniform blouse resembling that of a junior officer in the Waffen-SS.

SEPTEMBER 2–11

NAZI PARTY, *RALLIES*
Party Rally of Peace is held at Nuremberg without any sense of irony.

SEPTEMBER 3

SEA WAR, *NORTH SEA*
German ships start laying mines in the North Sea, concentrating on the defence of the German bight. Such mining operations continue through out the year, and become one of the navy's most important contributions to the war during its first winter.

EUROPE, *INTERNATIONAL RELATIONS*
Great Britain and France declare war on Germany. The Soviet Union invades Poland.

GERMANY, *LEGAL*
Jews are forbidden to be out of doors after 2000 hours in winter or 21:00 hours in summer. Confiscation of all radios from Jews is carried out.

SEPTEMBER 7

SEA WAR, *BALTIC*
Operational submarines are withdrawn from the Baltic Sea.

SEPTEMBER 16

SEA WAR, *ATLANTIC*
U-31, commanded *Kapitänleutnant* Hans Habekost, is the first U-boat to attack a British convoy.

SEPTEMBER 17

SEA WAR, *ATLANTIC*
The British aircraft carrier HMS *Courageous* is sunk by *U-29*, commanded by *Kapitänleutnant* Otto Schuhart.

SEPTEMBER 20

SEA WAR, *GERMANY*
The heavy cruiser *Blücher* is commissioned.

OCTOBER

EASTERN FRONT, *POLAND*
German armies advance rapidly through Poland. *Fall Gelb*, Operation Yellow, the invasion of France through the Low Countries, is planned.

The intention had been expressed in *Mein Kampf* in 1925 that Britain and France would stand in the way of German expansion to obtain *Lebensraum*, and thus the only solution was by force.

In 1939 began the subjugation of non-German-speaking nationalities to the totalitarian Nazi police state. When Germany started World War II, it came as the logical outcome of Hitler's plans. Thus, his first years were spent in preparing the Germans for the approaching struggle for world control and in forging that instrument which would enable Germany to establish its military and industrial superiority and thereby fulfil its ambitions. With mounting diplomatic and military successes, the aims grew in quick progression. The first aim was to unite all people of German descent within their historic homeland on the basis of "self-determination."

▲ *The British battleship* **Royal Oak** *was sunk in Scapa Flow in a daring attack by Günther Prien's* **U-47.**

The next step foresaw the creation of a *Grosswirtschaftsraum* (Large Economic Unified Space) or a *Lebensraum* (Living Space) through the military conquest of Poland and other Slavic nations to the East. Thereby the Germans would acquire sufficient soil to become economically self-sufficient and militarily impregnable. There, the German master race (*Herrenvolk*) would rule over a hierarchy of subordinate peoples and organize and exploit them with ruthlessness and efficiency.

At the beginning of October the Polish campaign was at an end. For the loss of 10,572 dead, Germany had conquered the Polish nation. The Poles lost 50,000 dead and 750,000 captured. The country was divided into two zones of occupation divided by the River Bug. The Blitzkrieg proved to be devastatingly effective.

OCTOBER 4

SEA WAR, *ATLANTIC*
The war against Allied merchant shipping is intensified by the German Naval Command, which lifts various restrictions on the types of vessels that can be attacked.

OCTOBER 13

SEA WAR, *SCAPA FLOW*
U-47, commanded by Günther Prien, penetrates the Royal Navy defences of Scapa Flow during the night of 13/14 October on a mission that is near-suicidal considering the strong currents, shallow draft, mine nets and other defensive measures. The 31-year-old Prien, commanding his first submarine, surfaces on a moonless night. Beginning his attack on the morning of the 14th, he selects as his first target the battleship HMS *Royal Oak*. He fires three of his four bow torpedoes, of which one hits and the other two miss or are duds. He then fires his stern tube, knowing that he may have already been sighted, but this also misses. By this time two of his bow tubes had been reloaded. These two, plus his remaining one, are then fired, all of which hit the aged Royal Navy battleship.

The *Royal Oak* quickly sank, taking 883 men and officers with her. Prien also hit and damaged the aircraft carrier HMS *Pegasus* and mistakenly reported it as the *Repulse*. Hitler awarded Prien the Knights Cross of the Iron Cross, which earned him the distinction of becoming the second naval officer to be so decorated. This victory was a great boost to German morale.

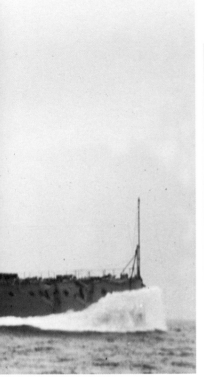

NOVEMBER 9

GERMANY, *RESISTANCE*

A bomb explodes in the Bürgerbräukeller in Munich shortly after Hitler leaves the hall on the 16th anniversary of the Munich *Putsch*.

▼ *French sailors parade in Paris, 1939. Great Britain and France failed to launch attacks to relieve pressure on the Poles.*

WESTERN FRONT, *FRANCE*

There is little military activity on the Western Front. This is the period of the "Sitzkrieg" or phoney war.

NOVEMBER 20

SEA WAR, *GREAT BRITAIN*

First mines are dropped in British waters by German aircraft.

▲ *Hitler in the Bürgerbräukeller on November 9, 1939. Moments after he left the hall, a bomb exploded.*

NOVEMBER 30

EASTERN FRONT, *FINLAND*

Russia attacks Finland, but the invasion only penetrates the border areas and is carried out so inefficiently that Germany and the world thinks the Red Army is of poor quality. But the Soviet Union had purged its officer corps three years before, on suspicion of political disloyalty, and had not

▲ *French troops near the German border in September 1939. The French Army adopted a defensive posture in the West.*

yet completed the training of enough new officers.

DECEMBER

SEA WAR, *NORWAY*

Admiral Raeder, commander of the German Navy, urges Hitler to seize Norway to make sure that Britain does not block the sea route from northern Norway, used to carry Swedish iron-ore to Germany. Rosenberg introduces Vidkun Quisling, leader of a Norwegian nationalist party with pro-Nazi views, to Hitler as a possible puppet leader for Norway.

When World War II broke out Norway, together with Sweden, Denmark and Finland, announced its neutrality. In September 1939 Germany assured Norway that it would respect its territorial integrity, but warned her that the Third Reich would not tolerate an infringement of that neutrality by a third power. Germany at this time was sincere about respecting Norwegian neutrality, but Raeder kept reminding Hitler that naval bases in Norway would be very useful in carrying the war to Great Britain. In addition, Raeder reminded the Führer, a British occupation of Norway would be disastrous for Germany because Sweden would then come entirely under British influence. This would interfere with iron-ore supplies and operations in the

Baltic. In addition, Allied aid that was being sent to the Finns might lead to an occupation of Norwegian ports. Hitler thus began to consider an invasion of Norway more carefully.

DECEMBER 1

SS, *WAFFEN-SS*

Gottlob Berger created the *Ergänzungsamt der Waffen-SS* (Waffen-SS Recruiting Office) within the *SS-Hauptamt* (SS Central Office). The remarkable growth of the

Waffen-SS must be attributed to Berger rather than Himmler. He had generally been able to outmanoeuvre and outwit his military counterparts with a cunning cocktail of diplomacy, threat and duplicity. His successes also encouraged him to undertake increasingly ambitious schemes to expand the wartime role of the SS, thus fulfilling the desires of his *Reichsführer-SS*. Berger, who had proved his organizational ability by directing the activities of the Henlien *Freikorps* during the 1938 Sudetenland crisis, was appointed by Himmler to command the new *SS-Hauptampt*, with responsibility, amongst other duties, for recruitment. One of the functions of the district leaders of the *Allgemeine-SS* had always been recruiting for the SS, but with the threat of impending war it became necessary to centralize and consolidate this increasingly important role.

The establishment of a nation-wide SS recruiting network was Berger's first task, and on December 1 he created the *Ergänzungsamt der Waffen-SS* within the SS-Hauptamt with himself as its chief, with an order he prepared and signed by Himmler. In each of the 17 *SS-Oberabschnitte* (Higher Sections), an *SS-Ergänzungsstelle* (Recruiting Centre) was established. Since the *Wehrkreise* (Army Defence Districts) were coterminous with these SS districts, Berger possessed a

▼ *French troops in the Ardennes in the winter of 1939–40. French and British inactivity would cost them dear in 1940.*

◀ *Gottlob Berger worked tirelessly to establish recruiting centres for Reichsführer-SS Himmler's Waffen-SS.*

▲ *The Admiral Graf Spee burns in Montevideo harbour after being scuttled by her crew in December.*

recruiting organization which geographically paralleled that of the army. The *Oberkommando der Wehrmacht* (OKW), High Command of the Armed Forces, at the same time issued an order to military district commanders explaining the function of the new bureaus and ordering them to deal directly with the *SS-Ergänzungsstelle* in all SS personnel matters.

DECEMBER 13

SEA WAR, *ATLANTIC*
The British submarine HMS *Salmon* scores torpedo hits on the cruisers *Leipzig* and *Nürnberg*.

DECEMBER 15

SEA WAR, *ATLANTIC*
The damaged *Leipzig* is torpedoed again, this time by HMS *Ursula*.

DECEMBER 17

SEA WAR, *ATLANTIC*
The Battle of the River Plate. After sinking several merchant ships in the

Atlantic, the *Admiral Graf Spee* was sighted on December 13, 1939, off the Río de la Plata estuary by a British search group consisting of the cruisers *Exeter*, *Ajax* and *Achilles*, commanded by Commodore H. Harwood. At 06:14 hours Harwood's three ships attacked, but in a little more than an hour the *Admiral Graf Spee* had damaged the *Exeter* and driven off the other two cruisers. The *Admiral Graf Spee* then made for Montevideo, Uruguay, where its commander, Captain Hans Langsdorff, obtained permission to stay for four days to repair damage. The British devoted the period to intense diplomatic and intelligence activity in order to keep the *Admiral Graf Spee* in harbour while they brought up heavy reinforcements. On December 17, however, when the *Admiral Graf Spee* put to sea again, only the *Cumberland* had arrived to reinforce the *Ajax* and the *Achilles*. The fight that the British had anticipated never took place: Captain Langsdorff, believing that a superior force awaited him, had his crew scuttle their ship; three days later Langsdorff shot himself.

1940

This year Germany maintained her series of military victories by defeating the combined armies of Great Britain and France in a quick campaign. The victory against Poland had been won against a foe that was inferior to the German Army, but in the West in 1940 the *Wehrmacht* defeated opponents who were technologically equal, and who actually had more tanks and aircraft. But the German Army used its weapons and men more imaginatively. At sea, meanwhile, the U-boat campaign in the Atlantic gathered momentum.

▲ The Altmark *photographed after the incident with HMS* Cossack *in mid-February 1940.*

JANUARY 10

WESTERN FRONT, *BELGIUM*

News received from the German embassy in Brussels puts *Luftwaffe* headquarters into turmoil when it learns of the crash-landing of a German military plane near the Belgian town of Mechelen-sur-Meuse. The aircraft, on a flight from Münster to Cologne, became lost in thick cloud. After it came down, one of the passengers jumped out and raced for a clump of bushes, where

he set fire to papers he had taken from his briefcase. Belgian soldiers closed in and retrieved the partly burnt papers. The man has been identified as Major Helmut Reinberger, a *Luftwaffe* staff officer, and the papers are operational plans, complete with maps, for a German airborne attack on the West, to begin on January 14 with saturation bombing attacks on French airfields. When distraught aides gave news

▼ *Great Britain's lifeline: an Atlantic convoy bringing supplies from the United States, now under U-boat threat.*

the gloves off in the battle to stop essential supplies of food and war materials reaching Great Britain from the United States. Any ship which is likely to come under British control can now be torpedoed without warning.

The policy was already in effect, as was made evident by the sinking of Danish, Dutch, Norwegian and Swedish ships in the days that preceded the order. Danish newspapers protested loudly at the sinking of one of their ships, the *5177*, to Chastine Maersk by a U-boat.

FEBRUARY 16

SEA WAR, *BALTIC*

The destroyer HMS *Cossack* rescues some 299 British seamen held prisoner on the

▼ **The Altmark after having been driven farther into the Norwegian fjord following the engagement with HMS Cossack.**

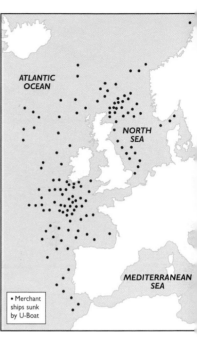

▲ *This map shows the success the U-boats enjoyed against merchant shipping between September 1939 and May 1940.*

ATLANTIC
OCEAN

NORTH
SEA

MEDITERRANEAN
SEA

• Merchant ships sunk by U-Boat

of the lost plans to Hitler, the Führer exploded in anger and retorted: "It's things like this that can lose us the war."

FEBRUARY

GERMANY, *ANTI-SEMITISM*

First deportations of Jews from Germany begin, mainly from Pomerania.

FEBRUARY 15

SEA WAR, *ATLANTIC*

Hitler gives the order for unlimited U-boat war. U-boat commanders are ordered to take

▶ *A German U-boat in the Atlantic in February 1940. Hitler gave his submarines licence to attack any potential enemy.*

Altmark. The *Altmark* was the supply ship for the German pocket battleship *Admiral Graf Spee*, and the prisoners had been taken from merchant ships captured by her. After the sinking of the *Admiral Graf Spee*, the *Altmark* sailed for Europe, taking a route near the Arctic to avoid detection. Incredibly, the Norwegians, who stopped and searched her, found neither her

▲ *Airborne troops were used extensively by the Germans in Norway and Denmark to seize airfields and strongpoints.*

concealed guns nor the prisoners. Two British destroyers then chased her into Jossing Fjord. The *Cossack* lowered two boats, but they could not move through the ice. The *Altmark* then made two attempts to ram the *Cossack*. As the two ships scraped together, several members of a boarding party leapt aboard the German ship. The *Altmark* then ran aground and the rest of the Royal Navy party scrambled over the side, opening fire with their rifles and charging with fixed bayonets. Four German crewmen were killed. One prisoner said: "It was a hit-and-run affair along the decks and round corners, more of a rathunt than anything. You can imagine our joy when we heard an English voice shouting down 'The Navy's here!'"

The captain of the *Altmark* had denied the existence of prisoners right up to the end. One prisoner told how they had shouted, hammered and blown SOS whistles to attract the attention of the Norwegian search party at Bergen. The Germans turned a fire hose on them to stop them, and to drown the noise they turned on a winch. Even so, the prisoners found it difficult to understand why the Norwegians had not noticed something of their presence. Afterwards the Germans told them that their behaviour was mutiny and put out a notice saying: "On account of today's behaviour of the prisoners, they will get bread and water tomorrow instead of their regular meals."

FEBRUARY 22

SEA WAR, *NORTH SEA*
The Dutch destroyers *Leberecht Maass*, commanded by *Korvettenkapitän* Fritz Bassenge, and *Max Schultz*, commanded by *Korvettenkapitän* Claus Trampedach, while trying to avoid an attack by German aircraft, run onto mines laid by a British submarine.

MARCH 11

EASTERN FRONT, *FINLAND*
Finland signs a peace treaty with the Soviet Union, ceding territory around the Baltic to

▼ *The* Admiral Hipper *sinks the Royal Navy destroyer HMS* Glowworm *after the latter had rammed her.*

▲ *The German plan for the attack on the West in May 1940 compared to the Schlieffen Plan of World War I.*

improve Soviet defences. The war has not been a great success for the Red Army. It has lost 200,000 men, while the Finns lost only 25,000.

NORTHERN FRONT, *SCANDINAVIA*
Hitler, convinced of his military planning ability after the victory against Poland in 1939, orders an attack on Norway. Denmark is also included in the plan. He takes personal charge, issuing orders through Keitel and his OKW rather than planning through *Oberkommando des Heeres* (OKH), the Army High Command.

MARCH 31

SEA WAR, *ATLANTIC*
The auxiliary cruiser *Atlantis*, commanded by *Kapitän zur See* Bernhard Rogge, leaves German coastal waters, the first auxiliary cruiser to do so. The many days at sea stretched into months, and the total shipping tons of enemy vessels sunk reaches 93,803. Rogge went on to become

▼ *The Blitzkrieg in operation in Norway. German troops go into the attack following an artillery barrage.*

▲ *Major-General Eduard Dietl (centre) commanded the German 3rd Mountain Division at Narvik in northern Norway.*

the most successful and famous of the auxiliary cruiser commanders. His success is directly attributed to the courage displayed by the men of his command, the manoeuvring tactics, and his ability to disguise his ship. In recognition of the outstanding success achieved by the ship, Rogge was awarded the Knights Cross of the Iron Cross on December 7, 1940.

APRIL 6

SEA WAR, *ATLANTIC*
The *Orion* under the command of *Kapitän zur See* Weyher, becomes the second auxiliary cruiser to leave Germany.

APRIL 8

SEA WAR, *NORWAY*
The British lay mines off Norway. The *Admiral Hipper* sinks the British destroyer HMS *Glowworm*.

APRIL 9

NORTHERN FRONT, NORWAY
The invasion of Denmark and Norway, codename *Fall Weserübung* or Operation Weser Exercise, begins in the early dawn. The operation is characterized by lightning speed, meticulous planning and total secrecy. In Denmark it is met with virtually no resistance. Two German aircraft are shot down and a few armoured cars damaged.

Thirteen Danish soldiers are killed and another 23 wounded. It is nothing more than a skirmish.

Before the Danes had had breakfast, it was all over. There was no "fifth column". The *Volksdeutsche* (ethnic Germans) and the pro-German Danes were as surprised as any by the fate which literally fell from the sky upon them. It was the first example in any war of a successful airborne operation. Once they had recovered from their shock, the North Schleswig Germans welcomed the arrival of "their" army. They offered hospitality, directed traffic and in some cases even took it upon themselves to round up and guard Danish prisoners of war. But nowhere did any Danish citizen indulge in any act of premeditated sabotage. Before the invasion the Germans had dispatched a small commando unit to Pagborg to ensure that the Danes did not try to impede their advance by blowing up the important bridge there – an unnecessary precaution, as the Danes had not even mined it.

The German Navy sailed into Norwegian ports from Oslo to Narvik in the north and landed troops. German naval losses were heavy, with three cruisers, *Karlsruhe*, *Königsberg* and *Blücher*, being sunk and a battleship badly damaged. In southern Norway German troops were also landed by air. *Luftwaffe* units took over airfields and gained air superiority over Norway. The

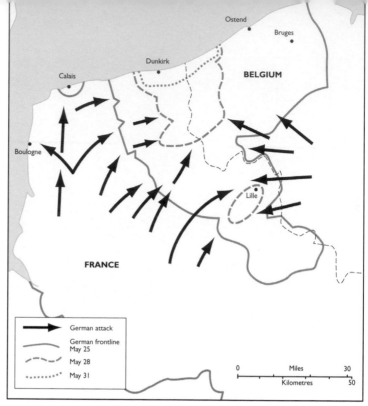

German attack

German frontline
May 25

May 28

May 31

0   Miles   30

Kilometres   50

▼ *The Belgian fortress of Eben Emael, reckoned to be impregnable, was captured by German paratroopers in gliders.*

▲ *The fight to hold the Dunkirk perimeter was fierce, though Hitler did not permit his panzers to attack the port.*

next morning the lookouts spotted the outline of the *Blücher* approaching in the darkness. Two 280mm shells hit her director control tower, and lighter guns demolished the bridge. Wrecked and ablaze, the *Blücher* tried to creep out of range, but as she passed the fortress, two torpedoes were fired by the fixed tubes ashore. Both hit the mark and she rolled over and sank. The guns then turned on the *Brummer*, and within a few minutes the whole of the force was in retreat down the fjord. In Norway the Germans were not a moment too soon; the British Navy was almost simultaneously mounting Operation Wilfred, the laying of mines off the

▲ *Hitler poses with some of those paratroopers who captured the fortress of Eben Emael in May 1940.*

▶ *Rotterdam burns following the devastating Luftwaffe attack on the city, which demoralized the citizens.*

heavy cruiser *Blücher* was part of a task force which tried to seize Oslo by surprise on April 8. With the pocket battleship *Lützow*, the light cruiser *Emden* and the gunnery training ship *Brummer*, she went up Oslo Fjord that night. The arrival of the force had been reported to the coastal fortress of Oskarsborg on the Island of Kalholmen and although the guns were old and the gunners were elderly reservists, both were adequate to the task for which they had been designed. At 03:30 hours

◀ *General Erwin Rommel (centre), commander of the 7th Panzer Division, led the panzers to the Channel in May 1940.*

Norwegian coast. But in the terminology of the "Gun fighter" the Germans had the drop on the British. It was the *Kriegsmarine*, not the Royal Navy, that sailed first into Norwegian waters. In spite of all the ominous portents, the Norwegian authorities were taken completely by surprise. The campaign lasted 62 days and cost the lives of 5000 casualties on both sides. Eduard Dietl, the "Hero of Narvik", stated later: "Had the British held on for another two hours I would have withdrawn." But they did not and the conquest of Norway was assured. For his decisive leadership during the battle of Narvik, he was awarded the Knights Cross of the Iron Cross on May 9, 1940. No SS troops were used in either of these countries, which is a little surprising

considering Himmler's eagerness to test his racial warriors. With the occupation of these strategic countries complete, Hitler was free to make his next move.

APRIL 10

SEA WAR, *NORWAY*
The light cruisers *Karlsruhe* and *Königsberg* are sunk in Norwegian waters. *Königsberg*'s presence at Bergen was noted by British reconnaissance aircraft and word was passed to a group of 15 Skua dive-bombers based at Hatston in the Orkneys by the carrier HMS *Ark Royal*. At their maximum range the Skuas took the cruiser by surprise and sank her at her moorings with three 500lb bombs. The *Karlsruhe* was torpedoed off Kristiansund by the British submarine HMS *Truant* shortly after landing troops during the invasion of Norway, and had to be sunk by her escort after the crew had been rescued.

APRIL 14

NORTHERN FRONT, *NORWAY*
Anglo-French troops are landed at Narvik and near Trondheim, but are unable to do more than hold some of their landing areas.
SEA WAR, *ATLANTIC*
U-49, commanded by *Kapitänleutnant* Johann Egbert von Gossler, is sunk by HMS *Brazen* and HMS *Fearless*. Secret documents, probably connected with the German "Enigma" cyphering machine, float to the surface and are then captured by the British.

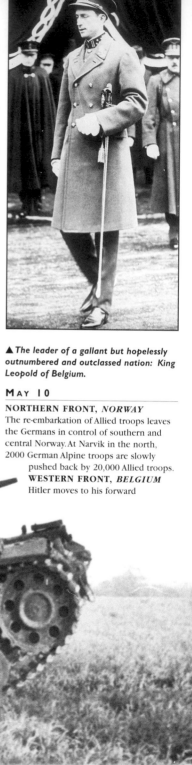

▲ The leader of a gallant but hopelessly outnumbered and outclassed nation: King Leopold of Belgium.

MAY 10

NORTHERN FRONT, *NORWAY*
The re-embarkation of Allied troops leaves the Germans in control of southern and central Norway. At Narvik in the north, 2000 German Alpine troops are slowly pushed back by 20,000 Allied troops.
WESTERN FRONT, *BELGIUM*
Hitler moves to his forward

▲ Field Marshal Walther von Brauchitsch, commander of Germany's forces in the attack on the West in May 1940.

▶ The spearhead of the Blitzkrieg: a Panzer III tank races through the French countryside in May 1940.

artillery pieces in four casements and three revolving turrets. The field of fire from these guns allowed them to cover Maastricht to the north and Vise to the south, as well as the three bridges across the Albert Canal that were also to be taken. The two 120mm guns were encased in a huge rotating steel dome. All the artillery positions were connected by 4.5km (2.8 miles) of corridors, stairs and lifts, and officers even used bicycles to move around the complex. Some 500 Belgian artillery troops manned the large guns, with an additional 500 men manning the immediate defences on the flat roof of the fortress, consisting of 60mm antiaircraft guns, searchlights and heavy machine guns. Two heavy machine-gun bunkers sat atop the surface. Eben Emael also had dummy installations to fool any attacker. The only downside to Eben Emael was the lack of surface trenches and defences against infantry attack.

Before the Netherlands are attacked, a key frontier bridge is taken by "Brandenburgers'", small groups of Dutch-speaking and sometimes Dutch-uniformed troops. Parachute troops are landed near The Hague and communications are soon in German hands. "Brandenburgers" dressed as tourists pass into Luxembourg,

▲ *The lucky ones: some of the 300,000 Allied troops taken off the beaches of Dunkirk by British ships.*

▶ *Behind them they left all their heavy equipment and vehicles. These are spiked British antiaircraft guns on the Dunkirk beaches.*

headquarters, Felsennest (Cliff Nest) at Bad Munstereiffel, about 48km (30 miles) from the Belgian frontier, and issues the codeword Danzig which sets *Fall Gelb*, Operation Yellow – modified by General Erich von Manstein in operation – a strike through the Ardennes towards the English Channel to defeat the British and French.

On May 10 aircraft hit pre-arranged targets, while paratroopers prepared to seize vital objectives, one of these being the Belgian fort of Eben Emael. It was a well-situated, well-armed and well-defended strongpoint built into the side of the Albert Canal, with the natural defences on one side and an antitank ditch and barbed-wire defences on the other. Eben Emael was considered to be virtually impregnable due to its location. It measured approximately 700m (2296ft) east to west and 900m (2952ft) north to south. It had a formidable arsenal of 16 75mm and two 120mm

clearing minefields and roadblocks and keeping bridges intact.

MAY 11

WESTERN FRONT, *BELGIUM*
Fort Eben Emael, guarding a bridge on the Belgian border, is taken by German troops landing gliders on top of the caissons. Two panzer divisions move into Belgium.

MAY 14

WESTERN FRONT, *ARDENNES*
Rotterdam is heavily bombed on the fourth day to hasten the Dutch surrender. Rundstedt's Army Group A moves through southern Belgium, with a panzer corps under Guderian moving through the Ardennes' hills and forests. The French, taken by surprise at armour coming through the "unpassable" Ardennes, wait for them to halt at the River Meuse. But Rommel's 7th Panzer Division crosses the river. The same day, all of Guderian's panzers are across and racing through the open country beyond, with Junkers Ju 87 Stuka dive-bombers clearing opposition before them. This is classic Blitzkrieg strategy: to sustain the momentum of the advance by avoiding centres of resistance to strike the enemy's rear areas and his lines of communication and supply. Bold commanders take advantage of new opportunities as they arise.

▲ *Panzers parade in Paris. The Blitzkrieg in the West took just six weeks, and established German military prowess.*

MAY 15

WESTERN FRONT, *HOLLAND*
The Dutch Army surrenders. One of Guderian's divisions is 64km (40 miles) beyond the Meuse and still advancing west.

MAY 17

WESTERN FRONT, *BELGIUM*
The Belgian capital, Brussels, is taken.

▼ *The Waffen-SS in the West. These are troops of the Totenkopf Division moving through northern France.*

▲ The leader of Vichy France, Marshal Pétain. He felt it was his duty to establish a new regime after the French defeat.

◀ In 1940 French military defeat was accompanied by humiliation as German troops took possession of Paris itself.

MAY 19

FRANCE, *POLITICS*
French Premier Reynaud appoints Marshal Pétain as Vice Premier.

MAY 20

WESTERN FRONT, *FRANCE*
The German Army reaches the English Channel, cutting the Allied forces in two. The commander-in-chief, von Brauchitsch, wants to round up the trapped Anglo-French and Belgian troops, but Rundstedt decides to halt and regroup his forces; Hitler confirms these orders to give Göring's *Luftwaffe* the chance to distinguish itself by destroying the Allied armies in the Dunkirk Pocket. However, the sands reduce the effect of aircrafts' bombs.

MAY 27

WESTERN FRONT, *DUNKIRK*
British start evacuations of troops, including French and Belgian, from beaches of Dunkirk to England. The Belgian King Leopold of Belgium surrenders.

▶ Under the terms of the Armistice the Germans left Vichy areas, but they retained control of he vital Atlantic ports.

SEA WAR, *PACIFIC*
The German auxiliary cruiser *Orion* passes Cape Horn on her outward voyage.

JUNE 3

WESTERN FRONT, *DUNKIRK*
The Dunkirk evacuation ends; over 300,000 soldiers are taken to England, but without their equipment and weapons. Another 200,000 are evacuated from other ports.

JUNE 5

WESTERN FRONT, *FRANCE*
The German Army resumes its offensive, moving south and west into France. Guderian takes the French defensive Maginot Line in the rear and encircles a

large part of the remaining French Army, which is now totally demoralized.

JUNE 7

NORTHERN FRONT, *NORWAY*

The Norwegian King and Government are taken to Great Britain on board a British destroyer, and a government-in-exile is formed. In Norway, Quisling is proclaimed sole political head with a state council of 13 Nazi-appointed commissioners. Josef Terboven, *Gauleiter* of Essen, is made Reich Commissioner as the effective ruler.

JUNE 8

NORTHERN FRONT, *NORWAY*

The last British troops are evacuated from Narvik in northern Norway as the Anglo-French military position disintegrates in France.

SEA WAR, *ATLANTIC*

The British aircraft carrier HMS *Glorious* is sunk by the *Scharnhorst* and the *Gneisenau*.

JUNE 10

WESTERN FRONT, *FRANCE*

Italy declares war on Great Britain and France, and moves troops into southern France. The French Government leaves

▶ *Stockpiling supplies and ammunition at the Channel ports for the proposed amphibious invasion of Great Britain.*

▼ *German troops practice with landing craft for Operation Sea Lion, the German invasion of southern England.*

SEA WAR, *ATLANTIC*
Great Britain announces a total blockade of the Continent.

JULY

GERMANY, *ALLIES*
Romania, attacked by the Soviet Union, becomes an ally of Germany.

JULY 3

SEA WAR, *PACIFIC*
The German auxiliary cruiser *Komet* leaves Gotenhafen in the Baltic for the Pacific Ocean, sailing under the command of *Konteradmiral* Robert Eyssen, around the North Cape of Norway and heading east via the Siberian Sea passage.

JULY 19

BERLIN, *PARADES*
A victory parade is held in Berlin to celebrate the stunning victory in the West. The *Leibstandarte-SS Adolf Hitler* takes part, and for the first time the achievement of the Waffen-SS is brought to the attention of the German public at large.

However, what was not disclosed was that the SS dash and élan had resulted in disproportionately high casualty rates among its members. In addition, the fact that the SS had committed atrocities during the campaign was also kept secret. The army is angry at these outrages.

▲ With the fall of France the danger to Atlantic convoys increased as the U-boats started using French ports.

Paris, first to Tours, then to Bordeaux, but defeat is only a matter of time.

JUNE 14

WESTERN FRONT, *FRANCE*
German troops enter Paris.

JUNE 17

SEA WAR, *FRANCE*
The first U-boats arrive in France to use the French Atlantic ports for refuelling.

JUNE 21

WESTERN FRONT, *FRANCE*
The French surrender is signed at Compiègne, the same railway carriage where the Germans surrendered in November 1918. France is divided into occupied and unoccupied "Vichy" zones. After the fall of France, Hitler is secure in Western Europe. He imminently expects the surrender of Great Britain, which will enable him to turn his attention to the East. Meanwhile, the Soviets move into Estonia, Latvia and Lithuania and make them Soviet Republics.
SEA WAR, *BALTIC*
The German auxiliary cruiser *Pinguin*

▶ The aftermath of a German air raid on London in September 1940 during the Battle of Britain.

passes through the Denmark Strait on her outward voyage.

JUNE 25

WESTERN FRONT, *FRANCE*
The ceasefire in France comes into effect at 01:35 hours. French casualties are 85,000, British 3475 and the Germans 27,074.

AUGUST

AUGUST

EASTERN FRONT, *SOVIET UNION*
Hitler secretly orders his staff to prepare a plan for the invasion of the Soviet Union, to be codenamed "Otto", while making provisional plans for an invasion of Britain. The attack on Russia will be two-pronged: against Moscow and Kiev. Nazi Germany always intended to attack the Soviet Union, regarded as the centre of Jewry and Bolshevism and thus the ideological enemy.

AUGUST 1

SEA WAR, *GERMAN NAVY*
The heavy cruiser *Prinz Eugen* is commissioned.

AUGUST 8

AIR WAR, *GREAT BRITAIN*
Adlertag or Eagle Day, the codename for the first day of the air offensive against Great Britain, is launched. The Germans need to establish air superiority over Great Britain before they can launch an invasion. *Luftwaffe* attacks occur on British targets, first Royal Air Force (RAF) bases, developing later in the year into night attacks on London and other cities – the "Blitz" – in an effort to destroy civilian morale.

▼ *Surprisingly cheerful Greek civilians watch Italian bombers fly overhead towards their targets.*

AUGUST 17

SEA WAR, *ATLANTIC*
Germany announces a total blockade of Great Britain and an area in which all ships are to be sunk without prior warning.

AUGUST 20

MEDITERRANEAN, *GIBRALTAR*
The German High Command plans to capture Gibraltar with a plan codenamed Operation "Felix".

AUGUST 24

SEA WAR, *GERMAN NAVY*
The battleship *Bismarck* is commissioned.

AUGUST 27

WESTERN FRONT, *GREAT BRITAIN*
The plan to mount an initially large-scale invasion of Great Britain is abandoned in favour of landings on a small front from Eastbourne to Folkestone.

AUGUST 30

WESTERN FRONT, *GREAT BRITAIN*
With the failure of the *Luftwaffe* to clear the skies of the RAF, the invasion of Great Britain is postponed indefinitely.

SEPTEMBER 27

POLITICS, *AXIS*
The Axis Treaty is joined by Japan. Germany, Italy and Japan pledge to fight any state that declares war on an Axis nation. This is the central element of the Tripartite Pact.

OCTOBER 7

FRANCE, *NAZI IDEOLOGY*
Deportations of "non-Germans" from Alsace-Lorraine, Saar and Baden take place.
EASTERN FRONT, *ROMANIA*
Germany invades Romania, seizing the vital oilfields at Ploesti. The pretext is the training of the Fascist Iron Guard.

OCTOBER 9

SEA WAR, *ATLANTIC*
The start of one of the most important and critical convoy battles: 21 ships are sunk from convoy SC7 and another 12 from convoy HX79, making this also one of the most successful U-boat "wolf pack" attacks.

OCTOBER 23

SEA WAR, *ATLANTIC*
The pocket battleship *Admiral Scheer* leaves Gotenhafen for the Atlantic under the command of *Kapitän zur See* Theodor Krancke. Some of the German heavy cruisers were classed as pocket battleships before the war.

OCTOBER 23

SPAIN, *DIPLOMACY*

Reichsführer-SS Himmler visits Spain to discuss various questions to include those arising out of the shared frontier between France and Spain, now that France has been occupied.

OCTOBER 28

BALKANS, *GREECE*

Hitler did not want a conflict on his southern flank in the Balkans, and had restrained his Axis partner Mussolini on several occasions during the spring and summer of 1940 from initiating plans for an Italian invasion of Yugoslavia and Greece. Mussolini reluctantly accepted Hitler's wishes as he was dependent on Germany for raw materials needed for armaments. On this morning, though, Italian forces based in Albania crossed the frontier into Greece to initiate one of the most surprising campaigns of World War II.

To understand why the Italian dictator finally ignored Hitler's directives and drew Germany into the conflict it is necessary to view the situation through Mussolini's eyes. Benito Mussolini proclaimed the birth of a "New Roman Empire" that was to take shape under his direction and would recreate the ancient glories of Roman history, celebrated in the rhetoric of the Fascist poet D'Annunzio. He was a man obsessed with thoughts of personal greatness and this proclamation was to satisfy his belief that he was indeed a genius. He had no master plan, unlike Hitler, to make his dream a reality. His decisions were frequently coloured by the prevailing condition of his health, which

▲*November 1940. Italian artillery pounds Greek positions from Albania during Mussolini's ill-fated campaign.*

was affected by the aftermath of syphilis contracted in his youth, as well as a duodenal ulcer. His arbitrary behaviour added to his intensely vain and theatrical nature. On occasions he exercised great shrewdness, on others he acted on impulse. Under Mussolini's rule Italy had already overrun two weak states: Abyssinia in 1936 and Albania in March 1939. Mussolini was a realist and recognized that he did not possess the raw materials to wage war on a grand scale. This realization did not,

however, prevent him before the outbreak of World War II from uttering bellicose sentiments illuminating the fact that Italy was ready to fight by Germany's side. Privately he considered it folly to wage war at this time, and he attempted unsuccessfully to persuade Hitler not to attack Poland. In March 1940, an official German communiqué roundly presenting Germany's military achievements, after only six months of war, brought Mussolini's

▼ *Italian heavy bombers on their way to Greece. Italy was confident of victory, but Greek resistance stunned the world.*

grudging admiration and deep envy. He had nothing to show in comparison to Hitler's territorial gains. He felt his prestige as Europe's first Fascist dictator demanded that he should occupy the stage and bask in the limelight the Führer now enjoyed. In May 1940, Mussolini's frustration was further heightened when the German armies drove the British forces off the

▲ *Romanian leader Ion Antonescu listens glumly as Hitler dictates the terms of Romania's alliance with Germany.*

continent and brought France to her knees. It now seemed certain to him that Germany would win the war. He had an understanding with Hitler that in the "New Europe" Italy would be rewarded with pickings from the French Empire. To reinforce this right and give Italy these spoils by force of arms, Mussolini announced on June 10, 1940, her declaration of war on Great Britain and France. Unfortunately, *Il Duce* was caught in

what his Foreign Minister Ciano ironically called "an outbreak of peace".

OCTOBER 31

SEA WAR, *ATLANTIC*
The German auxiliary cruiser *Widder* arrives in Brest after a cruise in American waters.

NOVEMBER

GERMANY, *TREATIES*
Hungary, Romania and Slovakia, a puppet state taken from the dismemberment of Czechoslovakia, sign treaties with Germany. The resettlement treaty between Germany

▼ *RAF Sunderland flying boats were operating against U-boats in November.*

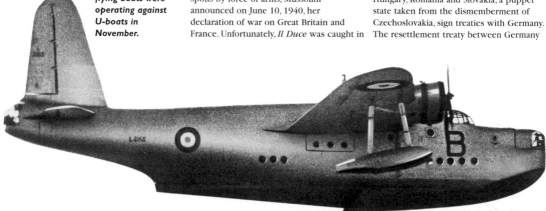

SEA WAR, *ATLANTIC*
The first U-boat located, but not sunk, by
radar fitted in a Sunderland flying boat.

SEA WAR, *ATLANTIC*
The German auxiliary cruiser *Komet*
returns to Hamburg after 516 days at sea.

EASTERN FRONT, *SOVIET UNION*
Directive No 21 calling for an invasion on
or about May 15, 1941, is issued. Operation
Barbarossa (named after a medieval German
emperor nicknamed "Redbeard") mapped
out a lightning attack by three million
troops organized in 186 divisions equipped
with 2500 tanks, 28,800 aircraft and 6000
artillery pieces. The assault would be three-
pronged. Army Group North under Field
Marshal von Leeb would strike through the
Baltic states to Leningrad where it would

and the Soviet Union in regard to ethnic
Germans living in Soviet-annexed
Bessarabia and northern Bukovina has to be
completed by November 1940. Throughout
October, some 45,000 settlers make the
long and so-called "final trek" to reception
camps in Pomerania, Eastern Prussia and
Warthegau before leaving for permanent
settlement in the newly incorporated Polish
territory. Each family was limited to 50kg
(110lb) of personal possessions or two
wagonloads. On arrival at the reception

▲ *Field Marshal Wilhelm Keitel (wearing
gloves), chief of OKW, was deeply involved
in the planning of Barbarossa.*

camp at Galatz, settlers are screened and
processed before proceeding by train. Types
of ethnic Germans from Bessarabia were
given identity tags, but many families
become separated.

This policy was part of the grand Nazi
scheme to colonize the conquered Eastern
territories with "Nordic" blood.

link up with Finnish forces allied with
Hitler. Army Group Centre under Field
Marshal von Bock, including panzer groups
under Generals Guderian and Hoth, would
strike through central Poland and
Belorussia all the way to Moscow itself.
Army Group South under Field Marshal von
Rundstedt, including two Romanian armies
and one Hungarian corps, would smash into
the Ukraine and beyond into the Crimea
and Caucasus to conquer the USSR's vast
agricultural lands and its richest oilfields.

▼ *Troops of the Totenkopf Division on
their way east to take part in the
forthcoming attack on the Soviet Union.*

1941

Hitler launched his invasion of the Soviet Union, and thus fulfilled his ideological dream of locking horns with the home of Bolshevism and Jewry. At first the German armies carried all before them, but as the campaign continued, his armies seemed to be swallowed up by the endless Russian terrain. The panzers began to falter, and the attack on Moscow in December failed. Then came the Red Army counterattack; for the first time in the war, the *Wehrmacht* was on the defensive.

JANUARY

GERMANY, *TREATIES*
Germany signs trade and frontier pacts with the Soviet Union, to import from the Soviets essential commodities, such as rubber and petroleum.

NORTH AFRICA, *GERMANY*
The *Afrika Korps* is formed for the Libyan campaign. Italy's forces under the command of Marshal Rodolfo Grazziano have suffered a series of heavy defeats at the hands of the British in Cyrenaica. Indeed, the remaining Italian troops are in no condition to defend Mussolini's remaining North African possessions, and Hitler is therefore forced to come to the aid of his ally.

FEBRUARY

EASTERN FRONT, *BULGARIA*
Hitler, pre-empting a suspected Soviet move, occupies Bulgaria from his Romanian bases.

NORTH AFRICA, *TRIPOLI*
Hitler issues Führer Directive No 22 to create a special force: the 5th Light Division, later renamed 21st Panzer Division, as the nucleus of an *Afrika Korps* under the command of General Erwin Rommel, which lands at Tripoli in Libya.

◀ *The cuff band of Rommel's* **Afrika Korps,** *which arrived in North Africa in February 1941.*

▼ *The Focke Wulf Fw 200 Condor long-range bomber, which operated against Allied ships in the Atlantic.*

▲ The Afrika Korps *arrives at the port of Tripoli in February, just in time to reverse Axis fortunes in North Africa.*

FEBRUARY 4

AIR WAR, *ATLANTIC*
Some 40 Focke Wulf Fw 200 Condor long-range bombers come under the direct control of the U-boat arm, to be used for reconnaissance purposes in the Atlantic.

FEBRUARY 25

SEA WAR, *GERMAN NAVY*
The battleship *Tirpitz* is commissioned.

MARCH 2

EASTERN FRONT, *BULGARIA*
German troops march into Bulgaria. To control the Balkans, Hitler persuades

Yugoslavia to join the Axis treaty. Hitler makes his intentions clear to the German Army by briefing 250 senior officers on his plans for war against the Soviet Union.

GERMANY, *IDEOLOGY*
Some 5000 ethnic Germans from Bukovina were presented with Reich citizenship in Breslau by *Reichsführer-SS* Himmler. Such gestures are the physical manifestation of the Nazis' racial purity theories.

MARCH 3

GREAT BRITAIN, *ESPIONAGE*
The British capture an "Enigma"-type cipher machine from an E-boat.

MARCH 6

GERMANY, *IDEOLOGY*
Reichsführer-SS Himmler visits the Austrian concentration camp at Mauthausen in which the "scum of mankind were exploited for the good of the great folk community by breaking stones and baking bricks so that the Führer can erect his grand buildings". Himmler views the prisoners, already weakened by undernourishment and exploitation, who negotiate the *Totensteige*, where in cold or heat in a continuous column five prisoners wide, they carry stones up 148 steps hour after hour, day after day, year after year. They carry the stones until they die, or are killed by their guards.

MARCH 17

SEA WAR, *ATLANTIC*
HMS *Vanoc* locates *U-100* on the surface with radar, the first success with the Type 286 radar, which leads to the sinking of

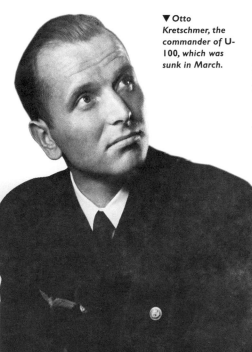

▼ *Otto Kretschmer, the commander of U-100, which was sunk in March.*

▲ *Yugoslav troops surrender to German forces during the invasion. Belgrade was bombed heavily.*

▼ *The Waffen-SS in Greece. The standing figure is "Sepp" Dietrich, commander of the Leibstandarte Division.*

▲ *German panzers enter the Greek port of Thessalonika in April. Greece's mountains did not hinder the panzers.*

U-100, commanded by Joachim Schepke, and *U-99*, commanded by Otto Kretschmer.

APRIL 6

BALKANS, *YUGOSLAVIA AND GREECE*

Invasion and occupation of Yugoslavia and Greece by Germany. Hungarian troops also attack Yugoslavia, and its government surrenders. German troops occupy Greece, brushing aside the small British Army. Germany has been forced into the Balkans by events inside Yugoslavia. Following the *Anschluss* of 1938, the Yugoslav Government attempted to sustain a position of

independence while being pressured to ally itself ever more closely with Germany. When, on March 25, 1941, the government succumbed to Axis pressure and signed the Tripartite Pact, the news was greeted by demonstrations of protest, especially in Belgrade. On March 27 the regency was replaced in a coup headed by senior officers, who declared the majority of Prince Peter and repudiated the pact. Belgrade was immediately bombarded and

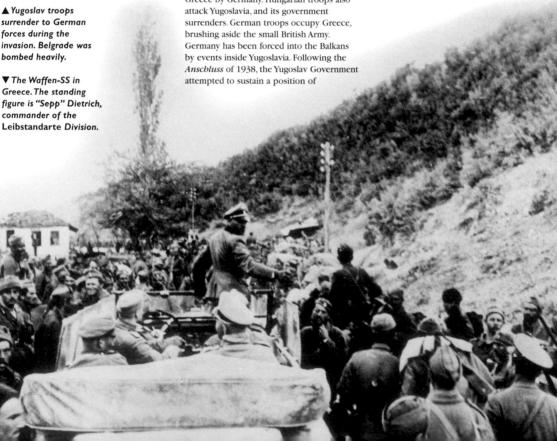

the country invaded by Germany and its allies. Resistance collapsed with surprising speed in view of the size, reputation, and equipment of the Yugoslav Army. On April 14 the king and government fled to Athens.

NORTH AFRICA, *LIBYA*

With three reinforced Italian Army corps and the German 15th Panzer Division, Rommel moves on through Libya towards Egypt, bypassing Tobruk, where the 1st Australian Division holds him off and is left in a state of siege.

APRIL 23

SEA WAR, *ATLANTIC*

The German auxiliary cruiser Thor, commanded by *Kapitän zur See* Otto Kähler, arrives in the Bay of Biscay after a successful cruise in the South Atlantic.

APRIL 27

BALKANS, *GREECE*

The advance guard of the *Leibstandarte-SS Adolf Hitler* crosses the gulf of Corinth in requisitioned Greek fishing boats. German troops occupy Athens as Commonwealth troops are evacuated to the island of Crete. The Greeks have lost over 15,000 men in the campaign; German losses are 1518.

▲ *One of Rommel's Panzer III tanks advancing east towards Egypt during the Afrika Korps' first offensive.*

▼ *An early German casualty in North Africa: the grave of an Afrika Korps soldier killed on April 26, 1941.*

APRIL 30

SEA WAR, *ATLANTIC*

The German auxiliary cruiser *Thor* arrives in Hamburg from France after 329 days at sea.

MAY

GERMANY, *IDEOLOGY*

Heydrich prepares the SS for its part in the forthcoming war in the Soviet Union, instructing the leaders of the *Einsatzgruppen* (Special Task Force) on their work of murdering all Jews, "Asiatics", communist officials, intellectuals, professionals and gypsies.

MAY 7

SEA WAR, *ATLANTIC*

The German floating weather station *München* is sunk by a British cruiser force. Men from the destroyer HMS *Somali* manage to get aboard her before she goes down. In the event, they capture valuable radio equipment and a naval cipher machine of the "Enigma" type, plus various important related documents.

MAY 8

SEA WAR, *ATLANTIC*

The auxiliary cruiser *Pinguin* is sunk.

137

KEY PERSONALITY

Hess

He served in World War I in the same regiment as Hitler. After the war he served in the *Freikorps*. He was seduced by the oratory of Hitler and joined the NSDAP in 1920. He marched in the 1923 *Putsch* and was imprisoned at Landsberg with Hitler. By 1932 he had been appointed chairman of the central political commission of the party. With Hitler coming to power, Hess became Deputy Leader, and in June 1933 Reich Minister without portfolio. In 1935 Hess was a selector of all senior Nazi officials. By 1939 his great days had been eclipsed by the generals and admirals on one hand and Göring and Himmler on the other. He felt himself estranged from Hitler and excluded from the centre of the web. It was his loyalty to Hitler which led to his flight to Britain in May 1941 with the intention of recovering his position with Hitler. He was incarcerated for the rest of his life, and committed suicide in 1987.

MAY 10

SEA WAR, *ATLANTIC*
U-110, commanded by Fritz Julius Lemp, is captured by British forces. Valuable secret material falls into British hands, including a working model of the secret cipher machine set up with the code of the day.
NAZI PARTY, *POLITICS*
Rudolf Hess flies to Great Britain. Hess believes a diplomatic coup is possible if he can have an audience with George VI, whom he might persuade to dismiss Churchill. Peace could then be implemented between the two countries and they could act in concert against a common enemy: the Soviet Union. The piloting of the aircraft and the final roll to allow his parachute descent was masterful. On landing he gave his name as Captain Horn and asked to be escorted to the Duke of Hamilton, whom he had met at the 1936 Berlin Olympic Games. The British, however, immediately imprison Hess.

MAY 19

SEA WAR, *ATLANTIC*
The *Prinz Eugen* and *Bismarck* leave Gotenhafen for the *Bismarck*'s first and only operational cruise.

MAY 20

BALKANS, *CRETE*
German paratroopers land on Crete and, despite heavy casualties, conquer the island in a daring air assault.

MAY 21

SS, *WAFFEN-SS*
Reichsführer-SS Himmler attends the oath-taking ceremony of the Norwegian SS in Norway, where he addresses the assembled volunteers: "The formation of the *Norges* SS is a new and important step forward for the Germanic community. The honour of its foundation will fall upon Norway."

▼ *The cuff band worn by those who took part in the airborne assault on Crete, where one in four paratroopers died.*

MAY 24

SEA WAR, *ATLANTIC*
The British battlecruiser HMS *Hood* is sunk by the *Bismarck*.

MAY 27

SEA WAR, *ATLANTIC*
The *Bismarck* is sunk during a battle with Royal Navy ships, with the Fleet Commander and the entire Fleet Command on board.
BALKANS, *GREECE*
"Sepp" Dietrich accepts the surrender of Greek General Tsolakaglu's Centre and Epirus Armies.

JUNE 4

SEA WAR, *ATLANTIC*
The German tanker *Gedania* is abandoned and scuttled when the British auxiliary cruiser *Marsdale* appears. Royal Navy personnel manage to get on board before the tanker sinks and capture secret material relating to the "Enigma" cipher machine.

KRETA

JUNE 22

EASTERN FRONT, *SOVIET UNION*

Operation Barbarossa, the German invasion of the Soviet Union, begins. The "Commissar Order" is issued to the army, under the signature of Hitler's chief of staff, Keitel. It states that Red Army political commissars are to be killed on capture. General orders are addressed to all troops to be ruthless against the "Bolshevik" Russians. Despite reports from his own intelligence agents and from the British that an attack is imminent, Stalin refuses to believe them. The Russian news agency TASS issues a statement seven days before the invasion: "To counter absurd rumours, responsible bodies in Moscow judge it necessary to declare that these rumours are sheer propaganda put out by the forces opposed to the USSR and Germany, attempting to spread and intensify the war."
Accompanying German forces are Romanian, Finnish, Hungarian and Slovak troops. Italian and volunteer Spanish and French troops were to follow. The Russian command is taken by surprise, in spite of warnings from British intelligence and their own agents in Germany, the *Rote Kapella*.

JUNE 15

SEA WAR, *ATLANTIC*

The German supply ship *Lothringen* is captured by the British cruiser *Dunedin*. Once again, secret documents fall into British hands. By this time, Great Britain has captured vital documents and machinery for deciphering German secret codes, which is unknown to the Germans.

▲ *U-boats in the Atlantic. Dönitz forbade attacks on US warships in order not to provoke Washington.*

▼ *German troops in June 1941 during the opening phase of Operation Barbarossa.*

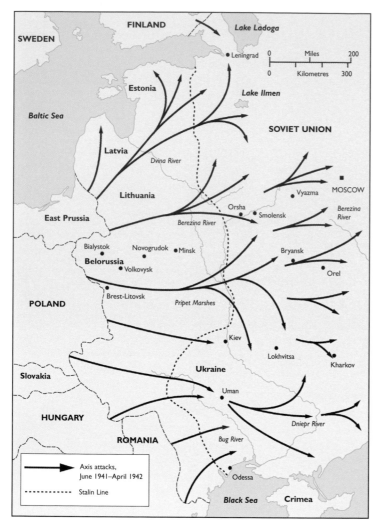

was the most successful commander, but he commanded two different boats and *U-48* was responsible for sinking more tonnage than either of the two. During this month, U-boat command began to suspect that some Allied convoys were being deliberately routed around the German submarine "wolf packs".

JUNE 23

GERMANY, *MEDIA*
Dr Goebbels announces on the radio at 05:30 hours the invasion of the Soviet Union.

JUNE 30

SEA WAR, *ESPIONAGE*
The German floating weather station *Launenburg* sinks in the North Atlantic. Men from the British destroyer HMS *Tartar* manage to get on board before she goes down and capture yet more top-secret German documents.

JULY

EASTERN FRONT, *SOVIET UNION*
Göring orders Heydrich to clear the occupied lands in the Soviet Union of Jews. The SS *Einsatzgruppen* follow the German armies according to plan, and begin executing Jews and "sub-humans". German troops enter the Ukraine. By the end of the month the German Army has occupied Latvia, the River Dnieper is reached and Smolensk captured. Nearly 750,000 prisoners are taken. Most will die as slave labourers or starve to death.

◀ *During the first weeks of Barbarossa the Germans experienced phenomenal success in the Soviet Union.*

▼ *Waffen-SS soldiers in the Soviet Union during Barbarossa. Himmler's racial warriors fought a savage war in Russia.*

The British immediately declare themselves as allies of the Russians.

SEA WAR, *ATLANTIC*
An incident occurs between the USS *Texas* and *U-203*, commanded by Rolf Mötzelburg. As a result, Dönitz forbids German submarines attacking American warships, even if they appear inside the blockade area around the British Isles.

U-48, the most successful U-boat of the war, returns to port from her last operational war cruise. She is subsequently used for training.

It has been stated that *U-99* was the most successful U-boat of the war; however, this is not so. Her commander, Otto Kretschmer,

▲ *German troops on the outskirts of Uman in August 1941. Entire Soviet armies were being destroyed by the Wehrmacht.*

JULY 5

SEA WAR, *ARCTIC*
U-boats start to operate in the Arctic seas.

AUGUST

EASTERN FRONT, *SOVIET UNION*
The German advance in the East continues. Estonia is occupied and incorporated into a new territory, subject to the Third Reich, called *Ostland*. The British and Soviets move into Iran to secure Russia's southern flank and prevent any German linkup in the Middle East.

AUGUST 23

SEA WAR, *ATLANTIC*
The German auxiliary cruiser *Orion* returns to France after a successful voyage that lasted 511 days.

AUGUST 28

SEA WAR, *ATLANTIC*
British forces capture the *U-571* which later becomes HMS *Graph*.

▶ *A Red Army soldier captured during Barbarossa. He and his comrades were regarded by his captives as a "sub-human".*

SEPTEMBER 1

GERMANY, *LEGAL*
Yellow star becomes compulsory attire for Jews living in Germany. The general deportation of German Jews to concentration camps starts.

SEPTEMBER 3

NAZI PARTY, *PERSONALITIES*
Heydrich, perhaps in reward for his efforts, certainly in recognition of his considerable

talents, is appointed to succeed Neurath as Protector of Bohemia and Moravia. His administration of the territory is masterful. It begins in brutality, but within months adroitly combines stick and carrot.

Czech industrial production began to rise. Fuelled with this, Heydrich issued additional ration cards on a productivity basis. The message was unequivocal: collaborate and prosper, or resist and perish. Heydrich was shown the crown jewels of Czechoslovakia

by President Hacha, who told him of an intriguing legend that surrounded them. It is said that any person not the true heir who put the crown on his head is sure to die. It is said that he laughed and tried it on.

SEPTEMBER 19

EASTERN FRONT, *UKRAINE*

German troops take Kiev, having already occupied most of the Ukraine and begin siege of Leningrad. The Shah of Iran is

▲ *An ammunition ship explodes en route to the Soviet Union as part of American and British aid to Stalin.*

▶ *Reinhard Heydrich, the new Protector of Bohemia and Moravia. His reign would be characterized by brutality and cleverness.*

▼ *The hazardous Arctic convoy routes, which were prey to German air and naval attack from bases in Norway.*

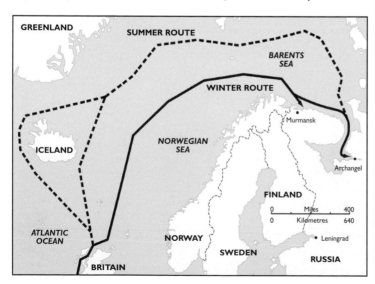

forced to abdicate and two zones of control, Soviet and British, are established in Iran. The specially equipped and trained 90th Light Division reinforces the *Afrika Korps*. U-boats experience difficulties in finding and attacking enemy convoys.

OCTOBER 1

EASTERN FRONT, *SOVIET UNION*
The German Army begins Operation Typhoon, the offensive against Moscow. Meanwhile, Hitler in Berlin speaks to the German public and describes the extent of his victory: 2.5 million prisoners, 22,000 guns captured, 18,000 tanks destroyed and 145,000 Russian aircraft eliminated. After such losses he may wonder why the Red Army is still in existence.

OCTOBER 11

SS, *WAFFEN-SS*
Dutch volunteers join in the SS parade in The Hague before leaving for training in eastern Prussia. German stupidity, broken promises and contempt for the nationals of countries they had defeated has adversely affected recruitment, though, and many volunteers return home disillusioned. This is an inauspicious beginning for Himmler's brotherhood of "Nordic" nations.

NOVEMBER 14

SEA WAR, *MEDITERRANEAN*
The British aircraft carrier HMS *Ark Royal* is sunk by *U-81* commanded by *Kapitänleutnant* Friedrich Guggenberger.

NOVEMBER 15

SEA WAR, *GERMAN NAVY*
U-459, the first purpose-built supply submarine, is commissioned by *Korvettenkapitän* Georg von Wilamowitz-Möllendorf.

NOVEMBER 19

SEA WAR, *PACIFIC*
The German auxiliary cruiser *Kormoran*, after a successful career in the South Atlantic and the Indian Ocean that lasted 350 days at sea, falls in with the Australian cruiser HMAS *Sydney*. Apparently the cruiser was taken in by the disguised raider's pretence of being an innocent Dutch freighter and came too close. The concealed guns quickly inflicted serious damage and a torpedo hit damaged the *Sydney* seriously. The cruiser replied effectively with her guns, but both ships caught fire and were heavily damaged. The *Sydney* drifted away and was never seen again, and the *Kormoran* sank. Nothing was

▲ *A German Jew complete with yellow Star of David, the wearing of which was made compulsory in September.*

known about the action until months later, when a few of the *Kormoran*'s survivors were found on a South Pacific island. It was the only case of a mercantile auxiliary cruiser sinking a regular warship of any size during the war.

NOVEMBER 22

SEA WAR, *ATLANTIC*
The German auxiliary cruiser *Atlantis*, after being at sea for 622 days and sailing over 160,000 km (100,000 miles), is intercepted and sunk by HMS *Devonshire*.

NOVEMBER 27

EASTERN FRONT, *MOSCOW*
The German drive towards Moscow begins to falter. In November, a new Hitler directive ordered the resumption of the Moscow drive. And so the Germans pushed on. The plan this time was for Guderian's Second Panzer Army to take Tula, then move north and loop around behind Moscow. In the north the Ninth Army and the Third Panzer Army would cross the Moscow-Volga canal and swing south for Moscow. In the centre, the Fourth Army and the Fourth

centre north of Moscow, littering the road to the west for 40km (25 miles) with the charred and frozen remnants of tanks and men from two panzer divisions. On that day the Siberians killed 3000 German soldiers. South of Moscow, the Red Army's cavalry corps crossed frozen rivers. Tanks pulled armoured sleds packed with more infantry. Soldiers fought on the run, carrying sacks of dry bread crusts and raw vegetables, and feeding their horses with straw stripped from thatched roofs. The Red Army forced

▲ *The Kriegsmarine suffered mounting U-boat losses in 1941, and the Bismarck (above), pride of the fleet, was sunk.*

Panzer Group would make a frontal attack on the city. It was an ambitious plan for German troops who were hungry and sick with fatigue. The offensive is slowed by heavy rains then halted by severe frost, although German tanks eventually reach to within 32km (20 miles) of Moscow. The intense cold halts the Germans, who are not equipped for a winter campaign.

DECEMBER 5

EASTERN FRONT, *SOVIET UNION*
To the surprise of the German General staff and the bewilderment of the frontline

▶ *A case study in folly: the Reichstag salutes Hitler following his unnecessary declaration of war on the United States.*

troops, Russian counterattacks come through the snow using reserves fresh from training in Siberia and signalling the commencement of the Soviet Union's effort to drive the German Army from the outskirts of Moscow. In the days that were to follow, the Siberians distinguished themselves. Kept warm by sheepskin coats, as well as quilted pants, fur hats and felt boots, they could travel almost silently over the snow and wait patiently for hours in snow before launching an attack at night.

The Siberians broke through on December 14 near Klin, a transportation

▼ *The British aircraft carrier* **Ark Royal** *photographed just before she sank after being torpedoed.*

the Germans back 160–240km (100–150 miles) before stabilizing the line.

Stalin, gambling that Japan would not attack Russia in the East, moved the Siberians across Asia to the European theatre. In the south Rundstedt was forced to evacuate Rostov, which he had just taken. Shocked by the news of his first major military setback ever, Hitler dismissed Brauchitsch and assumes his role. Other army commanders are dismissed, including Rundstedt and Guderian.

DECEMBER 7

PACIFIC, *PEARL HARBOR*
The Japanese attack Pearl Harbor and part of the US Pacific Fleet is destroyed.

DECEMBER 11

GERMANY AND ITALY, *TREATIES*
Germany and Italy declare war on the United States, an absurd gesture of solidarity with Japan which is to have significant consequences for Germany.

DECEMBER 14

SEA WAR, *ATLANTIC*
A dramatic and very significant convoy

▼ *German troops trudge through the snow as they retreat from Moscow. Suddenly the Supermen appeared fallible.*

▲ *Red Army soldiers escort Germans into captivity during the Red Army's counteroffensive of December 1941.*

battle takes place in the Atlantic Ocean. Swordfish aircraft from the British escort carrier *Audacity* succeed in keeping U-boats away from convoy HX76. *U-751*, commanded by *Korvettenkapitän* Gerhard Bigalk, manages to sink the *Audacity* after a ferocious battle. However, Dönitz records in his war diary: "The risk of being sunk is greater than the possible success. The presence of aircraft make 'wolf pack' tactics impossible." U-boat High Command now issues standing directives to U-boat commanders telling them to make the location and destruction of aircraft carriers their prime objective.

1942

This year marked the high point of the Third Reich. Hitler's armies were at the gates of Cairo and were on the Volga in the Caucasus. However, two military defeats turned the tide of war against Germany. In North Africa Rommel was decisively defeated at El Alamein, while at Stalingrad Hitler refused to allow the Sixth Army to withdraw from the city when faced by encirclement. The Third Reich was suddenly on the defensive.

▲ *Adolf Eichmann, head of the Gestapo's "Jewish Evacuation Department" and organizer of the "Final Solution".*

JANUARY 1

POLITICS, *ALLIES*

"United Nations" conference in Washington, Britain, USA and Soviet Russia agree on no separate peace with Germany.

JANUARY 20

GERMANY, *ANTI-SEMITISM*

Reinhard Heydrich hosts a conference of Nazi Party and government officials in the SS RHSA headquarters at Wannsee, a Berlin suburb. The meeting is chaired by Heydrich and attended by 15 SS and government officials, including Stukart, Heinrich Müller, Adolf Eichmann, head of the "Jewish Evacuation Department" of the Gestapo, and Freisler.

In July 1941, Heydrich had been appointed the officer in charge of planning the "Final Solution" of the Jewish "problem". In the early years of the Nazi regime, they promoted the idea of achieving Aryan racial purity. They decided that undesirables – Slavs, Gypsies, homosexuals, and the handicapped and mentally ill – were to be disposed of. But the chief target of the regime's campaign was the Jewish population of Germany; later, of all Europe. A policy of consistent persecution was

▼ **Afrika Korps officers watch an artillery bombardment of the garrison of Tobruk, which fell to Rommel in June.**

followed during the 1930s, but a more ambitious programme was crafted under the cover of the war. Hitler announced that about 11 million European Jews yet remained to be dealt with. He had decided that a "Final Solution" to the Jewish problem must be implemented while the war was going on.

The Wannsee Conference, as it was known, lasted only a few hours, and proposed the "Final Solution". The idea of mass deportation was ruled out as impractical, considering the ongoing war. Forced sterilization was discussed, but no decision was made at the conference. But as a result of it, directives were sent to move Jews to the East as part of the "territorial solution". No doubt was left that this meant the physical destruction of all Jews, accelerating the process that had already started. The *Einsatzgruppen* had already been in action for six months and the first extermination camp, at Chelmno, was by then in operation. The conference decided that the best policy was to round up the Jews from all parts of Europe and send them eastward to work in labour gangs. Hard enough work, it was believed, would result in significant loss of life. Within a few weeks the first poison gas chambers in concentration camps were built in Poland.

▲ **Afrika Korps** *infantry and armour on the advance in Libya during Rommel's drive towards the Egyptian frontier.*

▲ *A German E-boat badge. These vessels accompanied German warships during the so-called "Channel Dash" in February.*

Responsibility for carrying out the policy of extermination was given to *Reichsführer-SS* Heinrich Himmler. The conference gave Eichmann the necessary authority for his actions in the various ministries, and 30 copies of the conference records were distributed to them. At no point was killing mentioned. Recipients were expected to understand the meaning of "final solution" and "deportation to the East". The policy of extermination went forward until the end of the war. Accurate numbers are impossible to obtain, but the estimates run as high as 15 million people, including six million Jews. They were liquidated in the camps or by mass executions in isolated places.

JANUARY 21

NORTH AFRICA, *LIBYA*

Rommel, having retreated, allowed the British Eighth Army into Libya again. Two Australian divisions are moved from Egypt to the Pacific theatre of war to hold Japanese advances, while Rommel receives reinforcements from Germany. Rommel then attacks and smashes the British armour. Benghazi falls by the 29th.

FEBRUARY 4

NORTH AFRICA, *LIBYA*

Rommel again nears Tobruk, though his lines of communications are stretched.

▲ *The German Wound Badge, which was awarded to soldiers, and, on the insistence of Goebbels, later civilians hurt in air raids.*

FEBRUARY 11

SEA WAR, *ENGLISH CHANNEL*
The start of the "Channel Dash". The *Gneisenau*, *Scharnhorst* and *Prinz Eugen* sail through the English Channel from Brest in France to Germany and Norway. This is a major embarrassment for the Royal Navy and Royal Air Force (RAF), and a great propaganda victory for the *Kriegsmarine*.

FEBRUARY 26

SEA WAR, *ENGLISH CHANNEL*
The *Gneisenau* is put out of action by bomb damage, but manages to make her way to Kiel.

◀ *The Funeral Pillow of Reinhard Heydrich during his funeral in Berlin, showing his various awards.*

▼ *In commemoration of Heydrich, the 11th SS Gebirgsjäger Regiment was formed. This is the unit's cuff band.*

▶ The German Order, the Party's highest decoration. Hitler pinned the medal on Heydrich's funeral pillow.

▲ The coffin of Reinhard Heydrich, draped in the swastika flag, at his funeral in Berlin, June 8, 1942.

MARCH 13

SEA WAR, *ATLANTIC*
The German auxiliary cruiser *Michel* passes through the Strait of Dover on the outward voyage of her first operational cruise.

APRIL 4

SEA WAR, *BALTIC*
The *Gneisenau* is moved to Gotenhafen.

APRIL 24

SEA WAR, *KRIEGSMARINE*
The motor torpedo-boats, which previously had been under the jurisdiction of the Flag Officer for Destroyers, are given their own autonomous command under *Kapitän zur See* Rudolf Petersen.

MAY 8

EASTERN FRONT, *CRIMEA*
Manstein's army enters the Crimea and besieges Sevastopol, which falls in July.

Satisfied with this, Hitler moves Manstein north to tackle the siege of Leningrad, which has been going on since September 1941. Bock's Army Group South defeats Russian tank forces in the Ukraine and takes Kursk, but when Bock pauses in his attack on Voronezh, Hitler dismisses him.

MAY 12

SEA WAR, *BALTIC*
The *Stier* leaves Kiel on her first war cruise as an auxiliary cruiser.

MAY 26

NORTH AFRICA, *LIBYA*
Rommel's *Afrika Korps* outflanks the British and attacks towards Tobruk, and although delayed by Free French outpost at Bir Hacheim, takes the offensive, driving British out of Libya.

AIR WAR, *GERMANY*
British air raids on German cities intensify.

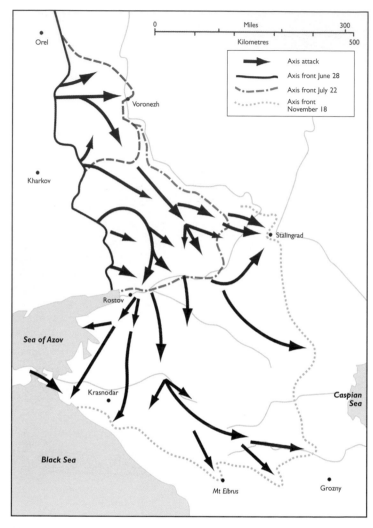

The German 1942 summer offensive in the East was initially very successful, but the Soviets were trading space for time.

▲ German Army soldiers hear the Führer's words on the eve of their summer offensive on the Eastern Front.

hostages from amongst the Czech intelligentsia and to shoot 100 of the most important that same night.

JUNE 4

CZECHOSLOVAKIA, *RESISTANCE*
Heydrich dies from septicemia - caused by foreign bodies - in Prague at the Bulov hospital. Himmler's first act after he has recovered from the shock of Heydrich's death is to locate the key to the safe in which Heydrich kept his "personal" files.

Heydrich's coffin lay in state in the main courtyard of Hradcany Castle and the people of Prague filed by in resemblance of homage, some giving the Nazi salute.

JUNE 8

NAZI PARTY, *PERSONALITIES*
At 15:00 hours, Heydrich's coffin is carried into the courtyard of the Reich Chancellery for the state funeral. Hitler and 600 of Germany's leading officials and industrialists attend to pay homage to him. In addition, there is evidence that the Czech puppet government, headed by President Emil Hácha and his staff, was supporting the Nazi attitude that a great

MAY 27

CZECHOSLOVAKIA, *RESISTANCE*
A plan, implemented in London for the assassination of Heydrich, is carried out by British-trained Czech assassins.

This decision has always caused speculation, as he was the only Nazi leader thus targeted. In late spring of 1942, a section of Czech soldiers flew from England and were dropped outside Prague. Heydrich, possibly through bravado, rode in an open-topped, unprotected car on his way from his residence to the palace. The assassination team struck during the journey. His car was machine-gunned on the Kirchmayer Boulevard. Heydrich was

injured and drew his pistol. Then the Czech Sten gun jammed. Heydrich was about to pursue the assassin when a grenade, thrown by another member, Kubis, exploded, impregnating him with horsehair stuffing and pieces of metal springs from the car seat. At 21:10 hours that evening, Karl Hermann Frank, former deputy leader of the Sudeten German Party, Secretary of State and Chief of Police in Bohemia and Moravia under Heydrich, was ordered by Himmler via telegram to arrest 10,000

crime had been committed when Heydrich was killed. Hitler bestows upon him the German Order, the highest party and state award. It is well known that Heydrich kept files on all the leading Nazis, even on Hitler himself, and many are relieved to see him dead. However 50,000 Czech workers march in protest in Prague on the day of the funeral, angry about the assassination. Heydrich is buried with full military honours at the Invalidenfriedhof cemetery.

JUNE 10

CZECHOSLOVAKIA, *ATROCITIES*
Karl Frank, Heydrich's deputy, immediately threatens reprisals unless the assassins are found. Although there is very little evidence to support his assumption, Frank decides that Lidice should be punished for having harboured the assassins. Hitler orders that this mining village be "wiped from the face of the earth" in retaliation.

During the night of 9/10 June, SS troops surrounded Lidice and at 02:00 hours the

▼ *As they head east once more, the morale of these Germans is high. The easy advance was like a repeat of Barbarossa.*

villagers were woken and driven to the main square. The men were separated from the women and children. They were told to take food to last for three days and any valuables if they so wished. This was for an "inspection" they were told, and then they would be returned. The women and children were taken to the schoolhouse and the men to the farm of the Horak family. At the school there were two SS men with two suitcases where they were told to deposit their valuables. Then they assembled in the classroom and were checked against their police identity cards to ensure all were present. Trucks to the city of Kladno then transported the women

▲ British infantry capture one of Rommel's Panzer IIIs near El Alamein in July 1942.

▶ Rommel near El Alamein. Though he was near Alexandria, his supply lines were long and his troops were exhausted.

▶ Field Marshal Wilhelm List commanded an army group during the German offensive into the Caucasus.

and children. Some 197 men were killed and the women and children were sent to concentration camps. On June 12 it was announced that the village of Lidice had been destroyed. The village was then bulldozed and it took volunteers almost a year to raze it completely.

JUNE 18

CZECHOSLOVAKIA, *RESISTANCE*
The Czech Orthodox Church of Saints Cyril and Methodius in Prague is where the Czech assassins of Heydrich and their helpers have taken sanctuary. The chaplain Vladimir Petrek hid them in the crypt under the floor. Here, members of the Czech Fire Brigade have had to pump water into the crypt in an attempt to flush out

their countrymen after they had been engaged in a heroic battle against SS units. The remaining parachutists take their own lives with their last rounds of ammunition.

JUNE 21

NORTH AFRICA, *LIBYA*

The British retreat into Egypt, losing Tobruk to the *Afrika Korps* following an intense battle to the south of the port. Rommel is promoted to field marshal.

▶ *The aftermath of the Dieppe raid: British prisoners are led away into captivity. It was a total disaster.*

JULY 1

SEA WAR, *BALTIC*

The battlecruiser *Gneisenau* is decommissioned.

JULY 4

EASTERN FRONT, *CRIMEA*

The Germans take Sevastopol.

JULY 13

EASTERN FRONT, *UKRAINE*

Hitler moves to his Ukraine headquarters at Vinnitsa, called "Werewolf", to supervise the the summer offensive and the Sixth Army's advance on Stalingrad and the Caucasus. The Germans make great initial advances

AUGUST 11

SEA WAR, *ATLANTIC*

The British aircraft carrier HMS *Eagle* is sunk by *U-73*, commanded by *Kapitänleutnant* Helmuth Rosenbaum.

AUGUST 17

AIR WAR, *FRANCE*

18 American Boeing B-17E "Flying Fortresses", personally led by General Ira Eaker, bomb Rouen-Sotteville, France, and return to England without loss. It is the modest beginning of the United States Army Air Force's (USAAF's) daylight bombing operations in Europe. The USAAF under its Commanding General H.H.

The *Africa Korps* reaches El Alamein in Egypt, within 96km (60 miles) of the Nile Delta. The *Afrika Korps* now has three divisions with supporting units, and under Rommel are three Italian corps, including élite Italian armoured forces. The British have divisions from South Africa, India, New Zealand and Australia. Rommel is at the end of a very long and vulnerable supply line. The British, on the other hand, are receiving fresh supplies on a daily basis.

POLAND, *FINAL SOLUTION*

Mass gassings begin at Auschwitz concentration camp in Poland.

▶ *Men of the Sixth Army near Stalingrad in August 1942. During this offensive the Red Army yielded space for time.*

Arnold had until now favoured daylight attacks by well-armed bombers. The rationale of the policy was that they could deliver higher degrees of industrial damage and lower civilian casualties than the RAF's night attacks. They were convinced that unescorted daylight bombing could be successful if the bombers were sufficiently well armed.

The American four-engine bombers "bristled" with .50-calibre heavy machine guns and flew in a formation designed for mutual defence and maximum combined firepower. Although the Rouen raid was insignificant in itself, it argued ill for the future of the *Luftwaffe* in the West.

AUGUST 19

WESTERN FRONT, *FRANCE*
5000 Canadian and 1000 British troops raid Dieppe in France as part of a "reconnaissance in force". It is a total disaster, with almost 4000 men being captured or killed.

GERMANY, *ESPIONAGE*
The *Rote Kapelle* communist spy network in Germany is uncovered by the *Abwehr*.

SEPTEMBER 1

EASTERN FRONT, *CAUCASUS*
German troops enter Stalingrad and reach the Elbruz Mountains in the Caucasus. Hitler had, however, hoped to reach the oilfields at Baku. He dismisses Field Marshal List for not advancing fast enough. At "Werewolf" there are arguments between Hitler and his military advisors, who claim

▲ American B-17 bombers in the skies over Germany. US daylight raids resulted in heavy losses in bombers.

that his strategy has stretched out his forces too widely. When General Halder, the chief of the army general staff, warns that the Soviets with growing strength could soon counterattack, he too is dismissed and eventually sent to the concentration camp at Dachau. Paulus' Sixth Army takes most of Stalingrad and with control of the air seems to be on the way to break through the town to the river. But the Red Army holds on, its backs to the river, artillery supporting it from the other bank.

NORTH AFRICA, *EGYPT*
A strengthened British Eighth Army, now commanded by Bernard Montgomery, halts Rommel's offensive at Alam Halfa.

SEPTEMBER 12

SEA WAR, *ATLANTIC*
The liner *Laconia* is torpedoed and sunk by *U156* commanded by *Korvettenkapitän* Werner Hartenstein. More than 1400 of the 2491 men and sailors on boards are drowned, despite Hartenstein's efforts to help the survivors.

SEPTEMBER 27

SEA WAR, *ATLANTIC*
The German auxiliary cruiser *Stier* is scuttled after damage inflicted by action with the American armed freighter *Stephen Hopkins*.

▼ *Cologne Cathedral and its surrounding buildings after a bombing raid. Air raids failed to break German civilian morale, but did hit industry hard.*

SEPTEMBER 28

SEA WAR, *BERLIN*

The German Naval High Command, including leaders of the U-boat arm, meet with Hitler in Berlin to discuss new trends in the Battle of the Atlantic and the deterioration of the U-boat impact on Allied convoys.

OCTOBER 8

SEA WAR, *NORTH SEA*

The German auxiliary cruiser *Komet* leaves Hamburg for her second war cruise, under the command of *Kapitän zur See* Ulrich Brocksien.

OCTOBER 9

SEA WAR, *PACIFIC*

The German auxiliary cruiser *Thor* arrives at Yokohama in Japan at the end of her second cruise.

OCTOBER 14

SEA WAR, *ATLANTIC*

The German auxiliary cruiser *Komet* is torpedoed by a British torpedo boat.

AIR WAR, *GERMANY*

The catastrophic raid by 291 American Boeing B-17E "Flying Fortresses" on Schweinfurt to destroy its ball-bearing factories demonstrated that daylight bombing is bedevilled with practical

▼ **Luftwaffe** *personnel direct fighters against Allied bombers. Ground defence of cities was in the hands of the* **Gauleiters.**

difficulties. The "Flying Fortresses" are attacked by continuous waves of German fighters, and by the time the American force returned to England, 60 bombers have been shot down and 138 suffer heavy damage. Such a loss rate cannot be sustained.

OCTOBER 23

NORTH AFRICA, *EGYPT*

The British defeat Rommel at El Alamein.

By mid-October the British Eighth Army had 230,000 men and 1230 tanks ready for action, while the German–Italian forces numbered only 80,000 men, with only 210 tanks of comparable quality ready; and in air support the British enjoyed a superiority of 1500 to 350. Allied air and submarine attacks on the Axis supply lines across the Mediterranean, moreover, had prevented Rommel's army from receiving adequate fuel, ammunition, and food; and Rommel was convalescing in Austria.

The British launched their infantry attack at El Alamein, but found the German minefields harder to clear than they had foreseen. Two days later, however, some of those tanks were deploying 9.6km (six miles) beyond the original front. When Rommel, ordered back to Africa by Hitler, reached the front in the evening of October 25, half of the Germans' available armour was already destroyed. Nevertheless, the impetus of the British onslaught was stopped the next day when German antitank guns took a heavy toll of British armour. During the night of October 28,

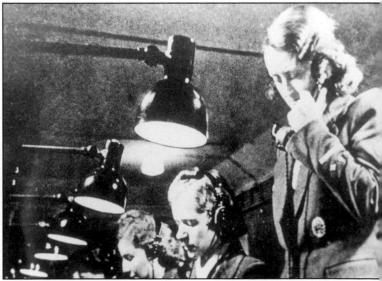

DECISIVE MOMENTS

Stalingrad

During the summer of 1942 the Germans advanced to the suburbs of Stalingrad but failed to take the city itself against a determined defence by the Red Army, despite repeated attacks by the Sixth Army under Friedrich Paulus and part of the Fourth Panzer Army under Ewald von Kleist. By September they reached the city's centre, where they encountered stiff resistance from the Soviet Sixty-Second Army under General Vasily I. Chuikov. The city's Soviet defenders had been driven almost to the Volga by mid-October, but the Germans' supplies were beginning to run low and their tanks were of little value in the constant street fighting.

On November 19 the Soviets launched a counterattack in the form of pincer movements north and south of the city, and by the 23rd they had encircled the Sixth Army and part of the Fourth within Stalingrad. A German attempt to relieve Paulus failed in mid-December. Under orders from Hitler, Paulus continued to fight on, but in early January 1943 he surrendered, and on February 2 the last of his remaining 91,000 troops turned themselves over to the Soviets. The Soviets recovered 250,000 German and Romanian corpses in and around Stalingrad, and total Axis losses are estimated to have been 800,000 dead. Official Russian military historians estimate that 1.1 million Soviet soldiers lost their lives in the campaign.

▶ *Stores are loaded onto one of Göring's Junkers Ju 52 transport aircraft for the relief of the Sixth Army at Stalingrad.*

Montgomery turned the offensive northwards, but this too failed. In the first week of their offensive the British lost four times as many tanks as the Germans but still had 800 available against the latter's remaining 90. Rommel had no choice but to order a withdrawal, or see his *Afrika Korps* destroyed where it stood.

OCTOBER 24

GERMANY, *POLITICS*

Hitler holds a meeting with Marshal Pétain, which gives rise to secret accords known as *Montoir*. Pétain agrees to support Germany in every way short of military involvement: "The Axis Powers and France have an identical interest in seeing the defeat of England as soon as possible." In return for Vichy support, France is to be accorded "the place to which she is entitled" in the new Europe. Pétain possibly has no choice but to pay lip service to Hitler's ambitions. However, the aged Pétain has succeeded at Montoire in keeping France out of the war.

▼ *German heavy artillery in Tunisia in December. The Germans now faced a war on two fronts in North Africa.*

NOVEMBER 8

NORTH AFRICA, *MOROCCO*

Anglo-American troops land in Morocco.

NOVEMBER 9

EASTERN FRONT, *STALINGRAD*

The Russian counterattack at Stalingrad begins. Hitler is in Munich at the annual celebration of the 1923 Beer Hall *Putsch*

when news comes of the counteroffensive that threatens to encircle the Sixth Army. The new chief of the Army general staff, Zeitzler, suggests a withdrawal to the River Don, but Hitler insists that he will not leave the Volga.

NOVEMBER 23

EASTERN FRONT, *STALINGRAD*

The whole of the German Sixth Army, a quarter of a million men, is encircled. If they do not withdraw now, while they still can, they face annihilation. The Germans are forced to eat horses' bones, and as temperatures drop to minus 30 degrees Centigrade the German bread ration, already as low as 100 grammes (4oz) a day, is reduced to just 50 (2oz). The starving German soldiers are forced to slaughter their horses and later still to dig up their frozen carcasses to eat the bones. Despite the desperate situation and the urgent advice of his military commanders,

Hitler refuses to contemplate a withdrawal. However, after General Manstein's attempts to relieve them in December failed, Paulus's men have neither the supplies nor the strength to break through the Soviet lines.

DECEMBER 31

SEA WAR, *ARCTIC*

Battle of the North Cape. Hitler threatens to "throw the surface fleet into the dustbin" as a result of the failure of the German North Norway Naval Squadron to drive home its attack on convoy JW51B.l

EASTERN FRONT, *STALINGRAD*

Göring's *Luftwaffe* fails to drop adequate supplies to the trapped Sixth Army.

▶ The poor weather, combined with Red Army antiaircraft gun, made the airborne relief operation at Stalingrad a failure.

1943

The disasters on the Volga and in North Africa threw the Third Reich onto the defensive, while in the Atlantic the U-boats began to lose the war against the convoys. Worse still for the German population, the Allies continued their strategic bombing campaign, bringing death and destruction on a daily basis. And with the German defeat at Kursk in July, Hitler lost all hope of winning the war on the Eastern Front.

JANUARY 1

EASTERN FRONT, *CAUCASUS*

A Red Army offensive retakes Voronezh on the River Don. A Soviet drive might have cut off the *Wehrmacht* in the Caucasus, but the retreat of the Germans from the southeast is well managed and they elude the Soviet net.

JANUARY 30

SEA WAR, *BERLIN*

Grand-Admiral Erich Raeder resigns as Supreme Commander-in-Chief of the *Kriegsmarine* and is replaced by Karl Dönitz.

FEBRUARY 2

EASTERN FRONT, *STALINGRAD*

Paulus surrenders with his army at Stalingrad and with the 90,000 survivors becomes a prisoner of the Soviets. Hitler is furious: "The man should have shot himself just as the old commanders threw themselves on their swords. That's the last field marshal I shall appoint in this war." From now on, Hitler gives preference to the Waffen-SS over the regular army.

Relying on the original six SS divisions as his élite troops, he allows the Waffen-SS to take in conscripts and double in size. The Red Army now retakes Kursk although the Germans, hoping to begin a spring offensive this year, hold Kharkov and Orel.

GERMANY, *ECONOMY*

Hitler orders Albert Speer, minister of armaments, and Heinz Guderian, inspector

▲ *A haggard Field Marshal Paulus surrenders his remaining troops at Stalingrad to the Red Army.*

general of tank forces, to improve the production and design of tanks. The successful Soviet Yak-9 fighter plane becomes operational.

FEBRUARY 12

HOLLAND, *TECHNOLOGY*

The "Rotterdam Radar", as it was known, falls into German hands after being taken

▼ *Red Army troops in the ruins of Stalingrad in February 1943. This battle cost the Germans their finest field army.*

▲ *Axis troops retreat following the disaster at Stalingrad, a defeat that put the southern Eastern Front in jeopardy.*

▲ *Karl Dönitz, the new Grand-Admiral of the Kriegsmarine. After Hitler's death in 1945 he would be Führer for a few days.*

from a crashed British aeroplane near Rotterdam in Holland.

FEBRUARY 14

NORTH AFRICA, *TUNISIA*
Rommel retreats into Tunisia, but then makes a stand at Mareth and launches an attack He defeats green American units at Kasserine Pass, but lacks the reserves to effect a decisive breakthrough. His attacks eventually run out of momentum and he is forced to retreat. Meanwhile, Montgomery closes in from the southeast.

FEBRUARY 22

GERMANY, *RESISTANCE*
The execution of Hans and Sophie Scholl of the White Rose resistance takes place in Munich. They were found guilty of distributing traitorous literature and beheaded.

MARCH 2

SEA WAR, *PACIFIC*
The German auxiliary cruiser *Michel* arrives at the port of Kobe in Japan to end her first war cruise.

MARCH 13

GERMANY, *RESISTANCE*
The Smolensk Plot, an attempt to assassinate Hitler, was organized by General von Treschow, a Prussian officer who fought with

▲ *Red Army antiaircarft guns deployed at Stalingrad. Batteries such as this one shot down many Luftwaffe transports.*

distinction in Poland and France, but who became convinced that Germany would face ruin in the war with Soviet Russia. The plan, involving Gördeler, Tresckow, General Friedrich Olbricht and Fabian von Schlabrendorff, was for Hitler to be enticed to army headquarters in the Smolensk area, where Tresckow was serving, and there murdered. In the event it was decided to place two bombs, disguised in a parcel to look like bottles of brandy, on the Führer's plane. But technical problems with the bombs meant that the conspirators waited in vain for news of the explosion. When Hitler landed safely at Rastenburg the bombs were removed by Schlabrendorff and a new date was fixed, a week later, for another attempt, this time at the memorial day for World War I heroes at the Zeughaus in Berlin.

▼ *German panzers advance to meet American forces at Kasserine Pass, Rommel's last victory in North Africa.*

159

MARCH 14

EASTERN FRONT, *KHARKOV*

German tanks and infantry enter Kharkov. After two months of bitter fighting, the SS Panzer Corps manages to hold the German line, recapture Kharkov and encircle and destroy part of the Soviet First Guards Army and an army group. But in doing so it has lost 11,500 dead, wounded and missing.

Two of the young Waffen-SS officers that were instrumental in the fighting were Joachim Peiper and Fritz Witt; the latter was to become the youngest general in the German Army. Prisoners of war and the inhabitants of the city were immediately put to work cleaning up the mess and restoring vital services. To commemorate the recapture of the city of Kharkov the Red Square was renamed "Platz der Leibstandarte" in honour of the SS Panzer Corps' exploits.

MARCH 16

SEA WAR, *ATLANTIC*

The start of the largest convoy battle of World War II, with U-boats attacking convoys HX229 and SC122.

MARCH 25

SEA WAR, *ATLANTIC*

The battle for convoy HX231, which lasted until April 8, was the first time since the fighting began that a convoy had managed to cross the Atlantic Ocean and beat off all the attacking U-boats, despite the "air-gap" still being 724km (450 miles) wide.

APRIL 1

SS, *WAFFEN-SS*

The Waffen-SS victors of the battle of Kharkov – Buchner, Jüttner, Kraas, Macher and "Panzer" Meyer – are received by Dr Goebbels in Berlin. At the same time, *Generaloberst* Heinz Guderian visits the SS Panzer Corps' repair shops in the former tractor factory in Kharkov. The Eastern Front has been stabilized.

▲ *The Close Combat Bar, nicknamed the "Eyeball-to-Eyeball" medal, was regarded as the highest German infantry award.*

▼ *A Tiger tank of the Das Reich Division, SS Panzer Corps, west of Kharkov prior to Manstein's attack in March.*

▲ Fritz Witt, one of the young Waffen-SS officers who distinguished himself in the battle to retake Kharkov.

▲ Kharkov's battled-scarred Red Square following the German recapture of the city after Manstein's counterattack.

▼ Joachim Peiper was an officer in the élite Leibstandarte Division during the fighting in Kharkov in early 1943.

APRIL 19

RESISTANCE, *WARSAW*

The Jews of the Warsaw ghetto rise. The defence has been organized by the Jewish Combat Organization.

The Germans expected to liquidate the ghetto in three days. However, the fighters held off attacks for four weeks, some survivors fighting on in the ruins for months. By mid-May the ghetto no longer existed, and around 60,000 Jews had been killed. However, they had inflicted 1300 casualties on their German tormentors

RESISTANCE, *YUGOSLAVIA*

In the Balkans, the Yugoslav partisans grow in strength and increase from 20,000 men at the beginning of the year to nearly 250,000 by the end. They are led by Tito.

MAY 13

NORTH AFRICA, *TUNISIA*

Some 150,000 *Afrika Korps* and Italian troops surrender to Allied forces at Tunis. Only Rommel and a small number escape.

MAY 21

SEA WAR, *PACIFIC*

The German auxiliary cruiser *Michel* leaves Yokohama in Japan after fitting out.

MAY 23

SEA WAR, *ATLANTIC*

U-boat losses rise dramatically, and Grand-Admiral Karl Dönitz admits defeat in the Battle of the Atlantic by withdrawing U-boats from the troubled waters. Up to May there were 40 U-boats in place each day in the Atlantic, but between February and May 91 U-boats have been lost and such losses cannot be sustained. A combination of long-range bombers, radar and submarine hunter groups have made the Atlantic a hazardous place for U-boats.

MAY 29

AIR WAR, *GERMANY*

On a single night, 90 percent of Barmen-Wuppertal is destroyed by the RAF in a bombing raid. The reaction of the Nazi leaders differs greatly. Hitler, despite requests from the *Gauleiters* of bomb-damaged cities, refuses to visit them to see for himself the extent of the damage (in Berlin he even arranges for his chauffeur to avoid bombed areas of the city while driving him around). Göring, who said that if the RAF ever raided Berlin "you can call me Meier", makes fewer and fewer public appearances as civilian casualties mount.

KEY PERSONALITY

Göring

Born in Rosenheim, Bavaria, to minor gentry, he joined an infantry regiment in World War I, but arthritis made him unfit for his duties. By pulling strings he became a fighter pilot and established himself as one of Germany's aces with 22 victories. During 1939 he was made Chairman of the Reich Council for National Defence and named as Hitler's successor. He planned the *Luftwaffe's* role in the invasions of Poland, Norway and France. In 1940, when Hitler made nine of his generals field marshals, Göring was given the unique rank of *Reichsmarshall*. He had reached the height of his career. Self-indulgence softened him and more ambitious Nazis, Himmler, Bormann, Goebbels and Speer, began to bypass him and reduce his importance. At the Nuremberg trial he was found guilty on all counts and condemned to death. He cheated the hangman by taking cyanide on October 15, 1946.

▲ *In the Jewish ghettos the inhabitants organized their own services: this is a postage stamp from Litzmannstadt.*

MAY 31

GERMANY, *ECONOMY*
U-boat construction is handed over completely to Albert Speer's Department of Military Armaments.

JUNE 4

SEA WAR, *PACIFIC*
The last German auxiliary cruiser still operational, *Michel*, leaves Yokohama, Japan, for her second cruise under the command of *Kapitän zur See* Günther Gumprich.

JULY 5

EASTERN FRONT, *KURSK*
Unsuccessful German assault on the Soviet salient around the city of Kursk. The salient is a bulge in the Soviet lines that stretches 240km (150 miles) from north to south and protrudes 160 km (100 miles) westwards

▼ *A British warship escorting an Atlantic convoys opens fire against attacking German aircraft, probably Condors.*

The RAF is under the command of Arthur Harris. Made an air commodore in 1937, he was named air vice marshal in 1939 and rose to air marshal in 1941 and commander-in-chief of the RAF bomber command in February 1942. As a firm believer in mass raids, Air Marshal Harris has developed the "saturation" technique of mass bombing: concentrating clouds of bombers in a giant raid on a single city, with the object of completely demolishing it, a tactic he used to the end of the war.

successes encouraged them to develop a broad offensive that recovered the nearby city of Orel on August 5 and Kharkov on August 23. The Battle of Kursk was the largest tank battle in history, involving some 6000 tanks, two million troops and 4000 aircraft. It marked the decisive end of the German offensive capability on the Eastern Front and cleared the way for the great Soviet offensives of 1944–45.

JULY 10

MEDITERRANEAN, *SICILY*
Anglo-American forces comprising General Montgomery's British Eighth Army and General George Patton's US Seventh Army

▲ *Jews of the Warsaw ghetto are lined up against a wall prior to being executed.*

◄ *Artillery and mortar rounds pound the Warsaw ghetto as the Jews fight back.*

▶ *The RAF's "saturation" bombing in action: incendiaries being dropped on Kiel.*

▼ *Some of the tens of thousands of Axis prisoners captured by the Allies in North Africa.*

into the German lines. In an attempt to recover the offensive on the Eastern Front, the Germans launch a surprise attack on the salient from both north and south, hoping to surround and destroy the Soviet forces within the bulge. Hitler orders Kluge in the north and Manstein in the south to attack. The object is to encircle and destroy the Russian armies and then move on to Moscow. The German assault forces consist of almost 50 divisions containing 900,000 troops, including 17 motorized or armoured divisions having 2700 tanks and assault guns.

However, the Soviets had realized the German attack beforehand and had withdrawn their main forces from the obviously threatened positions within the salient. The Germans soon encountered deep antitank defences and minefields, which the Soviets had emplaced in anticipation of the attack. The Germans advanced only 16km (10 miles) into the salient in the north and 48km (30 miles) in the south, losing many of their tanks in the process. At the height of the battle on July 12, the Soviets began to counterattack, having built up by then a preponderance of both troops and tanks. Their subsequent

land on the shores of southern Sicily. The landings are codenamed Operation Husky, and are opposed by General Guzzoni's Sixth Army: 230,000 Italian and 40,000 German soldiers.

JULY 11

ITALY, *POLITICS*

Mussolini is dismissed as Prime Minister of Italy, overthrown and imprisoned. The King regains temporary power and Marshal Badoglio forms a government. Italy is in turmoil, and it looks as if the whole

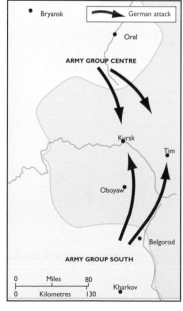

▲ Tiger tanks being shipped to the Eastern Front. Not even the mighty Tiger could give the Germans victory at Kursk.

country will fall into Allied hands. Against the advice of his generals, Hitler withdraws the *Leibstandarte* from the fighting at Kursk and rushes it to Italy that day. He justifies the weakening of the line in a vital sector by saying that, "down there I can only accomplish something with élite formations that are politically close to Fascism. If it weren't for that I could take a couple of army panzer divisions, but as it is

▲ An officer of the élite **Grossdeutsch-land** *Panzer Division* in the turret of his tank at the Battle of Kursk.

▶ The German attack plan at Kursk. The Red Army obstructed the German assault routes with mines and antitank guns.

▲ *The aftermath of a bombing raid on Hamburg, one of many cities to be targeted by the British and Americans.*

▶ *The German Tank Assault Badge, awarded to drivers, radio operators, gunners and commanders after combat.*

I need a magnet around which to gather the people together." Meanwhile, German forces in Italy take over the country and disarm Italian troops.

JULY 29

AIR WAR, *GERMANY*
Goebbels is active in visiting bomb-damaged areas of Germany and sees for himself the horrifying extent of the destruction meted out by Allied air attacks. He writes in his diary this day following one of the heaviest single raids on Hamburg: "1000 bombers, *Gauleiter* Kaumann spoke of a catastrophe

▼ *Propaganda Minister Goebbels visiting the victims of Allied bombing in Essen. He toured bombed cities tirelessly.*

▲ *Waffen-SS troops of the **Das Reich** Division take part in Germany's last great offensive on the Eastern Front: Kursk.*

the extent of which blunts the imagination. A city of one million people has been devastated in a manner unknown before in history; problems almost impossible to solve; food for a million people shelter, clothing, 800,000 homeless people wandering the devastated streets."

AUGUST 4

EASTERN FRONT, *UKRAINE*
The Red Army recaptures Orcl. The Germans are in general retreat in the East.

▼ *Men and vehicles pour ashore during Operation Husky, the Allied invasion of Sicily in July.*

SEPTEMBER 12

SEPTEMBER 12

MEDITERRANEAN, *ITALY*

Mussolini is rescued from imprisonment by a raiding squad under German commando leader Otto Skorzeny and installed as head of a new government in Northern Italy by the Germans. Earlier, on the 9th, the Allies landed on the Italian mainland at Messina, Calabria and Salerno, south of Naples.

Italy had surrendered on the 8th, but German troops under Field Marshal Albert Kesselring, already commander in southern Europe, occupied Rome and moved south.

▼ *Following the rescue of Mussolini (in black coat), he poses for photographs with his rescuers. Skorzeny is to his right.*

▲ *German troops in retreat on the Eastern Front in the autumn of 1943 following he Wehrmacht defeat at Kursk.*

Rommel was transferred to northwest Europe. Many disbanded Italian soldiers took to the hills to form partisan units.

GERMANY, *RESISTANCE*

The "Solf tea-party" resistance group, mostly German diplomats, is broken up by Gestapo.

SEPTEMBER 26

SEA WAR, *NORWAY*

British midget submarines known as X-craft launch a successful attack on the German battleship *Tirpitz* as she lays at anchor in Alten Fjord in Norway.

OCTOBER 13

POLITICS, *ITALY*

Italy declares war on Germany. Hitler orders a line to be held south of Rome.

GERMANY, *RESISTANCE*

Claus von Stauffenberg takes over the planning for the 1944 anti-Hitler coup.

▼ *The Tiger tank could defeat any Soviet tank in 1943, but the panzer divisions never had enough to regain the initiative.*

▲ *The Scharnhorst test-fires some of its guns prior to setting sail on her fateful journey in December.*

OCTOBER 17

SEA WAR, *PACIFIC*
The last German auxiliary cruiser *Michel* is sunk by the American submarine *Tarpon*.

NOVEMBER 6

EASTERN FRONT, *UKRAINE*
The Soviets recapture Kiev.

DECEMBER 26

SEA WAR, *ATLANTIC*
Admiral Dönitz told Hitler on December 19 that the *Scharnhorst* would attack a convoy soon if the circumstances were favourable. However, the circumstances were far from favourable, for the convoy they chose to attack this day in the Battle of the North Cape were covered by the flagship of the British Home Fleet, the battleship HMS *Duke of York*, and a strong force of cruisers and destroyers. The British had decoded the orders to the *Scharnhorst* and so she ran into a hot reception. The cruisers with the convoys damaged her radar and fire control, but she was still a formidable adversary. While her attention was distracted in a gun-duel with the *Sheffield* and *Norfolk*, the *Duke of York* approached unobserved to within 11km (6.8 miles) before opening fire. The *Scharnhorst*'s aim was not good, and she scored only two minor hits on the *Duke of York*, whereas she herself was hit repeatedly. She was attacked by four destroyers, which hit her with four torpedoes, slowing her down for the *Duke of York*. Finally the cruiser *Jamaica* torpedoed the *Scharnhorst*, which sunk with the loss of her entire crew, except for 36 men.

The year 1943 ended badly for the Germans. The qualitative improvement in the Red Army was matched by a marked

▼ *A Panther in Russia. The supply of the new Tiger and Panther tanks did not offset German manpower shortages in the East.*

▲ *A Tiger sheds a track during the German withdrawal in the East in the second half of 1943.*

increase in the supply of materiel from beyond the Urals. Tanks and artillery became increasingly available to Soviet commanders, and problems of mobility were largely overcome by the supply of American trucks. On the German side, the year's end saw serious shortages of manpower which could not be disguised by fielding divisions at half-strength.

1944

The Third Reich suffered a series of crippling blows in 1944. Having lost the initiative on the Eastern Front in 1943, the Red Army destroyed Army Group Centre in June 1944 when it launched Operation Bagration. In addition, the Western Allies finally landed in France on June 6, thereby opening the Second Front. Only in Italy did the German Army have any degree of success in slowing the Allied advance.

EASTERN FRONT, *LENINGRAD*
The siege of Leningrad is lifted. The German blockade and siege has claimed around one million Leningraders, mostly from starvation, exposure, disease, and shelling from German artillery. Sparse food and fuel supplies reached the city by barge in the summer and by truck and ice-borne sled in winter across

Lake Ladoga. These supplies kept the city's arms factories operating and its inhabitants barely alive, while one million more of its children, sick, and elderly were evacuated.

JANUARY 15

SEA WAR, *ATLANTIC*
U-377, commanded by *Oberleutnant zur See* Gerhard Kluth, is sunk by an acoustic

torpedo fired from *U-972*, commanded by *Oberleutnant zur See* Klaus König, who was to suffer a similar fate later in the month.

JANUARY 21

ITALY, *ANZIO*
The Allies land at Anzio, south of Rome, by means of an Anglo-American amphibious

▼ Men and equipment pour ashore following the amphibious landings at Anzio, south of Rome, in January.

▲ *German troops in Rome. Following the Italian capitulation to the Allies, the Germans took control of the country.*

assault. The Anglo-American armies in Italy, which had invaded a year earlier, are stalemated on the Gustav Line, the key point of which is Monte Cassino. General Mark Clark, commanding the US VI Corps, plans to mount an assault from the sea, at Anzio, to break the Gustav Line by linking up with the British attack due to strike in the centre, particularly the Abbey of Monte Cassino. It is hoped that the Anzio assault, by cutting the German Tenth Army's lines of communication, will oblige Kesselring to order the evacuation of the Gustav Line and allow the Anzio and Cassino attackers to link up, march on Rome and thus break the German hold on Italy.

▼ *The Allied plan to bypass the German defence line by landing at Anzio was sound, but relied on speed to succeed.*

▲ *The key to the Gustav Line was the hilltop monastery at Monte Cassino, seen here following bombing and shelling.*

▼ *German paratroopers during the defence of Monte Cassino. The Germans retreated from Cassino in good order.*

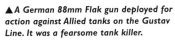

▲ *A German 88mm Flak gun deployed for action against Allied tanks on the Gustav Line. It was a fearsome tank killer.*

The Cassino attack quickly succeeds in attracting the German reserves. But the American General Lucas, though he gets his Anglo-American force easily ashore at Anzio, fails to profit from the temporary weakness around his bridgehead by pressing an advance from it. As a result, the Germans are able to rush forces to contain the bridgehead.

JANUARY 30

ITALY, *ANZIO*

When Lucas attempts a breakout from the Anzio bridgehead, he finds the Germans are very organized opposite him. He is obliged thereafter to conduct a static defence.

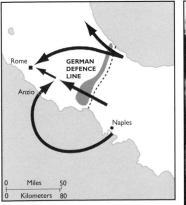

Rome

GERMAN
DEFENCE
LINE

Anzio

Naples

| 0 | Miles | 50 |
| 0 | Kilometers | 80 |

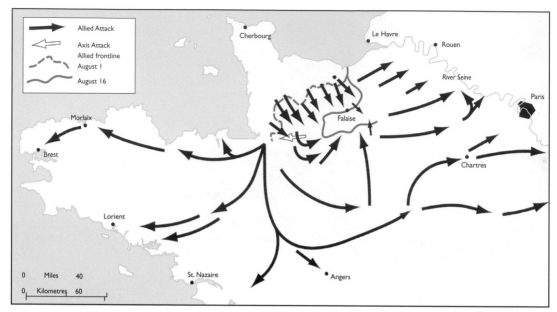

Legend:
- Allied Attack
- Axis Attack
- Allied frontline August 1
- August 16

(Map labels: Cherbourg, Le Havre, Rouen, River Seine, Paris, Morlaix, Falaise, Chartres, Brest, Lorient, St. Nazaire, Angers)

Scale:
0 Miles 40
0 Kilometres 60

▲ The Germans attempted to contain the Allied bridgehead after D-Day, but lacked the resources to do so.

◄ The battleship *Tirpitz* holed up in Kaa Fjord in July 1944. Note the antisubmarine net around the ship.

FEBRUARY 15

ITALY, *ANZIO*

The Germans, having gathered enough strength, attack and penetrate deeply into General Lucas' positions at the Anzio bridgehead. They are halted only by a desperate US counterattack on February 19. The Germans then seal the bridgehead and contain it. A general Allied offensive on May 11 permitted General Truscott, who had succeeded Lucas, to break out on May 23.

FEBRUARY 26

EASTERN FRONT, *BALTIC*

Germany's Army Group North loses Porkhov in the face of the Red Army offensive. Three German divisions are wiped out and another 17 badly mauled. Elsewhere on the Eastern Front Nikopol, with its manganese-ore mines, was abandoned on the 8th; and Krivoi Rog was lost before the end of the month.

MARCH 19

POLITICS, *HUNGARY*

As Soviet forces reach the Carpathians, Hitler orders the occupation of Hungary.

▲ The Defence Medal, instituted for work on Germany's fortifications, principally the Siegfried Line in the autumn of 1944.

APRIL 5

SEA WAR, *NORWAY*

The British mount a large-scale air attack on the *Tirpitz* moored in Kaa Fjord.

MAY 9

EASTERN FRONT, *CRIMEA*

The Crimea is cleared and Sevastopol recaptured by the Soviets. The Germans

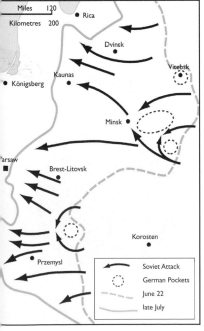

lose 100,000 men. Hitler dismisses Manstein to show where he places the blame for Germany's failures on the Eastern Front.

JUNE

GERMANY, *ESPIONAGE*

The *Abwehr*, the German military intelligence organization, is closed and absorbed into the SD under Walter Schellenberg. Admiral Canaris, head of the *Abwehr*, is dismissed on suspicion of being part of the anti-Hitler resistance, though nothing has been proved. In fact, Canaris was a member of the Resistance.

◄ *The Soviet frontline during Operation Bagration. Launched in June, it destroyed Germany's Army Group Centre.*

▼ *Red Army troops in the attack during Operation Bagration. The offensive took the Soviets to the gates of Warsaw.*

▲ *One of the Vergeltungwaffen (Reprisal Weapons) that Hitler believed would turn the tide of war: a V-1 rocket.*

JUNE 6

WESTERN FRONT, *NORMANDY*

Operation "Overlord", the D-Day Anglo-American landings, commences. The invasion begins before dawn with units of the US 82nd and 101st Airborne Divisions making night landings near the town of Sainte-Mère-Église, while British commando units capture key bridges and knock out Nazi communications. In the morning, the assault troops of the combined Allied armies land at five beaches along the Normandy coast codenamed Utah, Omaha, Gold, Juno and Sword. While four beaches

are taken easily and quickly, the forces landing at "Bloody Omaha" encounter stiff German resistance. By nightfall, sizeable beachheads have been secured on all five landing areas, and the final campaign to defeat Germany is underway.

JUNE 11

SEA WAR, *ATLANTIC*
The last remaining supply U-boat, *U-490*, is sunk.

JUNE 12

SEA WAR, *GERMANY*
The first electro-boat, *U-2321*, is commissioned. It is a Type XXIII, a small coastal submarine carrying two torpedoes.

JUNE 23

EASTERN FRONT, *BELORUSSIA*
Soviets launch their summer offensive, codenamed Bagration, concentrating on the White Russian fronts. The Red Army has

assembled 1,254,000 men, 2175 tanks, 1355 assault guns and 24,000 artillery pieces for the assault. Facing these forces is Army Group Centre, which has 500,000 men to defend 1120km (700 miles) of front. The Soviets smash through the German lines, advancing 240km (150 miles) in a week.

June was a bad month for the Third Reich. In addition to the landings in Normandy

▼ *German panzers make their way to the front in France, July 1944. The last vehicle in the column is a Panzer V Panther.*

▲ *Hitler after the attempt on his life at Rastenburg. Note the plaster on his left hand.*

◄ *Michael Wittmann, panzer ace, who fought in Normandy in 1944.*

▲ *Though the Germans lacked air cover in Normandy, they made skillful use of camouflage. This is an 88mm gun.*

and Bagration, the Allies captured Rome on the 5th and partisan strength in northern Italy reached 100,000. Also this month the Germans began V-1 attacks on Great Britain.

JUNE 27

SEA WAR, *GERMANY*

The first large Type XXI electro-submarine is commissioned: *U-2501*.

JULY 20

EASTERN FRONT, *BELORUSSIA*

Minsk falls; Army Group Centre is virtually destroyed. Total German losses exceed 200,000. Vilna falls and Soviet forces approach the East Prussian frontier.

The catalogue of German disasters continue as the Red Army continues its advance: Lvov falls to Koniev's army at the month's end.

GERMANY, *RESISTANCE*

Hitler moves to his East Prussian head-quarters at Rastenburg. An unsuccessful attempt is made to assassinate Hitler by Colonel Count Claus Schenk von Stauffenberg at the Wolf's Lair at Rastenburg, Hitler's headquarters in the East.

Stauffenberg had been drawn into the circle of military conspirators against Hitler but also quickly formed the opinion that they lacked resolution. Thus it was that he took it upon himself, as someone with access to Hitler's conferences but so disabled as to escape body search, to smuggle a bomb into the Führer's

conference room. Hitler and the other 24 occupants of the room suffer varying degrees of wounds, the most serious being the loss of life of Colonel Brant and Herr Berger, who die immediately, and *Generalleutnant* Schmundt and General Korten, dying subsequently from wounds they have received. The remaining 20 suffer superficial wounds and shock, save for General Buhle and *Generalmajor* Scherff, who are more seriously injured. Unfortunately, though Stauffenberg makes good his escape from the Rastenburg headquarters, the Berlin conspirators fail to act with resolution during his return flight to the city, and by the time he has arrived, they have lost irretrievable time. By the evening the coup has foundered and General Fromm, head of the Home Army, who hoped thereby to remove the evidence of his own complicity, shot Stauffenberg, with others, in the courtyard of the War Ministry.

The assassination attempt, codenamed Valkyrie, had failed, but coup signals had been sent out. The German command in Paris started to take over from the Nazis until news of the failure came through. Coup plotters and large numbers of suspects, including Canaris and Oster, were rounded up. General Ludwig Beck and

▲ *The special Wound Badge issued by Hitler following the July Bomb Plot. This particular one was awarded to Jodl.*

▼ *Roland Freisler (centre), head of the People's Court where most of the anti-Hitler conspirators were tried.*

others committed suicide. From July until April 1945 trials and executions of suspects continued.

WESTERN FRONT, *NORMANDY*

The American, British and Canadian forces have consolidated their D-Day beachheads and link up. For the loss of 5000 men killed, 750,000 have now been put ashore. The Americans to the west, on the Allied right wing, have cleared the peninsula south of Cherbourg. The British, holding the centre, face the city of Caen, and the Canadians on the Allied left have borne the heaviest weight of the German panzer attacks. In the air the Allies have complete superiority and are able to attack German army ground targets at will. Field Marshal von Rundstedt is dismissed when he expresses pessimism over the battle's outcome. The US First Army, with over 350,000 men and 1000 tanks, starts its advance south, while the British Second Army and the Canadian Army attack Caen. Field Marshal Rommel, German commander, is injured in a car crash and replaced by Field Marshal von Kluge.

Some 14 British and Canadian divisions are holding 14 German divisions and are engaged in heavy fighting for Caen. General Omar Bradley on the other wing has 15 US divisions facing a mixture of German units amounting to nine divisions. At the end of the month the Americans move out of the

◄ *To crush the Warsaw Jews the Germans used their most unsavoury characters, such as SS leader Oskar Dirlewanger, seen here.*

▼ *A German antitank gun in action in the Warsaw Ghetto. The destruction attests to the ferocity of the fighting.*

peninsula and reach Brittany, while the Canadians and British take Caen and slowly push the Germans back.

AUGUST 1

POLAND, *RESISTANCE*

The Polish resistance – the "Home Army" – in Warsaw rises as the Soviets approach. Commanded by General Tadeusz Bór-Komorowski, the Warsaw corps of 50,000 troops attacks the relatively weak German force and within three days gains control of

▲ *Poorly armed soldiers of the Polish Home Army. They fought with a courage and tenacity borne of desperation.*

most of the city. The Germans send in reinforcements and force the Poles into a defensive position, bombarding them with air and artillery attacks for the next 63 days. Meanwhile, the Red Army, which had been detained during the first days of the insurrection by a German assault, occupies a position at Praga, a suburb across the Vistula from Warsaw, and remains idle. In addition, the Soviet government refuses to allow the Western Allies to use Soviet airbases to airlift supplies to the beleaguered Poles. Without Allied support, the Home Army is split into small, disconnected units. It was forced to surrender when its supplies gave out (October 2). Bór-Komorowski and his forces

▲ *When fighting "sub-humans" the Germans ignored the rules of war. These are hostages hanged in the Warsaw Uprising.*

were taken prisoner, and the Germans then systematically deported the remainder of the city's population and destroyed the city block by block.

AUGUST 19

EASTERN FRONT, *BALTIC*

Russian troops surround 55 German divisions on the Baltic coast. The Red Army enters Bucharest. On August 23 Romania sues for peace. Hitler's Eastern Front is crumbling.

▲ *Field Marshal Walther Model (with monocle), the German commander in the West. He committed suicide in April 1945.*

WESTERN FRONT, *FRANCE*

By this time the Allies have landed 1.5 million soldiers and 300,000 vehicles. Now, 36 Allied divisions, each stronger and more liberally equipped that those of their opponents, now face the 20 German divisions. The British and Canadians advance south; US divisions sweep south

and turn east at great speed, threatening to surround the German forces. Kluge directs his army to move to the attack in obedience to Hitler's orders but is recalled to Paris to answer for his part in the "July Bomb Plot". Kluge commits suicide. Hitler replaces him with the general already in the frontline, Hausser, and gives command in the West to Field Marshal Model. German

◀ *A Panther outside Warsaw in August 1944. The Soviets made little effort to aid the Warsaw Jews in the ghetto.*

▼ *The German Auxiliary Cruisers Badge. These vessels sailed the oceans as part of the Kriegmarine's war.*

▲ *German paratroopers hitch a ride during the opening days of Hitler's gamble in the West, the Ardennes Offensive.*

▲ *US troops stand on "dragon's teeth" antitank defences on the Siegfried Line. Note the bullet holes in the concrete.*

forces. The French II Corps advances on Marseilles. On the last day of August Patton's Third Army reaches the Meuse.

AUGUST 20

NAZI PARTY, *AWARDS*

To commemorate the attempt on his life at the Wolf's Lair at Rastenburg on July 20, 1944, and his escape, Hitler introduces a special Wound Badge, which he awards to 24 recipients, or dependents in the case of the dead. He declines to award himself one of these medals.

The Recipients are:
KEITEL, Wilhelm *Generalfeldmarschall*
JODL, Alfred *Generaloberst*
WARLIMONT, Walter *General der Artillerie*
von PUTTKAMER, Jesko *Konteradmiral*

ASSMANN, Heinz *Kapitän Z See*
von BELOW, Nicolaus *Oberst*
VOSS, Hans-Erich *Konteradmiral*
GÜNSCHE, Otto *SS-Hauptsturmführer*
FEGELEIN, Hermann *SS-Gruppenführer*
HEUSINGER, Adolf *Generalleutnant*
BORGMAN, G. *Oberstleutnant*
BODENSCHATZ, Karl *General der Flieger*
BUHLE, Walter *General der Infanterie*
SCHERFF, Walter *Generalmajor*
KORTEN, Gunter *General der Flieger*
BRANT, Heinz *Oberst*
BERGER, Civilian
SCHMUNDT, Rudolf *Generalleutnant*

▼ *The bridge at Arnhem, scene of fierce fighting between the British and Germans during Operation Market Garden.*

forces are badly mauled in the Falaise Pocket, and afterwards the Americans advance 80km (50 miles) a day. In Paris the French resistance takes over part of the city, and within days the Free French 2nd Armoured Division, accompanied by US units, liberates the city. In the south of France, US forces land and move north against little opposition. Aix-en-Provence is taken by US

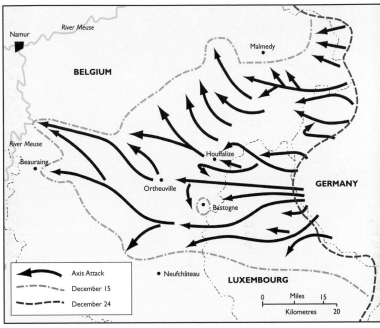

▶ *The Ardennes Offensive caught the Allies by surprise, but by the end of December it had run out of momentum.*

Axis Attack
December 15
December 24

von JOHN, *Oberstleutnant*
BÜCHS, G. *Major*
HAGAN
WEIZENEGGER, *Oberstleutnant*
HEWELL, Walter, *Civilian*
von SCHIMANSKI, *Hauptmann*

SEPTEMBER 17

WESTERN FRONT, *HOLLAND*
Operation Market Garden, Montgomery's plan for an armoured and airborne thrust through Holland, begins. General Eisenhower, supreme commander of the Allied forces, has taken over from Montgomery as commander of the Allied ground forces and decides to advance on a broad front towards the Rhine, notwithstanding Market Garden. Field Marshal von Rundstedt is given back command in the West. Allied forces now have a complete front from the Channel to Switzerland and move towards the German West Wall, the "Siegfried" line. France is almost totally liberated.

NOVEMBER 12

SEA WAR, *NORWAY*
The *Tirpitz* sinks at her anchorage, off

▶ *German King Tiger tanks. Used during the Ardennes Offensive, many ran out of fuel and had to be abandoned.*

Haakoy Island, when a force of Lancaster bombers surprise her without any defending fighters in the air. In perfect visibility the bombers hit her with three "Tallboys" and she capsizes.

DECEMBER 16

WESTERN FRONT, *ARDENNES*
The Ardennes Offensive is launched, Hitler's gamble to reach Antwerp and split the Allied armies in the West. The attack is made in the hilly and wooded Ardennes

region of southern Belgium. While Allied aircraft are hampered by bad weather, Rundstedt's Fifth and Sixth Panzer Armies launch two parallel attacks. The Fifth Army, under General Hasso von Manteuffel, bypasses Bastogne (which is held throughout the offensive by the US 101st Airborne Division), and has advanced by December 24 to within four miles (six kilometres) of the Meuse River. Germany's last reserves of men and tanks have been committed to the offensive.

1945

JANUARY 3

WESTERN FRONT, *ARDENNES*

The final German attack against Bastogne is defeated. Hitler's last offensive in the West has been stopped. The Allies regroup and launch a counterattack. By the 16th the US First and Third Armies have linked up at Houffalize.

JANUARY 27

EASTERN FRONT, *POLAND*

The Soviets liberate Auschwitz, the Third Reich's main death camp. The centre of a rail network, the first camp, Auschwitz I, was reserved throughout its history for political prisoners. In October 1941, work began on Auschwitz II, or Birkenau, located outside the nearby village of Brzezinka. There the SS later developed a huge concentration camp and extermination

With the failure of the Ardennes Offensive, defeat for Nazi Germany was only a matter of weeks. As her cities were pounded into rubble by fleets of Allied bombers, the Red Army closed in on Berlin for the final battle against National Socialism. Hitler decided to stay in his capital and committed suicide rather than risk capture by the Soviets. Behind him he left a country in ruins, and a people saddled with the great shame of being part of his horrific Final Solution, the evidence of which were found by Allied troops as they liberated the concentration camps.

▼ *Tired German troops are driven towards the front to meet the next Soviet offensive in early 1945. Few, if any, will return.*

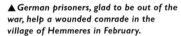

▲ *German prisoners, glad to be out of the war, help a wounded comrade in the village of Hemmeres in February.*

complex that included some 300 prison barracks; four large *Badeanstalten* (bathhouses), in which prisoners were gassed to death; *Leichenkeller* (corpse cellars), in which their bodies were stored; and *Einäscherungsöfen* (cremating ovens). Another camp (Buna-Monowitz), near the village of Dwory, later called Auschwitz III, became a slave-labour camp in May 1942.

Newly arrived prisoners at the death camp were divided in a process known as

▲ *US C-47 transport aircraft drop supplies to the besieged garrison of Bastogne during the Ardennes Offensive.*

Selektion. The young and the able-bodied were sent to work; young children and their mothers and the old and infirm were sent directly to the gas chambers. Thousands of prisoners were also selected by the camp doctor, Josef Mengele, for medical experiments, which were mostly sadistic. Experiments involving the killing of twins, for example, were meant to provide information that would supposedly lead to the rapid expansion of the "Aryan race".

Subject to harsh conditions – including inadequate shelter and sanitation – given minimal food, and worked to exhaustion, those who could no longer work faced transport back to Birkenau for gassing.

Between 1.1 and 1.5 million people died at Auschwitz; 90 percent of them were Jews, though other victims included a large number of Gypsies.

▼ *Dresden being bombed on February 14. Over 50,000 people were killed in the firestorm caused by the bombing.*

◄ *The town of St Hubert, Belgium, following its evacuation by German troops after the failure of the Ardennes attack.*

▼ *A veteran of the* **Grossdeutschland Division** *(left) instructs a young recruit in the use of a Panzerfaust antitank rocket.*

▲ *The bridge over the Rhine at Remagen, which was captured by US troops after demolition charges failed to go off.*

Russian army groups, both north and south of Warsaw, break through and take the city crossing the river Oder within 160km (100 miles) of Berlin. They reach the Baltic at Danzig and overrun industrial Silesia, seizing the last possible coal supplies of the Third Reich. The Soviet offensive in the East causes Hitler to move armoured forces from the West, including "Sepp" Dietrich's Sixth SS Panzer Army.

WESTERN FRONT, *FRANCE*
German losses in France since D-Day amount to 1.5 million men, over half of whom are prisoners of war.

FEBRUARY 14

EASTERN FRONT, *EAST PRUSSIA*
The *Kriegsmarine* evacuates German troops from Baltic ports, Danzig and East Prussia who have been trapped by the advance of the Red Army.

AIR WAR, *GERMANY*
Some 805 Royal Air Force (RAF) bombers attack the city of Dresden during the night. The raid causes a massive firestorm that kills 50,000 people. Then the Americans bomb the city during the day.

WESTERN FRONT, *THE RHINE*

The First Canadian Army, on the Allied left flank, attacks down the west bank of the Rhine, drawing the last German reserves on the Western Front.

MARCH 3

WESTERN FRONT, *FRANCE*

Patton's Third Army approaches the Rhine. His VIII and XII Corps make good progress.

MARCH 6

EASTERN FRONT, *HUNGARY*

Spearheaded by Dietrich's Sixth SS Panzer Army, Hitler launches Operation Spring Awakening to secure the oilfields at Nagykanizsa and retake Budapest. However, the offensive soon bogs down in the face of poor weather and Red Army resistance. Then the Third Ukrainian Front counterattacks and drives the Germans back.

MARCH 7

WESTERN FRONT, *GERMANY*

Hitler has given orders that not a single Rhine bridge must fall intact into Allied hands. What every Allied commander dreams of, a reconnaissance patrol of the US First Army achieves. The unit discovers a

◀ *Defeat in the West: dead Hitler Youth. The Führer was determined to fight to the last German boy.*

basically undamaged bridge across the Rhine at Remagen near Bonn.

Second Lieutenant Emmet J. Burrows appeared out of the woods above Remagen to find disorganized German troops fleeing across the Ludendorff railway bridge. Soon, a platoon of US tanks was charging down to the bridge. As it approached, a German engineer, *Hauptmann* W. Bratke, detonated charges on the bridge which created a small crater. The American pushed on, shelling the Germans on the east bank. One shell knocked out the engineer responsible for firing the demolition charge. When he came to and turned the key, nothing happened. He tried again and still the detonators failed. US troops, led by Sergeant A. Drabik of Holland, Ohio, raced onto the bridge amid a hail of gunfire. Then a powerful explosion lifted the bridge up; it settled back and, incredibly, was still standing. In less than 24 hours more than 8000 troops with tanks and self-propelled guns had crossed the Rhine.

MARCH 19

GERMANY, *ECONOMY*

Hitler issues the so-called "Nero Decree", ordering the destruction of Germany's bridges, industrial plants and railway lines.

▼ *The last photograph of Adolf Hitler, taken outside the bunker as he decorates a Hitler Youth member.*

▼ *Defeat in the East: a knocked-out German antitank gun and Panzer IV tanks on the outskirts of Berlin.*

The order is ignored by Albert Speer, who is now thinking of post-war Germany.

MARCH 22

WESTERN FRONT, *GERMANY*
Montgomery's Twenty-First Army Group crosses the Rhine to the north, then moves across north Germany towards Hamburg.

APRIL 2

WESTERN FRONT, *GERMANY*
The US First and Third Armies link up and complete the encirclement of the industrial Ruhr region.

APRIL 13

EASTERN FRONT, *AUSTRIA*
Vienna is taken by the Red Army. With Anglo-American forces driving east, Hitler's

▶ *Field Marshal Montgomery (right) negotiates the enemy surrender at the Twenty-First Army Group's headquarters.*

▼ *The Battle of Berlin. The black arrows depict Red Army attacks, which cut through German defences in five days.*

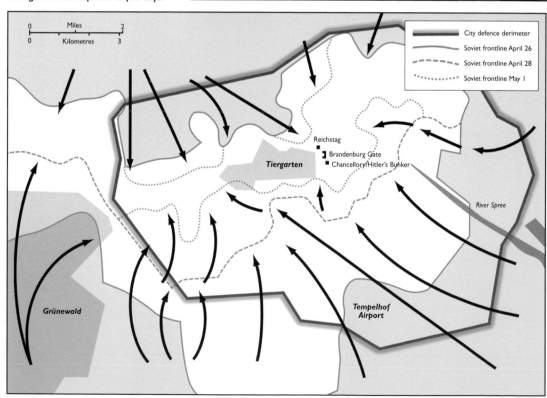

General Karl Wolff, governor of north Italy, negotiates with US agent Allen Dulles of the Office of Strategic Service (OSS) in Switzerland with a view to saving Italy's industry from unnecessary destruction. As a result of these negotiations, Kesselring surrenders German forces in Italy on May 2.

APRIL 30

NAZI PARTY, *BERLIN*

As Berlin is engulfed in explosives and fires, Hitler, having first married his mistress Eva Braun, commits suicide. Before he does so he dictates his political testament. In it he states: "I die with a happy heart, aware of the immeasurable deeds and achievements of our soldiers at the front, our women at

◀ *After the battle Berliners come out of their cellars to survey the damage. The first thing they met was choking smoke.*

◀ *Berlin, May 1945. This once-proud city lay in ruins, while an overpowering stench of dead flesh hung over its streets.*

Third Reich is crumbling rapidly. During this month American and Soviet troops meet on the Elbe at Torgau, and the British liberate Belsen.

APRIL 26

EASTERN FRONT, *GERMANY*

The Red Army assault on Berlin begins. Hitler is in the city, having decided to stay in his capital. He issues orders to non-existent armies to come to the city's relief. By the 27th German forces in Berlin have been restricted to an area 16km (10 miles) long by 5km (three miles) wide.

In Italy Mussolini tries to escape to Switzerland but is captured and shot by partisans on the 28th. Also in Italy, SS

▼ *A German prisoner reads a US forces newspaper heralding Hitler's death.*

▲ *With the war over the perpetrators of atrocities were arrested. This is Auschwitz guard Irma Grese, who was hanged in 1946.*

▶ *The V-2 was a supersonic rocket that had a range of 360km (225 miles). It came too late to save Hitler's Reich.*

home, the achievements of our farmers and workers and the work, unique in history, of our youth who bear my name." Eva Braun takes poison to be with her new husband in death. Grand Admiral Karl Dönitz becomes Head of State.

MAY 1

NAZI PARTY, *BERLIN*

Dönitz issues the following declaration to all members of the German armed forces still fighting the Allies: "I expect discipline and obedience. Chaos and ruin can be prevented only by the swift and unreserved execution of my orders. Anyone who, at this juncture, fails in his duty and condemns German women and children to slavery and death, is

a traitor and a coward. The oath of allegiance which you took to the Führer now binds each and every one of you to me, whom he himself appointed as his successor." But Dönitz realizes that further resistance is useless.

MAY 4

WESTERN FRONT, *GERMANY*

Admiral Friedeburg, head of the *Kriegsmarine*, is authorized by Dönitz to negotiate a separate but partial surrender to Montgomery of all German forces in northern Germany to take effect from 08:00 hours on the morning of May 5. The German delegation signs the surrender document at 18:30 hours in Montgomery's headquarters at Lüneburg Heath just south

▼ *German troops sought the Western Allies to surrender to, such as these paratroopers, to avoid Soviet retribution.*

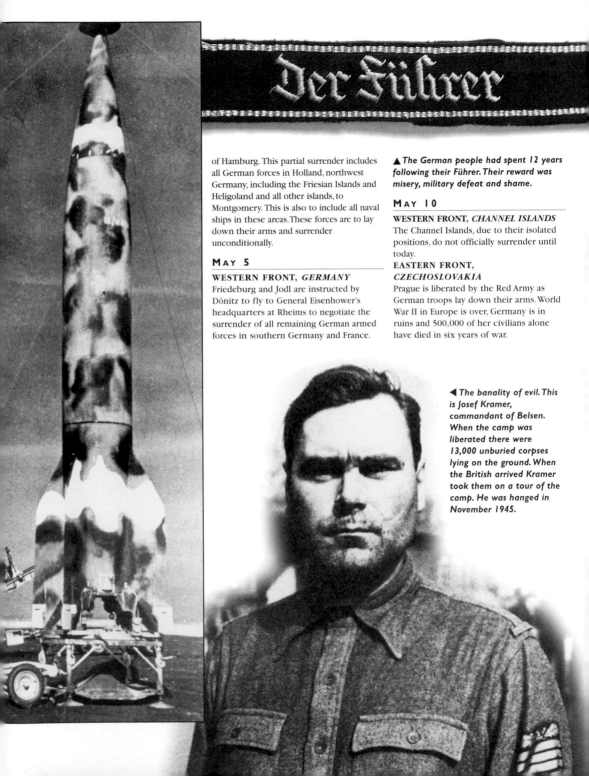

Der Führer

of Hamburg. This partial surrender includes all German forces in Holland, northwest Germany, including the Friesian Islands and Heligoland and all other islands, to Montgomery. This is also to include all naval ships in these areas. These forces are to lay down their arms and surrender unconditionally.

MAY 5

WESTERN FRONT, *GERMANY*
Friedeburg and Jodl are instructed by Dönitz to fly to General Eisenhower's headquarters at Rheims to negotiate the surrender of all remaining German armed forces in southern Germany and France.

▲ *The German people had spent 12 years following their Führer. Their reward was misery, military defeat and shame.*

MAY 10

WESTERN FRONT, *CHANNEL ISLANDS*
The Channel Islands, due to their isolated positions, do not officially surrender until today.

EASTERN FRONT, *CZECHOSLOVAKIA*
Prague is liberated by the Red Army as German troops lay down their arms. World War II in Europe is over, Germany is in ruins and 500,000 of her civilians alone have died in six years of war.

◀ *The banality of evil. This is Josef Kramer, commandant of Belsen. When the camp was liberated there were 13,000 unburied corpses lying on the ground. When the British arrived Kramer took them on a tour of the camp. He was hanged in November 1945.*

CONCLUSION
Adolf Hitler's Legacy

Hitler's European war was just as much a personal creation as the empire that the Führer built. Thus, it was with the nature of Hitler himself that world society had to deal after he came to power in 1933.

Nazism was first and foremost a conspiracy to win political power in Germany, yet it never evolved a coherent political philosophy of its own, merely borrowing social theories available in Germany or elsewhere. Nazism was in fact the creation of a band of men drawn together by a self-appointed leader who fired their frustrated national pride and personal ambitions. Without the individual magnetism of Hitler there would have been no Nazi Party, or at least not one capable of seizing power, and no Third Reich of the quite special kind. To his followers, Hitler had the historical personal greatness of

Caesar or Napoleon. Hitler certainly did possess certain attributes of personal greatness, but without the capacity to fulfil them. He was destitute of human quality; he lacked reliability or any recognizable moral standard. He refused to listen to advice, preferring to accept his intuition, which was to grow increasingly unsound from 1941 onwards. His stamina was derived from his monstrous egotism, the blind self-confidence that made him believe himself a man of destiny, chosen by an act of providence to lead the Nordic world.

Hitler may have believed himself to be unique, but his actions and traits shared certain similarities to other great dictators. To compare Hitler with Napoleon, for example, one can detect a similarity stemming from the nationalism born in

them and stemming from the revolutionary times they lived through.

The revolution that Hitler lived through had as its bloody overture the carnage of World War I. The alliances in Europe made World War I inevitable. When it erupted, it brought with it patriotism, nationalism and a sense of righting old wrongs. But four years of brutal warfare brewed a heady cocktail of barbarism on a scale never before witnessed, fuelled by mass industrial production that could deliver armaments on a scale that was previously unthinkable. Technology fed upon itself, inventing ever-more horrific methods of destruction. For the participants it was seared into their minds and in some cases it totally

▼ *German service chiefs salute their Führer. All military personal took an oath of personal allegiance to Hitler.*

dehumanized them. With the ending of the war they returned to alien worlds. This brought bitter dissatisfaction, and men with time on their hands proved fertile ground for the new political thinking, on one hand communism and the other fascism. The flowering of both creeds would inevitably give rise to intense antagonism.

In Germany there sprang up the *Freikorps*, groups of ex-soldiers who were loyal to the officers who led them, and very little else. They looked with disdain on Germany's Weimar government, which in their eyes had meekly caved in to the dictates of the Treaty of Versailles and had therefore been an accomplice to Germany's humiliation.

It was easy enough for Hitler and his Bavarian party to recruit *Freikorps* members, promising as he did to right Germany's wrongs and to win back her place in the sun. But the path was long and hard for the Nazis, for the German people did not embrace Nazism overnight. It took Hitler 14 years to gain power, and one can argue that he only did so because the world

▲ *The Japanese ambassador is welcomed to Japan. The Berlin-Tokyo Axis was an alliance in name only.*

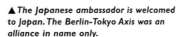

slump of 1929 made a desperate people more willing to listen to his simple solutions for Germany's ills. He was also aided by Germany's conservative élite, who believed that they could use Hitler to preserve their age-old status quo.

But Hitler had a separate agenda, one that was dominated by two concepts: race and space. Race was at the centre of his world view, and thus dictated the internal and external policies of the Third Reich once he had taken power in 1933. Hitler firmly believed in the racial superiority of the Aryan-Nordic race, whom he believed to be the founder and maintainer of civilization. The Jews, on the other hand, were destroyers of civilization. This anti-Semitism was by no means unique to him: many

▼ *"Ayran brothers": members of the Volunteer Labour Service for Flanders march out of camp into the fields.*

▲ *Norwegian RAD girls, part of the Nordic race that Hitler believed should have living space in the East.*

Europeans in the nineteenth and twentieth centuries had also believed this to be the case. Thus one can see this racial view in the laws introduced in Germany from the early 1935s.

Gradually Jews had their rights stripped away from them. Thus the 1935 Nuremberg Laws denied citizenship to German Jews, and slowly anti-Semitism was given a legal and state-sanctioned framework. It was the first step on the road to the Final Solution, in which the Nazis tried to exterminate European Jewry altogether.

Hitler and the Nazi hierarchy dreamed of a racially pure Germany, and so "racially pure" organizations were established, such as Heinrich Himmler's SS, whose members had to prove Aryan ancestry back to the eighteenth century.

Of course an Aryan "master race" by definition meant that other races were necessarily *Untermenschen* (sub-humans), an idea that was to have horrific consequences concerning Germany policy towards the conquered peoples of Eastern Europe and the Soviet Union.

Hitler's view towards Japan was curious. As they were Asiatics they did not fit into his racial scheme of things. Indeed, he once remarked to Ribbentrop: "One day the showdown with the yellow race will come." However, in the short term they were useful because they kept the British and Americans tied down in the Far East (though both Hitler and Goebbels had mixed feelings about the white man being defeated by the yellow race). Thus the Berlin–Tokyo axis was never anything more than a facade, one that neither party had much faith in. The real test came at the end

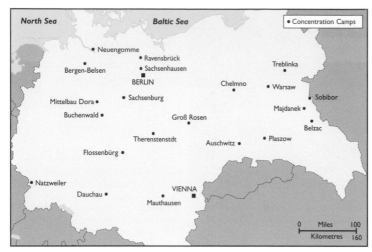

▲ The Nazi concentration camp system, designed for the systematic destruction of European Jewry and other "undesirables".

of 1941, when German armies stood before the gates of Moscow. The Japanese had no intention of attacking the Soviet Union in the Far East, a fact Stalin became aware of through his spy network in Japan, thus freeing up valuable reserves that he could ship from Siberia to the Eastern Front. Indeed, one can argue that the Japanese got more out of the axis than Germany, for Hitler's declaration of war on the United States brought him absolutely no benefits. The Japanese thus failed to aid Nazi Germany at a crucial time during the war on the Eastern Front.

The second concept that dominated Hitler's ideology was *Lebensraum* (Living Space). If the German race was to survive and grow strong, it needed space; space for industrial and agricultural output and space in which to raise future generations of "racially pure" Germans. And, like German leaders before him, Hitler looked to the East to fulfil his requirements. That the East was already populated by Slavs was of little consequence. The Slavs fulfiled no other purpose but to serve Germany, that or be eradicated. Above all, there should be no race mixing. Instead, the German race would become one of "pure blood". In this way Germany would remain strong and would not decay.

▶ Warsaw Ghetto Jews being rounded up for transportation to a concentration camp. Hitler described them as "chaff".

Space and race therefore defined Adolf Hitler and the Third Reich, and all that took place between 1933 and 1945 had to be placed within the quest for these two aims. Thus, the union with Austria and Czechoslovakia brought ethnic Germans back into the Reich. Having brought all his "children" back into the fold, Hitler then needed his living space. Thus he attacked Poland in September 1939. That Great Britain and France declared war on him in support of Poland was a great surprise, but did not deflect him from his plan. The defeat of these two countries in 1940 postponed his attack on the Soviet Union, but did not cancel it.

Hitler had always planned to attack the Soviet Union. To him it was a place full of Jews and other "undesirables". Moreover, it was the birthplace of Bolshevism, which he regarded as a "social criminality" that had to be eradicated. It was in the war against the Soviet Union that the concepts of space and race were fused into one, with the result that the war on the Eastern Front became a Nazi ideological crusade.

Seen in this context, some of the more inexplicable military decisions taken in the East are more easily understood. Hitler refused to retreat from Stalingrad because the city's name was that of the leader of the Soviet Union. Similarly, the Führer refused to sanction a withdrawal to a more defensible line following the failure of the attack against Moscow at the end of 1941 for no other reason that he refused to retreat in the face of "sub-humans".

It was therefore ironic that the "sub-human" Soviets should be the main agents in the destruction of the Third Reich, capturing Berlin itself in May 1945. With the fall of the Third Reich, that lasted but 12 turbulent years, not the 1000 Hitler boasted of, what did it leave? Certainly a new form of brutality that had never been witnessed on this scale. Atrocities had been committed before in war and will be in the future, but the systematic murder of millions of people in government-run camps heralded a new chapter in man's inhumanity to man.

In 1945 Germany was in ruins; indeed, never before had a nation been laid so low. However, Germany rose from the ruins, and became a state that today has one of the most democratic constitutions in the world. A nation that previously thrived on militarism now regards its armed forces in a defensive capacity only. This is an achievement that is given too little credit.

In Europe, the destruction of the Third Reich resulted in a continent that was divided for 50 years. As the Cold War developed, former allies became enemies and enemies became allies in weeks. The triploar world of fascism, communism and democracy was reduced to a bipolar stand-off between communism and democracy. The North Atlantic Treaty Organization (NATO) was created in 1949 in answer to the Soviet threat in Europe. Stalin, for his part, was determiined that never again would the Soviet Union be attacked from the West, and set about creating a buffer zone of satellite states in Eastern Europe. And to make sure they remained in the Soviet cam he left one million Red Army troops to garrison Eastern Europe. The

▲ *The consequences of Nazi racial ideology: the corpses of Jews at Belsen concentration camp.*

Warsaw Pact (which was created in 1955 and comprised the USSR and the states of Eastern Europe), though, was a paper tiger, an alliance that created an enormous economic strain on the USSR's finances and was only held together by Soviet coercion. It eventually collapsed, bringing down the Soviet Union with it.

For ordinary Germans, what were the benefits of living in the Third Reich? If you were a Jew you were singled out for persecution and, ultimately, extinction. The Jews were blamed for Germany's troubles, and thereby public opinion was aroused against them and their fate at the hands of the military and the police was condoned.

Nazi Germany was a totalitarian state where the police operated without the constraints of laws and regulations. Their actions were unpredictable and directed by the whim of Hitler. The Weimar constitution was never actually abrogated under Hitler, but an enabling act passed by the *Reichstag* in 1933 permitted him to amend the constitution at will, in effect nullify it. The role of lawmaker became vested in one man. Hitler did not allow change to become predictable, thus increasing the sense of terror among the people and repressing any dissent. Organizations like the Gestapo were everywhere, and its network of informers ensured that dissent and resistance were crushed.

In a positive light it can be stated that German advances in technology and medicine during the Third Reich were to revolutionize the world. The terror weapons of the V-1 and V-2 were eventually to place man on the moon. In the social field, the NSDAP made it possible for the ordinary person to indulge in sports, like

◄ *Erich von dem Bach-Zelewski, the SS general responsible for atrocities in Russia.*

tennis, ridding and gliding, that had until then been the preserve of the privileged classes. The arts and theatre were also thrown open. The provision of holidays through the "Strength through Joy" movement laid the ground for Butlins Holiday Camps in Great Britain and the package holiday enjoyed by millions today. (the camping sites on the Adriatic for the old Auto Union are still in operation).

And yet, in the final analysis, these benefits are insignificant when put beside the price the German people paid for Hitler's dreams. Over 10 million German service personnel were killed, wounded or posted as missing in World War II, while 500,000 were killed on the home front. The concentration camps murdered an estimated six million Jews in the name of Nazi racial doctrine, while millions of non-Germans died fighting one of the most evil regimes in world history. The Soviet Union, for example, lost an estimated 20 million killed in a war that really was one of national survival.

Hitler, and thus the Third Reich, rejected liberalism and democracy, the rule of law, human rights, and all movements of international cooperation and peace. He stressed instead instinct, the subordination of the individual to the state, and the necessity of blind and unswerving obedience to Nazi ideology. The result was horror on a grand scale.

▼ *One of the more brutal Nazi governors was Arthur Seyss-Inquart, Reichskommissar for the Netherlands.*

INDEX

Picture Credits

Christopher Ailsby Historical Archives: 1, 6, 8 (both), 9 (top), 10, 11 (both), 14-15, 15 (bottom), 19 (both), 21 (both), 22 (left), 23 (top), 24, 25 (top right), 26, 26-27, 27, 28, 28-29, 29 (both), 30 (both), 33 (both), 36, 36-37, 38, 44 (both), 45 (both), 46, 47, 48, 58 (bottom), 63 (bottom), 64, 65 (top), 66 (bottom), 77 (top), 78 (top & bottom), 79 (bottom), 90 (both), 91 (both), 92-93, 93, 95 (top right), 97 (top), 100 (bottom), 101 (both), 104 (top & bottom), 105 (top), 108 (top), 110 (both), 110-111, 111 (both), 112, 117 (bottom), 120 (top), 121 (top), 126 (both), 126-127, 133 (both), 134, 136 (bottom), 137 (bottom), 138 (bottom), 138-139, 140, 141 (top), 142-143, 143, 145 (top), 146 (top), 147 (both), 148 (all three), 149 (bottom), 150-151, 151, 154, 155, 156-157, 160 (top), 161 (top left & bottom), 162 (top), 164 (both), 165 (middle), 166 (both), 167 (top), 168-169, 169 (all three), 170 (bottom right), 172 (all three), 172-173, 173 (top), 174 (top), 175 (bottom), 176 (top & middle), 177, 178, 180 (bottom), 181 (top & bottom left), 184 (all three), 184-185, 185 (both), 186, 187 (all three), 189 (bottom left & right).

Robert Hunt Library: 7 (both), 9 (bottom), 12, 12-13, 13, 14, 15 (top), 16, 17, 18, 20, 22 (right), 23 (bottom), 25 (top left & bottom), 31 (both), 32, 34, 35, 39 (both), 40-41 (both), 42, 42-43, 43, 46-47, 48-49, 49 (both), 50, 51, 52, 52-53, 53, 54, 55 (both), 56, 56-57, 57, 58 (top), 59, 60, 60-61, 61, 62, 62-63, 63 (top), 64-65, 65 (bottom), 66 (top), 67, 68, 69 (both), 70, 70-71, 71, 72, 72-73, 73 (both), 74, 75 (both), 76, 76-77, 77 (bottom), 78 (middle), 78-79, 79 (both), 80, 81 (all three), 82, 82-83, 83, 84, 85 (top), 86, 87 (both), 88 (both), 89, 92, 94 (both), 95 (top left & bottom), 96, 97 (bottom), 98, 98-99, 100 (top), 102-103 (both), 103 (all three), 104 (middle), 105 (bottom), 106, 106-107, 107, 108 (middle & bottom), 109, 113 (both), 114-115, 115 (both), 116 (both), 117 (top), 118, 118-119, 119 (both), 120 (bottom), 121 (bottom), 122, 123 (middle & bottom), 124 (all three), 125 (both), 127, 128 (both), 129 (both), 130, 131 (both), 132 (both), 134-135, 135 (both), 136 (top left & right), 137 (top), 138 (top), 139, 141 (bottom), 142, 144 (both), 144-145, 145 (bottom), 149 (top), 152, 152-153, 153 (both), 154-155, 156, 157, 158, 159 (all four), 160 (bottom), 161 (top right), 162 (middle & bottom), 163 (all four), 164 (top left, top right, bottom left & bottom right), 166-167 (both), 167 (bottom), 168, 170 (bottom left), 171 (both), 173 (bottom), 174 (middle & bottom), 174-175 (both), 175 (top), 176 (bottom), 176-177, 179 (all four), 180 (top), 181 (bottom right), 182 (all three), 188, 189 (top).

Map artworks: John Woolford